W9-BEM-546

ARE YOU FAN ENOUGH TO FACE A MOUND OF TRIVIA QUESTIONS?

You're up! But be careful. Even a baseball-trivia pinch-hitter can strike out. . . .

1. Who pitched three doubleheaders in one month and won all six games, none of which lasted more than one hour and fifty minutes?
2. Who hit two game-winning home runs for the Giants against the Yankees in the 1923 series?
3. Who is the manager who is nicknamed the "White Rat"?
4. Who is the present-day pitcher who has won the American League ERA title with the lowest numbers?
5. Who hit the single that scored Enos Slaughter from first base for the winning run in the 1946 series?
   a) He won a batting title.
   b) His brother won one, too.
6. Who is the Met player who got married at home plate?

Answers
1. "Iron Man" Joe McGinnity of the 1903 Giants
2. Casey Stengel
3. Whitey Herzog
4. Ron Guidry (1.74 for the 1978 Yankees)
5. Harry Walker (Cards)
6. Mookie Wilson (Jackson, Miss., in 1978)

The Ultimate Baseball Quiz Book

Revised and Updated Edition

Dom Forker

A SIGNET BOOK

SIGNET
Published by the Penguin Group
Penguin Books USA Inc., 375 Hudson Street,
New York, New York 10014, U.S.A.
Penguin Books Ltd, 27 Wrights Lane,
London W8 5TZ, England
Penguin Books Australia Ltd, Ringwood,
Victoria, Australia
Penguin Books Canada Ltd, 10 Alcorn Avenue,
Toronto, Ontario, Canada M4V 3B2
Penguin Books (N.Z.) Ltd, 182–190 Wairau Road,
Auckland 10, New Zealand

Penguin Books Ltd, Registered Offices:
Harmondsworth, Middlesex, England

Published by Signet, an imprint of Dutton Signet,
a division of Penguin Books USA Inc.

First Printing, Revised and Updated Edition, March, 1988
First Printing, March, 1981
14 13 12 11 10

 REGISTERED TRADEMARK—MARCA REGISTRADA

Printed in the United States of America

To my lifetime heroes:
Ellen Gallagher Forker, my mother,
and Columb Forker, my father

Contents

Introduction

Forty-one summers have rolled by since that sudden spring when Jackie Robinson broke the color barrier of "organized" baseball, but I still fondly remember, as though it was yesterday, that unusually warm April afternoon of 1946 when he first crossed the foul line of a "white" diamond.

At the time I was an avid fan of Frank Hague, the larcenous mayor of Jersey City, and a bitter foe of Jackie Robinson, the felonious base thief of the Montreal Royals.

Looking back to that eventful day, however, I find it easy to justify the prejudices of my nine-year-old self.

First Mayor Hague had indirectly provided me with the ticket that gained me access to Roosevelt Stadium, which was filled with 26,000 pennant-waving fans on that historic occasion.

Little did I know, at the time, that Mayor Hague expected every city employee in Jersey City to buy a quota of tickets for the opening-day game every year in order to insure a sellout. He sold so many tickets, it seemed, that he could have turned people away from the Los Angeles Coliseum.

Fortunately for the grade-school baseball fans in the Jersey City–Bayonne area, not all of the people who bought tickets for the opener wished to attend it. Better still, many of them felt that they were getting at least part of their money's worth if they could give them away to appreciative young boys who would put them to their proper use. I was just one of many grateful youths who received free tickets for the 1946 opening-day game. We proudly presented our prized possessions to the good Sisters of St. Joseph's, and we promptly got excused from all afternoon classes on that special day.

Second, I was an ardent fan of the Jersey City Giants, the Triple-A International League farm team of the parent New York Giants.

Manager Mel Ott's players were, of course, the bitter

rivals of the Brooklyn Dodgers, who just happened to be the parent organization of the Montreal Royals. If you rooted for the Big Giants, you rooted for the Little Giants; if you cheered for the Dodgers, you cheered for the Royals. The rivalry was as simple as that.

So, when Jackie Robinson stepped into the batter's box in the first inning, I cheered the Jersey City Giants' pitcher and booed the Montreal Royals' second baseman. But Robinson, leaning forward like a cobra with his bat held straight up and down, seemed eager to give me a reception of his own.

And he did!

He led the Royals to a 14–1 victory with four hits, including a home run, two stolen bases, and four runs scored. By the time the game had ended, there seemed to be a lot of converts and very few Giants' fans left in the sparsely populated park.

That's the way it was back then, and in the 1950s, when we were growing up on the streets of Bayonne. From morning to night, we would form baseball comparisons that would inevitably lead to disputed deadlocks. Who's the best center fielder in New York: Joe DiMaggio, Willie Mays, or Duke Snider? Wow! Who's the best team in New York: the Yankees, the Dodgers, or the Giants? Dynamite! Who's the best manager in New York: Casey Stengel, Leo Durocher, or Charlie Dressen? Division!

I've never grown tired of talking about baseball: arguing the indefensible, conjuring up the possible, and predicting the might-have-beens. Facts, patterns, and ironic twists have always been especially appealing to me. Somehow none of it seems trivial. Anything that is connected with baseball is just too important to me.

Maybe you feel the same way! If you do, maybe you can help me. Who was that Jersey City Giants' pitcher whom I wanted to strike out Jackie Robinson, when I was young?

(Answer appears on page 321.)

Dom Forker
June 1, 1987

Chapter One

THE PRESENT-DAY PLAYERS

1. FROM ANDERSON TO YOUNT

How well do you know the accomplishments of the present-day players? Let's see how many of the following questions you can answer.

1. _____ Who is the pitcher who struck out a record 20 batters in one game?

2. _____ Who is the player who led the National League in triples his first three years in the majors?

3. _____ Who is the pitcher who holds the major league record of not yielding a home run in 269⅓ innings of pitching?

4. _____ Who is the only active player to have 200 or more hits in a season without batting .300?

5. _____ Who is the pitcher who held Rod Carew to a .100 mark in 1977 when the batting champ hit .388?

6. _____ Who is the only pitcher to win the Cy Young Award while hurling for a last-place club?

7. _____ Who is the player who appeared in a record 243 games before he reached the age of 20?

8. _____ Who is the player who stroked 184 singles, then an American League record, in 1980?

9. _____ Who is the player who ten times hit safely 200 or more times in one season?

10. _____ Who is the National League pitcher who uncorked a record-tying six wild pitches in one game?

11. _____ Who is the player who stole a major league record 38 consecutive times before he was thrown out?

12. _____ Who is the player, in addition to Julio Cruz, who stole an American League record 32 consecutive times before he was thrown out?

13. _____ Who is the player who became the first and only player to get caught stealing twice in one inning?

14. _____ Who is the pitcher who hurled a record 168⅓ innings in relief one year in the American League?

15. _____ Who is the pitcher who weaved a record eight shutouts in his rookie year?

16. _____ Who is the player who set a rookie record when he stole 72 bases?

17. _____ Who is the pitcher who led his league in losses a record four consecutive years?

18. _____ Who is the pitcher who lost a record 16 games in relief one year?

19. _____ Who is the player who has poled the most switch-hit homers in National League history?

20. _____ Who is the player whose 42 doubles in 1982 set a National League record for catchers?

21. _____ Who is nicknamed "Hit Man?"

22. _____ Who is the pitcher who tied a National League record for relief hurlers by striking out six consecutive batters?

23. _____ Who is the American League player who set a major league record when he was hit by his 244th pitch in 1987?

24. _____ Who is the pitcher who committed an American League record nine balks in one season?

25. _____ Who is the player who was thrown out stealing a record 42 times in one season?

26. _____ Who is the National Leaguer who won back-to-back RBI titles in 1982–83?

27. _____ Who is the major league manager who has two sons playing for him?

28. _____ From 1979–82 the Dodgers won four consecutive Rookie of the Year awards. Who is the pitcher, now with another team, who won the first?

29. _____ Who is the everyday player who won the fourth?

30. _____ Who registered a National League record 701 official at-bats in his rookie year?

31. _____ Who is the relief pitcher who won an American League record 17 games in one season?

32. _____ Who is the National League third baseman who hit 28 home runs in his rookie year?

33. _____ Who is the Met player who got married at home plate?

34. _____ Who was the former Met pitcher who once won two games in one day for the White Sox?

35. _____ Who is the Phillie who had a club-high .467 batting average in the 1983 playoffs and a club-low .050 in the World Series?

36. _____ Who is the first baseman who was traded to the Pirates and then sent to the Yankees for Jim Spencer and money, but was returned to the Bucs because Commissioner Bowie Kuhn said the deal violated cash restrictions?

37. _____ Who is the player who hit an American League record .349 as a rookie?

38. _____ Who is the pitcher who hurled 22⅓ consecutive no-hit innings, the second longest no-hit string in American League history? (Cy Young hurled 25⅓ consecutive no-hit innings for the 1904 Red Sox.)

39. _____ Who is the player nicknamed the "Human Rain Delay?"

40. _____ Who is the player who once hit for the cycle, getting each hit off a different pitcher?

41. _____ Who is the player who hit an American League record 37 home runs for a catcher?

42. _____ Who is the American League pitcher, recently with the Angels, who has posted five one-hitters?

43. _____ Who is the player who joins two former teammates as the only three members of the same club to hit 40 or more home runs in one season?

44. _____ Who is the Detroit pitcher who in 1983 became the first Tiger pitcher to win 20 games in a season since Joe Coleman did it and the first Bengal hurler to strike out 200 or more batters in a year since Mickey Lolich performed the feat?

45. _____ Who is the right-handed hitter who has connected for more single-season home runs than any other Yankee except Joe DiMaggio?

46. _____ Who is the National Leaguer who holds the all-time American League record for career home runs (333) by a third baseman?

47. _____ Who is the player who hit a club-record 16 home runs at shortstop for the Yankees one year?

48. _____ Who is the catcher who was the youngest player (20) ever to perform for the American League in an All-Star Game?

49. _____ Who is the pitcher whose win broke the National League's 11-year domination in the All-Star Game?

50. _____ Who is the player who has hit the only grand slam in the history of the All-Star Game?

51. _____ Who is the White Sox pitcher who became the youngest Pale Hose hurler to win 20 games since 1913?

52. _____ Who hit the "pine-tar" home run?

53. _____ Who is the relief pitcher who set the major league record for saves (46) in one season?

54. _____ Who holds the DH record for RBIs (133) in a season?

55. _____ Who is the Twin who homered in his first major league at-bat?

56. _____ Who is the reliever who struck out an American League record eight consecutive batters in one game?

57. _____ Who in 1981 became the first American League right-handed batter in 11 years to win the batting title?

58. _____ Who is the Yankee who became the first Bronx Bomber to win the batting title since Mickey Mantle did it in 1956?

59. _____ Who is the pitcher who, before Phil and Joe Niekro, was the only knuckleball thrower in the American League?

60. _____ Who is the Cub player who became the first Bruin since 1911 to surpass 20 homers and 20 steals in the same season?

61. _____ Who is the Expo pitcher who has fired a no-hitter and a one-hitter during his brief major league career?

62. _____ Who is the Gold Glove–Silver Bat winner who shared MVP honors with Willie Stargell in 1979?

63. _____ Who has been the only pitcher to hit two home runs in one game in the 1980s?

64. _____ Who is the pitcher who won both the Comeback of the Year Award and the Cy Young Award in the same season?

65. _____ Who is the player who has won four batting titles but has never started in an All-Star Game?

66. _____ Who is the Brave who was born in West Germany and played Little League baseball in Taiwan?

67. _____ Who is the Red who won three Gold Gloves for his outfield play for another team?

68. _____ Who is the Red pitcher who struck out 701 batters from 1982–84?

69. _____ Who is the player who replaced Pete Rose at third base for the Reds in 1979?

70. _____ Who is the Royal regular who struck out in 11 consecutive official at-bats in 1984?

71. _____ Who is the National League starter who posted a 1.69 ERA in 1981?

72. _____ Who was the 1987 Dodger who had three triples in one game for the Twins against the Rangers in 1980?

73. _____ Who is the pitcher who in 1983 threw a rain-curtailed 4–0 perfect game against the Cardinals?

74. _____ Who is the player who got a record-tying five long hits (two homers and three doubles) in one game?

75. _____ Who is the relief pitcher who set a National League record by striking out 151 batters in one season?

76. _____ Who have been the only pitching brothers to throw no-hitters?

77. _____ Who is the catcher who had only one passed ball in 152 games one year?

78. _____ Who is the second baseman who handled 473 chances in 89 games without making an error in 1982?

79. _____ Who is the Brewer who got a club-high 219 hits in 1980?

80. _____ Who is the manager nicknamed "Captain Hook?"

81. _____ Who is the Tiger who became the first player to have his salary cut—from $280,000 to $250,000 —by an arbitrator?

82. _____ Who is the player who scored 136 runs in 1982, the most in the American League since Ted Williams scored 150 in 1949?

83. _____ Who is the Astro outfielder who has fielded 1.000 in a season?

84. _____ Who is the pitcher who became the first lefty since Mel Parnell to lead the Red Sox in wins in back-to-back years?

85. _____ Who is nicknamed the "Candy Man?"

86. _____ Who is the pitcher who lost a record-tying three games in one World Series?

87. _____ Who is the player who tied a record by rookies when he homered twice in one World Series game?

88. _____ Who is the only player, in addition to Babe Ruth, Johnny Mize, and Larry Parrish to hit three home runs in a game in each league?

89. _____ Who is the one-time Indian who threw a perfect game?

90. _____ Who is the pitcher who broke Sparky Lyle's record when he posted 13 saves in 13 consecutive appearances?

91. _____ Who is the only player in Dodger history to hit at least 30 home runs and steal at least 20 bases in a season? (He's done it twice.)

92. _____ Who is the former White Sox pitcher who set a club record when he reeled off 14 straight wins over a two-year period?

93. _____ Who is the player who became the first graduate of the Royals' Baseball Academy to play in the major leagues?

94. _____ Who is the player who stole a record seven bases in two consecutive games in 1983?

95. _____ Who is the Ranger who has five times hit 20 or more home runs in a season?

96. _____ Who is the former Ranger outfielder who had 24 assists in one season, the most in the league since Stan Spence had 29 for the 1944 Senators?

97. _____ Who has been the most recent Cub to win a batting title?

98. _____ Who is the player who became the first Blue Jay to drive home 100 or more runs in a season?

99. _____ Who is the American League player who drove home 145 runs in 1985?

100. _____ Who is the Blue Jay who once hit seven home runs in a seven-day period?

2. FROM AIKENS TO YOUNT

Repeat the feat.

1. _____ Who is the Blue Jay pitcher who got a win by forfeit when Baltimore refused to continue the game because of field conditions in 1977?

2. _____ Who is the Angel slugger who hit three home runs in a game twice in one week?

3. _____ Who is the Angel who is the son of a former big-league infielder by the same name?

4. _____ Who is the player who became the youngest Pale Hose performer in history to drive in 100 runs (105) in a season?

5. _____ Who is the White Sox pitcher who led the league in strikeouts (209) with another team?

6. _____ Who is the manager who in 1983 got fired while he was the skipper of a first-place club and then assumed the reins of a last-place team in the same season?

7. _____ Who is the manager who has skippered five different teams?

8. _____ Who is the manager who once established a record for second basemen by hitting 43 home runs in one season?

9. _____ Who is the manager who homered in his first major league at-bat?

10. _____ Who is the Astro pitcher who three times won 1–0 games in 1981?

11. _____ Who is the pitcher who set a record for rookies when he struck out 276 batters in 1984?

12. _____ Who is the American Leaguer, in addition to Bo Jackson, who struck out a record-tying five times in a nine-inning game?

13. _____ Who is the second baseman who set an American League record at his position when he went 86 games without committing an error?

14. _____ Who is the Tiger outfielder who recorded more than 500 putouts in a season with the White Sox?

15. _____ Who is the other American League outfielder who has recorded 500 putouts in the 1980s?

16. _____ Who is the catcher who, in a 150 or more game season, fielded an American League high .995?

17. _____ Who is the American Leaguer who is one of three players to steal 300 bases before his 25th birthday?

18. _____ Who is the National Leaguer who has performed the same feat?

19. _____ Who is the player who went 0-for-21 in the last five games of the 1979 World Series and 2-for-16 in the first four games of the 1983 World Series?

20. _____ Who is the only present-day player to lead his league in walks and total bases in the same season?

21. _____ Who is the player who has two cousins connected with pro football?

22. _____ Who is the American League catcher who went errorless for 96 consecutive games in 1983?

23. _____ Who is the player who drove home ten runs in one game in his rookie year?

24. _____ Who is the American League catcher, once a National Leaguer, who threw out 50 percent of opposing base runners in 1982–83?

25. _____ Who is the player who has been named the World Series MVP with two different teams?

26. _____ Who wears the number "72," which represents the year in which he won the Rookie of the Year Award?

27. _____ Who is the White Sox player who drove home 100 runs in his rookie season?

28. _____ Who is the manager whose team had the best National League record in 1981 but finished second in both halves of the strike-tainted season?

29. _____ Who is the manager who lost his job after leading his team to a 103-win season?

30. _____ Who is the manager who played in four World Series with the Orioles?

31. _____ Who is the manager who was once traded for a player?

32. _____ Who is the manager who has won pennants with a record-tying three teams?

33. _____ Who is the pitcher who once won four 1–0 decisions in one season for the Rangers?

34. _____ Who is the present-day American League player who once hit three grand slams in one year for the Reds?

35. _____ Who is the pitcher who posted a club-high 52 shutouts for the Dodgers?

36. _____ Who is the manager who has a law degree?

37. _____ Who was the pitcher who struck out a single-season-high 289 batters for the Mets?

38. _____ Who is the Phillie who struck out a club-high 180 times in 1975?

39. _____ Who is the former Phillie pitcher who struck out a club-high 310 batters in one season?

40. _____ Who is the pitcher who twice saved 31 games in a season for the Pirates?

41. _____ Who is the pitcher who registered a National League-high 45 saves for the Cards in 1984?

42. _____ Who is the American League pitcher who also posted 45 saves in a season?

43. _____ Who is the pitcher who struck out 215 batters as a rookie for the Giants in 1975?

44. _____ Who is the skipper who has groomed managers Tony LaRussa, Rene Lachemann, Doug Rader, and Pat Corrales?

45. _____ Who is the pitcher who struck out 209 batters for the 1966 Dodgers?

46. _____ Who is the player, now in the American League, who set a National League record by drawing at least one walk in 15 consecutive games?

47. _____ Who is the player who has sprayed the most two-base hits (51) by a switch-hitter in a season?

48. _____ Who is the player who has bounced into the fewest double plays (1) by an American League switch-hitter in one season?

49. _____ Who is the first baseman who has led his league in most games played a record eight times?

50. _____ Who is the player who has legged out a record-tying 19 triples by a switch-hitter in one season?

51. _____ Who is the third baseman who set a record when he registered 412 assists in one season?

52. _____ Who is the outfielder who has led the American League in errors at his position a record-tying five times?

53. _____ Who is the National League player who tied a loop record in 1984 when he hit seven home runs in six consecutive games and at least one home run in six consecutive contests?

54. _____ Who is the manager who is nicknamed the "White Rat?"

55. _____ Who is the infielder who became the first switch-hitter to drill 100 or more hits from each side of the plate in a season?

56. _____ Who is the other player to get at least 100 hits from each side of the plate in a season?

57. _____ Who is called "Jack the Ripper?"

58. _____ Who is the player who hit 40-plus home runs while leading his league in hits in the same year?

59. _____ Who is the American League player who got at least 20 homers, 20 triples, and 20 doubles in the same season?

60. _____ Who is the player who hit three home runs in a Championship Series game?

61. _____ Who was the pitcher who became the first hurler to win the Cy Young Award without winning 20 games in that season?

62. _____ Who, in addition to Steve Carlton, is the only present-day hurler to be a unanimous choice for the Cy Young Award?

63. _____ Who is the pitcher who won 46 percent of his team's games one year?

64. _____ Who is the player who has struck out more than any other player in the history of baseball?

65. _____ Who is the player who had 662 at-bats in 162 games without stealing a base?

66. _____ Who is the pitcher who has recorded the highest winning percentage for a hurler who has won 20 or more games in a season?

67. _____ Who is the National League relief pitcher who won Fireman of the Year honors with two different teams in the American League?

68. _____ Who is the former Giant who holds the team's club record with 46 doubles in one season?

69. _____ Who is the Yankee who during a six-year period (1978–83) led the club in stealing five times?

70. _____ Who is the player who holds the White Sox single-season stolen base mark?

71. _____ Who is the present-day pitcher who has won the American League ERA title with the lowest numbers?

72. _____ Who is the player who won the Rookie of the Year Award the longest time ago?

73. _____ Who is the pitcher who committed a record 11 balks in one year?

74. _____ Who is the player whose first major league triple scored the winning run of a 1980 World Series game?

75. _____ Who is the player whose three-run homer, off Goose Gossage, wrapped up the 1980 pennant for the Royals?

76. _____ Who is the only player in history to win home run titles with three different teams?

77. _____ Who is nicknamed the "Italian Stallion" (the National League version)?

78. _____ Who is nicknamed the "Italian Stallion" (the American League version)?

79. _____ Who is nicknamed "Rags"?

80. _____ Who is nicknamed "Pudge"?

81. _____ Who is the 1986 pitcher who had the highest single-season winning percentage (.875) of any present-day hurler in the National League?

82. _____ Who is the Met who set a team record for rookies when he hit 26 home runs in his maiden season?

83. _____ Who is the Tiger who tied a major league record by hitting home runs in four consecutive plate appearances?

84. _____ Who is the player who has been the only shortstop to lead his circuit in hits and total bases in the same season?

85. _____ Who is the pitcher who in 1983 threw the first no-hitter for the Yankees since Don Larsen pitched his perfect game in the 1956 World Series?

86. _____ Who is the oldest player in the majors?

87. _____ Who is the catcher who holds club-high home run marks (26 and 37) at his position with two different teams?

88. _____ Who is the player who set a White Sox rookie record when he hit 35 home runs in one season?

89. _____ Who is the only player, in addition to Ty Cobb, who has won three league titles in hits and in triples?

90. _____ Who is nicknamed "Bye-Bye"?

91. _____ Who is the relief pitcher who set a record for rookies when he won 14 games in 1979?

92. _____ Who is the pitcher who threw a Ranger club-record 36 consecutive scoreless innings in 1983?

93. _____ Who is the former Expo who once hit two homers in one inning?

94. _____ Who is the Expo who homered in his first official at-bat?

95. _____ Who is the player who is second to Babe Ruth in leading his league (eight times) in home runs?

96. _____ Who is the player who has won two batting titles with each of two teams?

97. _____ Who is the Yankee who as a rookie for Oakland in 1974 batted .571 in the World Series?

98. _____ Who is the Red who has a .351 average in 15 National League Championship Series games?

99. _____ Who is the player who in 1983 became the only Tiger left-handed batter since Dick Wakefield to amass 200 hits (206) in a season?

100. _____ Who is the player who became the first rookie to lead either league in slugging (.566) percentage?

3. FROM AASE TO YOUMANS

1. _____ Who is the Cub whose 54 stolen bases in 1985 were the most by a Bruin since 1906?

2. _____ Who was the 1987 Cub who was named Rookie of the Year for the Giants in 1973?

3. _____ Who became the first Cubs' catcher in more than 40 years to hit more than 20 home runs in a year?

4. _____ Who is nicknamed "Thunder Pup"?

5. _____ Who is the Cub pitcher who went 16–1 during the stretch drive in 1984?

6. _____ Who broke Bruce Sutter's club career saves record with the Cubs?

7. _____ Who was the 1987 Cub who, in 1975, didn't allow an earned run in his first 28⅔ innings, a major league record for rookies?

8. _____ Who is the Expo backstop who had a .995 fielding percentage as a Met rookie in 1984?

9. _____ Who is the Expo who is called "Gran Gato" or "Big Cat"?

10. _____ Who is the Expo pitcher who was a boyhood friend of Dwight Gooden?

11. _____ Who is the Expo relief pitcher who tied the one-time major-league rookie record with 78 appearances?

12. _____ Who is the Twin reliever who went 94 games without a loss for the Mets in 1980–81?

13. _____ Who is the Expo who once stole 71 bases in 88 games?

14. _____ Who is the Met who hit his tenth grand slam in 1986?

15. _____ Who was the only National League player to hit 20 home runs and steal 20 bases from 1984–87?

16. _____ Who was the only American League player to do the same from 1984–86?

17. _____ Who is the Met who set a club record with at least one RBI in eight straight games?

18. _____ Who became the first pitcher to strike out 200 batters in his first three years?

19. _____ Who is the Met reliever who set a club record for wins out of the bull pen with 14?

20. _____ Who became the winningest Met lefty (18 wins) since Jerry Koosman in 1976?

21. _____ Who is the Met pitcher who didn't allow the Red Sox a run in four World Series appearances?

22. _____ Who earned his third MVP Award in 1986?

23. _____ Who is the Phillie who averaged 15 triples a year during his first three full seasons in the majors?

24. _____ Who is the Phillie relief pitcher who broke Jim Konstanty's single-season save mark for right-handers?

25. _____ Who, in 1985, became only the fourth catcher in 40 years to register 100 assists?

26. _____ Who is the Buc who is nicknamed "Rambo"?

27. _____ Who is the Buc who is the son of a former major leaguer?

28. _____ Who, in 1985, became only the seventh second baseman in major league history to top 100 RBIs?

29. _____ Who is the player whose batting average in 1985 was the highest ever by a National League switch-hitter?

30. _____ Who, in the 1985 National League Championship Series, hit his first left-handed home run in 3,009 pro at-bats?

31. _____ Who stole 110 bases in his rookie year?

32. _____ Who is the Card who set a Giant record with a 26-game hitting streak in 1978?

33. _____ Who is the Card pitcher who picked up three victories in post-season play in 1985?

34. _____ Who is the moundsman who became only the third European-born pitcher to start a World Series game?

35. _____ Who is the Card pitcher who has thrown two no-hitters?

36. _____ Who is the relief pitcher who was named the National League's Rookie of the Year in 1986?

37. _____ Who is the player whose consecutive-game streak of 740 contests was broken in 1986?

38. _____ Who is the Brave who participated in a triple play in only his second major-league game?

39. _____ Who is the Brave who set a personal single-season high for home runs in 1987?

40. _____ Who is the Brave who is a .313 hitter in nine Championship Series games?

41. _____ Who is the Brave relief pitcher who saved 24 games in 1986 after posting just one in 1985?

42. _____ Who is the pitcher who won 17 games in 1985 and lost 18 in 1986?

43. _____ Who averaged 112 RBIs a season for the 1984–86 Reds?

44. _____ Who is the Red who, in his first full season, hit three home runs in a 1986 game?

45. _____ Who is the Red whose 21-game hitting streak in 1984 is the team's longest since Pete Rose's record 44-game string?

46. _____ Who is the third baseman who is closing in on his dad's career total of 206 home runs?

47. _____ Who is the Red catcher who had a .333 batting average for the Phillies in the 1983 World Series?

48. _____ Who is the Red pitcher who, in 1985, reeled off 11 straight wins, the club's most in 30 years?

49. _____ Who is the player who became the first Astro to steal 40 bases since Cesar Cedeno in 1980?

50. _____ Who became only the fourth National League pitcher to whiff 300 batters in a season?

51. _____ Who was unable to hold 4–0 and 3–0 leads in the 1986 National League Championship Series?

52. _____ Who set the Houston record for the most wins by a rookie southpaw?

53. _____ Who is the Houston pitcher who won two games and saved 16 in his last 22 outings of 1986?

54. _____ Who is the Houston pitcher who allowed more than five hits in only two of his last 23 starts in 1986?

55. _____ Who is the Dodger whose All-Star Game average before 1987 was .600?

56. _____ Who is the Dodger who, in 1981, became the Pacific Coast League's first Triple Crown winner since Steve Bilko in 1956?

57. _____ Who was the 1987 Tiger who batted .375 in the 1979 World Series?

58. _____ Who is the Dodger who three times has hit more than 30 home runs in a season?

59. _____ Who struck out a record-tying five consecutive batters in the 1986 All-Star Game?

60. _____ Who is the Dodger pitcher known for his duels with Reggie Jackson in the 1978 World Series?

61. _____ Who played in 1,207 consecutive National League games?

62. _____ Who is the recent-day Padre who played six different positions for the Mets in 1986?

63. _____ Who is the Padre stopper who had 278 career saves entering the 1987 season?

64. _____ Who is the Padre pitcher who didn't allow a run in three 1984 Championship Series outings and just one in 12 World Series innings?

65. _____ Who is the Giant who hit a home run off Nolan Ryan in his first major-league at-bat?

66. _____ Who is called "Hac Man"?

67. _____ Who is the Giant who set a club record with 15 pinch-hits in 1986?

68. _____ Who, in 1986, became the Giants' first 20-game winner since 1973?

69. _____ Who is the Giant relief pitcher who limited left-handed batters to a .115 mark in 1986 and a .185 average in 1985?

70. _____ Who is the first official captain in the Orioles' modern history?

71. _____ Who topped American League shortstops in home runs and RBIs for the fourth straight year in 1986?

72. _____ Who is the Oriole who won a batting title with another club?

73. _____ Who is the Oriole who hit three home runs in one game against the Yankees in 1986?

74. _____ Who was the first Oriole to win the ERA crown and lead the league in victories?

75. _____ Who set the Oriole club record with 34 saves?

76. _____ Who was the 1987 Oriole pitcher who won the Cy Young Award in 1979?

77. _____ Who is the first player to get 200 hits and 100 walks in the same season since Stan Musial in 1953?

78. _____ Who is the player who has four 200-hit seasons and four 39 home runs-plus years?

79. _____ Who is the Red Sox player who established a record with 24 post-season hits?

80. _____ Who is the Twins player who has hit 25 or more home runs in a season for four different American League teams?

81. _____ Who is the Red Sox player who has moved into third place on the team's list of games played?

82. _____ Who won both the MVP and Cy Young awards in 1986?

83. _____ Who is the left-handed pitcher who threw all four of his shutouts at Fenway Park in 1986?

84. _____ Who became the first Indian to hit 20 home runs, steal 20 bases, and drive home 100 runs in the same season?

85. _____ Who is the Indian who collected at least 180 hits in each season from 1984–86?

86. _____ Who is the Indian who set a club record for most homers (17) by a switch-hitter?

87. _____ Who is the Indian who averaged 13 triples a season from 1983–86?

88. _____ Who broke Bobby Bonds's Indian club record for strikeouts (137) in a season?

89. _____ Who is the Indian who, in 1986, hit .326, the highest team mark since Miguel Dilone hit .341 in 1980?

90. _____ Who won his 300th career victory on the final day of the 1985 season?

91. _____ Who is the first Indian pitcher to have at least two seasons of 20 or more saves?

92. _____ Who was the first Indian pitcher to lead the league in complete games since Gaylord Perry did it in 1973?

93. _____ Who was the first Tiger left-handed-hitting home-run king since Ty Cobb in 1909?

94. _____ Who is the Tiger who was the World Series MVP in 1984?

95. _____ Who is the Tiger who was the Rookie of the Year in 1978?

96. _____ Who is the Tiger pitcher who is the major league leader in wins since 1979?

97. _____ Who is the Tiger pitcher who won the Cy Young Award?

98. _____ Who is the Brewer who was the first shortstop to lead the league in slugging percentage and total bases?

99. _____ Who struck out an American League record 186 times in 1987?

100. _____ Who in 1986 became the first Brewer to steal home since 1978?

4. FROM BALBONI TO WITT

Let's finish this chapter off in style.

1. _____ Who in 1986 became the third Brewer pitcher to win 20 games in a season?

2. _____ Who is the 1986 Brewer who is nicknamed "Horse"?

3. _____ Who set a Yankee record with 238 hits in 1986?

4. _____ Who is the Yankee who, except for 1987, has never failed to lead his league in stolen bases?

5. _____ Who is the Yankees' all-time leader in games played at his position?

6. _____ Who, in 1986, drove home 100 runs for the fifth straight year?

7. _____ Who is the Yankee pitcher who was the Rookie of the Year in 1981?

8. _____ Who is the Blue Jay who led American League outfielders with 20 assists in 1986?

9. _____ Who is the Blue Jay who is nicknamed "Shaker"?

10. _____ Who is the Blue Jay who hit a career-high 47 home runs in 1987?

11. _____ Who is the pitcher whose autobiography is titled *Tomorrow I'll Be Perfect*?

12. _____ Who became the first rookie to start in the All-Star Game since fan voting began in 1970?

13. _____ Who is the Angel infielder who hit 20 or more home runs in each season from 1984–86?

14. _____ Who is the Angel who ranks first on the club's all-time RBI list?

15. _____ Who is the first Angel to record three consecutive 30-plus stolen-base seasons?

16. _____ Who is the pitcher whose 18 wins in 1986 were the most by any Angel since Nolan Ryan won 19 in 1977?

17. _____ Who has had a record 21 consecutive seasons of more than 100 strikeouts?

18. _____ Who set a White Sox club record by hitting 20 or more home runs in six consecutive seasons?

19. _____ Who set a White Sox club record for the fewest errors (12) by a shortstop in 1985?

20. _____ Who ranks second to Yogi Berra in career homers by an American League catcher?

21. _____ Who became the first major leaguer to strike out the first seven batters he faced in a game?

22. _____ Who set a White Sox record with 32 saves in 1985?

23. _____ Who is the Royal who in 1986 was honored with his 11th consecutive All-Star selection?

24. _____ Who, in his first three years with the Royals, averaged 31 home runs a season?

25. _____ Who is the Royal switch-hitter who once led the league in hitting?

26. _____ Who is the Royal infielder who hit 22 home runs in both 1985 and 1986?

27. _____ Who is the Twin who had a club record-tying eight four-hit games in 1986?

28. _____ Who is the Twin who hit a career-high 34 home runs in 1987?

29. _____ Who is the Twin whose 108 RBIs in 1986 was the most by a Minnesota player since Larry Hisle plated 119 runners in 1977?

30. _____ Who is the Twin pitcher who holds the American League record of eight seasons with more than 200 strikeouts?

31. _____ Who is the A's player who was the Rookie of the Year in 1986?

32. _____ Who was the 1986 rookie who set the then American League record for strikeouts (185)?

33. _____ Who is the Texas player who became one of the select few to hit three home runs in a game in both leagues?

34. _____ Who is the Ranger pitcher who, in 1986, set a major-league rookie record with 80 appearances?

35. _____ Who became the first pitcher to win a major league game with no previous professional victories since David Clyde did it for Texas in 1973?

Ruth's Shadow

Babe Ruth captured the attention of the nation on October 2, 1932, for on that historic day he allegedly "called his shot."

The Yankees had won the first two games of the World Series before traveling to Chicago's Wrigley Field. The Cub fans and players were riding Ruth unmercifully for criticizing the Bruin players for failing to award former Yankee infielder Mark Koenig a full share of their series cut.

But Ruth relished the attention.

In the first inning Earle Combs reached second on a two-base throwing error by shortstop Billy Jurges. Bruin pitcher Charlie Root, obviously upset, proceeded to walk Joe Sewell, something he did not want to do with Ruth coming to the plate. On a 2–0 count, Ruth cracked a three-run homer.

The third time that Ruth came to the plate, in the fifth inning, the Yankees were leading, 4–3. In the interim, he had misplayed a ball in right field, much to the delight of the Cub supporters. Before Root got a chance to pitch to the Babe in the fifth, Ruth allegedly pointed his bat toward the center-field bleachers, saying, in effect, "This is where the ball is going to land." The stage had been set for one of the most dramatic moments in baseball history.

Ruth deliberately took two strikes, which he dutifully noted by raising first one finger and then a second one after the calls. Then he proceeded to deposit the ball in the exact spot to which he had pointed his bat. Coincidentally, that was the 15th and last home run that Ruth hit in series play.

Lost in the fanfare of that day were the exploits of another Yankee, who hit two home runs, including the game-winner.

Who was this Yankee great who played in the shadow of Ruth?

(Answer appears on page 321.)

Chapter Two

THE HITTERS

5. HOW GOOD IS .300?

Twenty of the following 40 players have won at least one batting title, though they have lifetime averages of less than .300; the other twenty players have lifetime averages of .300 or better, though they have never won a batting title. Put the batting champs in the left-hand column and the .300 hitters in the right-hand column.

Mickey Mantle	Lou Boudreau
Johnny Pesky	Mickey Vernon
Enos Slaughter	Debs Garms
Tommy Davis	Sam Rice
Norm Cash	Heinie Zimmerman
Joe Cronin	Dale Mitchell
Hal Chase	Pete Reiser
George Stirnweiss	Larry Doyle
Carl Yastrzemski	Hank Greenberg
Mel Ott	Ferris Fain
Bill Dickey	Alex Johnson
Pete Runnels	Eddie Collins
Bobby Avila	Phil Cavarretta
Lloyd Waner	Earle Combs
Harry Walker	Carl Furillo
Bob Meusel	Babe Herman
Joe Jackson	Kiki Cuyler
Hack Wilson	Frankie Frisch
Earl Averill	Pie Traynor
Dick Groat	Mickey Cochrane

Batting Champs

1. _____
2. _____
3. _____
4. _____
5. _____
6. _____
7. _____
8. _____
9. _____
10. _____
11. _____
12. _____
13. _____
14. _____
15. _____
16. _____
17. _____
18. _____
19. _____
20. _____

.300 Hitters

1. _____
2. _____
3. _____
4. _____
5. _____
6. _____
7. _____
8. _____
9. _____
10. _____
11. _____
12. _____
13. _____
14. _____
15. _____
16. _____
17. _____
18. _____
19. _____
20. _____

6. WHO DID IT TWICE?

National League

Five of the following ten players have won one National League batting title; the other five have won two. List the one-time winners in the left-hand column and the two-time winners in the right-hand column: Willie Mays, Lefty O'Doul, Tommy Davis, Harry Walker, Dixie Walker, Henry Aaron, Carl Furillo, Jackie Robinson, Ernie Lombardi, and Richie Ashburn.

1. _____   1. _____
2. _____   2. _____
3. _____   3. _____
4. _____   4. _____
5. _____   5. _____

American League

Five of the following ten players have won one American League batting title; the other five have won two. List the one-time winners in the left-hand column and the two-time winners in the right-hand column: George Kell, Al Kaline, Jimmie Foxx, Norm Cash, Luke Appling, Mickey Vernon, Mickey Mantle, Pete Runnels, Ferris Fain, and Harvey Kuenn.

1. _____   1. _____
2. _____   2. _____
3. _____   3. _____
4. _____   4. _____
5. _____   5. _____

7. THE FABULOUS FIFTIES

Ten players have hit a total of 50 or more home runs in one season: Willie Mays, Mickey Mantle, Hank Greenberg, George Foster, Jimmie Foxx, Roger Maris, Johnny Mize, Ralph Kiner, Hack Wilson, and Babe Ruth. The ten of them have done it a total of 17 times. One of them accomplished the feat four times. Four of them achieved it twice. Place them in the order of their single-season rank. Totals, years, and leagues are given as clues.

1. _____ (61) 1961 (AL)
2. _____ (60) 1927 (AL)
3. _____ (59) 1921 (AL)
4. _____ (58) 1932 (AL)
5. _____ (58) 1938 (AL)
6. _____ (56) 1930 (NL)
7. _____ (54) 1920 (AL)
8. _____ (54) 1928 (AL)
9. _____ (54) 1949 (NL)
10. _____ (54) 1961 (AL)
11. _____ (52) 1956 (AL)
12. _____ (52) 1965 (NL)
13. _____ (52) 1977 (NL)
14. _____ (51) 1947 (NL)
15. _____ (51) 1947 (NL)
16. _____ (51) 1955 (NL)
17. _____ (50) 1938 (AL)

8. THE (500) HOME RUN CLUB

There have been 14 players who have hit more than 500 home runs in their careers. See how many of them you can name. Their respective totals are listed in parentheses. Two of them were still active in 1987.

1. _____ (755)
2. _____ (714)
3. _____ (660)
4. _____ (586)
5. _____ (573)
6. _____ (563)*
7. _____ (536)
8. _____ (534)
9. _____ (530)
10. _____ (521)
11. _____ (521)*
12. _____ (512)
13. _____ (512)
14. _____ (511)

*Still active on July 1, 1987

9. THEY HIT FOR POWER AND AVERAGE

National League

Five National League players have won both the home run crown and the batting title in the same year. One of them did it twice. Match the following players with the year(s) in which they performed the feat: Joe Medwick, Johnny Mize, Heinie Zimmerman, Rogers Hornsby (2), and Chuck Klein.

1. _____ (1912)
2. _____ (1922)
3. _____ (1925)
4. _____ (1933)
5. _____ (1937)
6. _____ (1939)

American League

Do the same with the following nine American Leaguers: Ted Williams (3), Lou Gehrig, Nap Lajoie, Mickey Mantle, Babe Ruth, Ty Cobb, Jimmie Foxx, Carl Yastrzemski, and Frank Robinson.

1. _____ (1901)
2. _____ (1909)
3. _____ (1924)
4. _____ (1933)
5. _____ (1934)
6. _____ (1941)
7. _____ (1942)
8. _____ (1947)
9. _____ (1956)
10. _____ (1966)
11. _____ (1967)

10. THE 3000-HIT CLUB

The following 15 players have accumulated 3000 or more major league hits: Al Kaline, Tris Speaker, Carl Yastrzemski, Ty Cobb, Honus Wagner, Roberto Clemente, Eddie Collins, Stan Musial, Hank Aaron, Nap Lajoie, Pete Rose, Paul Waner, Cap Anson, Lou Brock, and Willie Mays. Their respective totals are included. Place the players in their proper order.

1. _____ (4256)
2. _____ (4192)
3. _____ (3771)
4. _____ (3630)
5. _____ (3515)
6. _____ (3430)
7. _____ (3419)
8. _____ (3311)
9. _____ (3283)
10. _____ (3251)
11. _____ (3152)
12. _____ (3041)
13. _____ (3023)
14. _____ (3007)
15. _____ (3000)

11. TRIPLE CROWN WINNERS

Eleven players have won the Triple Crown a total of 13 times: Ted Williams (2), Rogers Hornsby (2), Carl Yastrzemski, Mickey Mantle, Ty Cobb, Frank Robinson, Jimmie Foxx, Joe Medwick, Lou Gehrig, Chuck Klein, and Nap Lajoie. Fit them into the respective years in which they won the select award.

1. _____ (1901)
2. _____ (1909)
3. _____ (1922)
4. _____ (1925)
5. _____ (1933)
6. _____ (1933)
7. _____ (1934)
8. _____ (1937)
9. _____ (1942)
10. _____ (1947)
11. _____ (1956)
12. _____ (1966)
13. _____ (1967)

12. HIGHEST LIFETIME AVERAGE FOR POSITION

Identify the player, from the three listed at each position, who has hit for the highest lifetime average. At one position two players are tied for the lead.

National League

1B. _____ (.341) Bill Terry, Johnny Mize, or Stan Musial

2B. _____ (.358) Frankie Frisch, Jackie Robinson, or Rogers Hornsby

SS. _____ (.329) Arky Vaughan, Honus Wagner, or Travis Jackson

3B. _____ (.320) Joe Torre, Heinie Zimmerman, or Pie Traynor

OF. _____ (.336) Chuck Klein, Harry Walker, or Riggs Stephenson

OF. _____ (.333) Paul Waner, Babe Herman, or Zack Wheat

OF. _____ (.349) Kiki Cuyler, Stan Musial, or Lefty O'Doul

C. _____ (.310) Eugene Hargrave, Gabby Hartnett, or Roy Campanella

American League

1B. _____ (.340) Lou Gehrig, Jimmie Foxx, or George Sisler

2B. _____ (.339) Nap Lajoie, Charlie Gehringer, or Eddie Collins

SS. _____ (.314) Joe Cronin, Cecil Travis, or Luke Appling

3B. _____ (.307) George Kell, Frank Baker, or Jimmy Collins

OF. _____ (.367) Harry Heilmann, Tris Speaker, or Ty Cobb

OF. _____ (.356) Babe Ruth, Al Simmons, or Joe Jackson

OF. _____ (.344) Joe DiMaggio, Ted Williams,
or Heinie Manush
C. _____ (.320) Mickey Cochrane, Yogi Berra,
or Bill Dickey

13. HIGHEST SINGLE SEASON AVERAGE FOR POSITION

Identify the player, from the three listed at each position, who has hit for the highest average in a single season.

National League

1B. _____ (.401) Bill Terry, Johnny Mize, or Stan Musial

2B. _____ (.424) Frankie Frisch, Jackie Robinson, or Rogers Hornsby

SS. _____ (.385) Arky Vaughan, Honus Wagner, or Travis Jackson

3B. _____ (.372) Joe Torre, Heinie Zimmerman, or Pie Traynor

OF. _____ (.398) Paul Waner, Fred Lindstrom, or Lefty O'Doul

OF. _____ (.393) Stan Musial, Babe Herman, or Roberto Clemente

OF. _____ (.386) Chuck Klein, Zack Wheat, or Harry Walker

C. _____ (.358) Ernie Lombardi, Gabby Hartnett, or Chief Meyers

American League

1B. _____ (.420) Lou Gehrig, Jimmie Foxx, or George Sisler

2B. _____ (.422) Nap Lajoie, Charlie Gehringer, or Eddie Collins

SS. _____ (.388) Joe Cronin, Cecil Travis, or Luke Appling

3B. _____ (.390) George Kell, Frank Baker, or George Brett

OF. _____ (.420) Harry Heilmann, Tris Speaker, or Ty Cobb

OF. _____ (.408) Babe Ruth, Al Simmons, or Joe Jackson

OF. _____ (.406) Sam Crawford, Ted Williams,
                     or Heinie Manush
C. _____ (.362) Mickey Cochrane, Yogi Berra,
                     or Bill Dickey

14. THE YEAR THEY HIT THE HEIGHTS

Take the following ten hitters and match them up with their highest respective season's batting average: Babe Ruth, Jackie Robinson, Stan Musial, Rogers Hornsby, Charlie Keller, Ted Williams, Roberto Clemente, Ty Cobb, Joe DiMaggio, and Mickey Mantle.

1. _____ (.424)   6. _____ (.376)
2. _____ (.420)   7. _____ (.365)
3. _____ (.406)   8. _____ (.357)
4. _____ (.393)   9. _____ (.342)
5. _____ (.381)   10. _____ (.334)

15. MATCHING AVERAGES

Match the following ten players with their corresponding lifetime averages listed below: Rogers Hornsby, Babe Ruth, Honus Wagner, Ty Cobb, Stan Musial, Jimmie Foxx, Tris Speaker, Mickey Cochrane, Mel Ott, and Bill Terry.

1. _____ (.367)   6. _____ (.331)
2. _____ (.358)   7. _____ (.329)
3. _____ (.344)   8. _____ (.325)
4. _____ (.342)   9. _____ (.320)
5. _____ (.341)   10. _____ (.304)

16. ONCE IS NOT ENOUGH

Eight of the following sluggers have hit four home runs in a major league game: Babe Ruth, Lou Gehrig, Rocky Colavito, Hank Aaron, Gil Hodges, Pat Seerey, Mickey Mantle, Jimmie Foxx, Joe Adcock, Mike Schmidt, Willie Mays, Joe DiMaggio, Bob Horner, and Hank Greenberg. Who are they?

1. _____
2. _____
3. _____
4. _____
5. _____
6. _____
7. _____
8. _____

17. NATIONAL LEAGUE HOME RUN KINGS

Match the following National League home run champs with the number of times they have won the crown: Ted Kluszewski, Johnny Mize, Ralph Kiner, Duke Snider, Eddie Mathews, Johnny Bench, Mike Schmidt, and Mel Ott.

1. _____ (8)
2. _____ (7)
3. _____ (6)
4. _____ (4)
5. _____ (2)
6. _____ (2)
7. _____ (1)
8. _____ (1)

18. AMERICAN LEAGUE HOME RUN KINGS

Match the following American League home run champs with the number of times they have won the crown: Roger Maris, Lou Gehrig, Frank Howard, Babe Ruth, Tony Armas, Carl Yastrzemski, Jimmie Foxx, Joe DiMaggio, Jim Rice, Harmon Killebrew, Frank Baker, Hank Greenberg, George Scott, Reggie Jackson, Graig Nettles, Ted Williams, Gorman Thomas, Larry Doby, Mickey Mantle, and Dick Allen.

1. _____ (12)
2. _____ (6)
3. _____ (4)
4. _____ (4)
5. _____ (4)
6. _____ (4)
7. _____ (4)
8. _____ (4)
9. _____ (3)
10. _____ (3)
11. _____ (2)
12. _____ (2)
13. _____ (2)
14. _____ (2)
15. _____ (2)
16. _____ (2)
17. _____ (1)
18. _____ (1)
19. _____ (1)
20. _____ (1)

19. WOULD YOU PINCH-HIT?

Some of the best pinch-hitters in the history of the game are listed with their averages as substitute batters. Were their lifetime averages higher (Yes–No) than their pinch-hitting marks?

1. _____ (.320) Tommy Davis
2. _____ (.312) Frenchy Bordagaray
3. _____ (.307) Frankie Baumholtz
4. _____ (.303) Red Schoendienst
5. _____ (.300) Bob Fothergill
6. _____ (.299) Dave Philley
7. _____ (.297) Manny Mota
8. _____ (.286) Steve Braun
9. _____ (.283) Johnny Mize
10. _____ (.280) Don Mueller
11. _____ (.279) Mickey Vernon
12. _____ (.278) Gene Woodling
13. _____ (.277) Bobby Adams
14. _____ (.277) Ed Kranepool
15. _____ (.276) Jose Morales
16. _____ (.276) Ron Northey
17. _____ (.273) Sam Leslie
18. _____ (.273) Pat Kelly
19. _____ (.273) Debs Garms
20. _____ (.270) Peanuts Lowrey

20. DECADES OF BATTING CHAMPS

Listed below is one batting champ from each decade and the year in which he led the league. All you have to provide is the team for which he did it.

National League

1. _____ (1908) Honus Wagner
2. _____ (1917) Edd Roush
3. _____ (1929) Lefty O'Doul
4. _____ (1938) Ernie Lombardi
5. _____ (1945) Phil Cavarretta
6. _____ (1953) Carl Furillo
7. _____ (1968) Pete Rose
8. _____ (1970) Rico Carty
9. _____ (1982) Al Oliver

American League

1. _____ (1902) Ed Delahanty
2. _____ (1916) Tris Speaker
3. _____ (1923) Harry Heilmann
4. _____ (1936) Luke Appling
5. _____ (1945) George Stirnweiss
6. _____ (1951) Ferris Fain
7. _____ (1962) Pete Runnels
8. _____ (1970) Alex Johnson
9. _____ (1981) Carney Lansford

21. SUB-.320 BATTING LEADERS

Name the five players from the following ten who have won batting titles with averages that were less than .320: George Stirnweiss, Tony Oliva, Roberto Clemente, Rod Carew, Carl Yastrzemski, Ted Williams, Pete Runnels, Frank Robinson, Alex Johnson, and Elmer Flick.

1. _____ (.318) 1972
2. _____ (.316) 1966
3. _____ (.309) 1945
4. _____ (.306) 1905
5. _____ (.301) 1968

22. .390-PLUS RUNNERS-UP

Name the five players from the following ten who have failed to win batting titles with averages that were better than .390: Harry Heilmann, George Sisler, Babe Ruth, Joe Jackson, Ted Williams, Rogers Hornsby, Al Simmons, Ty Cobb, Babe Herman, and Bill Terry.

1. _____ (.408) 1911
2. _____ (.401) 1922
3. _____ (.393) 1923
4. _____ (.393) 1930
5. _____ (.392) 1927

23. STEPPING INTO THE BOX

In front of the 30 players who are listed, mark an "L" (left-handed), "R" (right-handed), or "S" (switch-hitter) for the way in which they hit.

1. _____ Mel Ott
2. _____ Ernie Lombardi
3. _____ Tom Tresh
4. _____ Tony Lazzeri
5. _____ Pete Rose
6. _____ Willard Marshall
7. _____ Jim Gilliam
8. _____ Wally Westlake
9. _____ Jim Gentile
10. _____ Bud Harrelson
11. _____ Granny Hamner
12. _____ Tommy Holmes
13. _____ George McQuinn
14. _____ Hector Lopez
15. _____ Smoky Burgess
16. _____ Wes Covington
17. _____ Phil Masi
18. _____ Sid Gordon
19. _____ Willie Miranda
20. _____ Maury Wills
21. _____ Nellie Fox
22. _____ Jimmie Foxx
23. _____ Red Schoendienst
24. _____ Eddie Waitkus
25. _____ Sam Mele
26. _____ Frankie Frisch
27. _____ Gino Cimoli
28. _____ Jim Rivera
29. _____ Mickey Mantle
30. _____ Roy White

The Shot Heard 'Round the World

Bobby Thomson's game-winning home run in the final playoff game of the 1951 season gave the Giants the most dramatic come-from-behind title in the history of baseball. It also provided trivia buffs with a gold mine of facts and questions.

Sal Maglie started the game for the Giants; Don Newcombe toed the mound for the Dodgers. They hooked up in a classic pitching duel until the eighth inning when the visiting Dodgers scored three runs to take a 4–1 lead. With Maglie departed from the scene and Newcombe mowing down the Giants in the bottom of the eighth, the Dodgers seemed virtually assured of winning their sixth National League pennant. But the Giants, who had fought back from a 13½-game deficit during the regular season, were not about to give up.

Al Dark led off the bottom of the ninth by singling to center. Charlie Dressen, the manager of the Dodgers, made a tactical mistake when he did not tell first baseman Gil Hodges to play behind the runner, for Don Mueller ripped a single to right, sending Dark to third. If Hodges had been playing deep, Mueller would have hit into a double play; and the Dodgers would have cinched the pennant, for Monte Irvin, the following batter, popped out. Whitey Lockman then ripped a double, scoring Dark and sending Mueller to third. Sliding into the base, Mueller broke his ankle and was replaced by pinch-runner Clint Hartung. That brought Thomson up to the plate with a free base at first. Had Dressen chosen to put the potential winning run on base, the Giants would have had to send a rookie up to the plate—Willie Mays.

Instead Dressen decided to change pitchers. He had Carl Erskine and Ralph Branca warming up in the bull pen. Erskine had looked the sharper of the two, but just before bull pen coach Clyde Sukeforth made his recommendation to Dressen, Erskine bounced a curve. That settled the matter: Branca got the call. When Branca walked in from the bull pen, some of the superstitious "faithful" from Flatbush must have got an ominous feeling when they noted the number "13" on the back of the pitcher's uniform. Coincidentally, Branca had 13 wins at the time. He also had 12 losses. After his second pitch to Thomson, which the "Staten Island Scot" hit for the pennant-winning homer, the 13's were balanced, all the way across.

Almost all of baseball's avid followers of the sport know that Branca was the losing pitcher in that fateful game. But I've run across very few baseball aficionados who know who the winning pitcher was. Do you?

(*Answer appears on page 321.*)

Chapter Three

THE PITCHERS

24. FAMOUS HOME RUN PITCHES

Match the following pitchers with the batters to whom they threw historic home run pitches: Don Newcombe, Bob Purkey, Bob Lemon, Ralph Terry, Howie Pollet, Robin Roberts, Ralph Branca, Jack Billingham, Al Downing, and Barney Schultz.

1. _____ He threw the home run pitch to Bill Mazeroski that gave the Pirates the 1960 World Series. The circuit clout gave Pittsburgh a 10–9 win.

2. _____ He threw the game-winning home run pitch to Joe DiMaggio in the top of the tenth inning in the second game of the 1950 World Series. The Yankees won, 2–1.

3. _____ He threw the home run pitch to Bobby Thomson in the final playoff game of the National League's 1951 season. The Giants outlasted the Dodgers, 5–4.

4. _____ He threw the three-run homer to Dick Sisler in the top of the tenth inning of the final game of the 1950 season. The home run gave Robin Roberts the margin of victory, and it gave the Phillies the National League pennant.

5. _____ He threw the pitch that Hank Aaron hit for home run number 714.

6. _____ He threw the pitch that Hank Aaron hit for home run number 715.

7. _____ He threw the tenth-inning home run pitch to Rudy York in the first game of the 1946 World Series. It gave the Red Sox a 3–2 victory.

8. _____ He threw the ninth-inning home run

pitch to Mickey Mantle in the third game of the 1964 World Series. It gave the Yankees a 2–1 victory.

9. _____ He threw the three-run homer to Dusty Rhodes in the bottom of the tenth inning in Game One of the 1954 World Series. The blow gave the Giants a 5–2 victory.

10. _____ He threw the ninth-inning home run pitch to Roger Maris in the third game of the 1961 World Series. The home run gave the Yankees a 3–2 win.

25. THE PITCHING MASTERS

Walter Johnson, Eddie Plank, Tom Seaver, Early Wynn, Cy Young, Lefty Grove, Warren Spahn, Christy Mathewson, Gaylord Perry, and Grover Alexander all won 300 or more games in their careers. Put them in their proper order. Also, identify the three 300-game winners who were still pitching in 1987.

1. _____ (511)
2. _____ (416)
3. _____ (373)
4. _____ (373)
5. _____ (363)
6. _____ (327)
7. _____ (314)
8. _____ (311)
9. _____ (300)
10. _____ (300)
11. _____ (still pitching)
12. _____ (still pitching)
13. _____ (still pitching)

26. THE PERFECT GAME

Ten of the following 20 pitchers have thrown perfect games: Walter Johnson, Tom Seaver, Carl Hubbell, Ernie Shore, Babe Ruth, Jim Hunter, Sal Maglie, Whitey Ford, Jim Bunning, Cy Young, Steve Carlton, Robin Roberts, Bob Feller, Addie Joss, Sandy Koufax, Wes Ferrell, Don Larsen, Charlie Robertson, Mike Witt, and Len Barker. Name them.

1. _____
2. _____
3. _____
4. _____
5. _____
6. _____
7. _____
8. _____
9. _____
10. _____

27. MULTIPLE NO-HITTERS

All of the 25 pitchers who are listed below have hurled no-hit games. Fifteen of them have done it more than once. In fact, one of them has done it five times; one of them, four times; two of them, three times; and 11 of them, twice. Match the pitcher with the number that denotes how many times he performed the feat.

Bobo Holloman
Mel Parnell
Johnny Vander Meer
Steve Busby
Rick Wise
Ken Holtzman
Don Wilson
Gaylord Perry
Dean Chance
Sandy Koufax
Jim Bunning
Juan Marichal
Bo Belinsky

Warren Spahn
Sam Jones
Milt Pappas
Bill Singer
Carl Erskine
Sal Maglie
Bob Feller
Virgil Trucks
Allie Reynolds
Jim Maloney
Don Larsen
Nolan Ryan

1. _____ (5)
2. _____ (4)
3. _____ (3)
4. _____ (3)
5. _____ (2)
6. _____ (2)
7. _____ (2)
8. _____ (2)

9. _____ (2)
10. _____ (2)
11. _____ (2)
12. _____ (2)
13. _____ (2)
14. _____ (2)
15. _____ (2)

28. BACK-TO-BACK 20-GAME WINNERS

Match the pitchers with the span of their careers when they recorded consecutive 20-game winning seasons.

1. _____ Tom Seaver		a.	1969–71
2. _____ Dave McNally		b.	1967–72
3. _____ Lefty Grove		c.	1910–19
4. _____ Paul Derringer		d.	1936–39
5. _____ Hal Newhouser		e.	1911–17
6. _____ Red Ruffing		f.	1968–69
7. _____ Warren Spahn		g.	1965–66
8. _____ Bob Feller		h.	1971–72
9. _____ Carl Hubbell		i.	1968–70
10. _____ Bob Lemon		j.	1963–66
11. _____ Denny McLain		k.	1933–37
12. _____ Vic Raschi		l.	1970–73
13. _____ Christy Mathewson		m.	1948–50
14. _____ Grover Cleveland Alexander		n.	1938–40
15. _____ Don Newcombe		o.	1903–14
16. _____ Juan Marichal		p.	1927–33
17. _____ Mike Cuellar		q.	1949–51
18. _____ Bob Gibson		r.	1942–44
19. _____ Walter Johnson		s.	1968–71
20. _____ Robin Roberts		t.	1939–41, 1946–47*
21. _____ Sandy Koufax		u.	1950–55
22. _____ Mort Cooper		v.	1956–61
23. _____ Ferguson Jenkins		w.	1944–46
24. _____ Jim Palmer		x.	1955–56
25. _____ Dizzy Dean		y.	1933–36
26. _____ Tommy John		z.	1979–80

* The pitcher's consecutive string of 20-win seasons was interrupted by the war.

29. THE FLAMETHROWERS

Name the 11 flamethrowers from the following 22 who have struck out 300 batters at least once in one season: Nolan Ryan, Tom Seaver, Sandy Koufax, Ferguson Jenkins, Mickey Lolich, Sam McDowell, Jim Lonborg, Bob Feller, Steve Carlton, Herb Score, Dwight Gooden, Jim Bunning, Walter Johnson, Don Drysdale, Bob Gibson, Red Ruffing, Rube Waddell, Vida Blue, Bob Turley, Carl Erskine, J. R. Richard, and Mike Scott.

1. _____
2. _____
3. _____
4. _____
5. _____
6. _____
7. _____
8. _____
9. _____
10. _____
11. _____

30. BLUE-CHIP PITCHERS

Ten of the 20 pitchers who are listed below have recorded winning percentages of .600 or better. Who are they?

Whitey Ford	Jim Perry
Ted Lyons	Vic Raschi
Early Wynn	Jim Kaat
Allie Reynolds	Don Drysdale
Jim Palmer	Sal Maglie
Robin Roberts	Dizzy Dean
Gaylord Perry	Sandy Koufax
Mort Cooper	Mickey Lolich
Tom Seaver	Claude Osteen
Waite Hoyt	Lefty Gomez

1. _____
2. _____
3. _____
4. _____
5. _____
6. _____
7. _____
8. _____
9. _____
10. _____

31. 200 TIMES A LOSER

Ten of the 20 pitchers listed below have lost 200 or more major league games. Name them.

Cy Young
Billy Pierce
Christy Mathewson
Bobo Newsom
Walter Johnson
Juan Marichal
Mel Harder
Warren Spahn
Grover Alexander.
Lefty Grove

Bob Feller
Red Ruffing
Milt Pappas
Carl Hubbell
Paul Derringer
Robin Roberts
Bob Gibson
Bob Friend
Early Wynn
Jim Bunning

1. _____
2. _____
3. _____
4. _____
5. _____
6. _____
7. _____
8. _____
9. _____
10. _____

32. WINDING UP

Mark "L" in the space provided for the pitchers who threw left-handed and "R" for the hurlers who threw right-handed. There are an even number of each contained in the list.

1. _____ Hal Newhouser
2. _____ Vernon Gomez
3. _____ Mike Garcia
4. _____ Eddie Lopat
5. _____ Virgil Trucks
6. _____ Ellis Kinder
7. _____ Billy Pierce
8. _____ Herb Score
9. _____ Bucky Walters
10. _____ Van Lingle Mungo
11. _____ Vic Raschi
12. _____ Johnny Sain
13. _____ Preacher Roe
14. _____ Dave Koslo
15. _____ Billy Loes
16. _____ Ned Garver
17. _____ Billy Hoeft
18. _____ Don Mossi
19. _____ Frank Lary
20. _____ Max Lanier
21. _____ Harry Brecheen
22. _____ Johnny Podres
23. _____ Larry Jansen
24. _____ Lew Burdette
25. _____ Mudcat Grant
26. _____ Vernon Law
27. _____ Mel Parnell
28. _____ Rip Sewell
29. _____ Tommy Byrne
30. _____ Ron Perranoski

The Asterisk Pitcher

The pitcher who threw the best game that has ever been spun lost the decision. If you don't believe me, you can look it up. Or, better still, you could ask Harvey Haddix.

On May 26, 1959, the Pirates' left-hander pitched a perfect game for nine innings against the host Braves. That puts him in the select company of Cy Young, Addie Joss, Ernie Shore, Charlie Robertson. Don Larsen, Jim Bunning, Sandy Koufax, Jim Hunter, Len Barker, and Mike Witt, the only other pitchers who have thrown a nine-inning perfect game in the modern era. But Haddix was not as fortunate as his select peers. Their teams gave them sufficient support to win the games. Haddix's club did not.

So "The Kitten" was forced to prove that he could pitch a game that had never been thrown before. He put the Braves down one, two, three in the tenth; he mowed them down in order in the eleventh; and he sailed through the lineup in sequence in the twelfth. But still his teammates, though they had touched Lew Burdette for 12 hits, could not dent the plate the one time that was needed to give their special southpaw instant immortality.

Inning 13 proved to be unlucky for Haddix. Felix Mantilla, the first batter, reached first when third baseman Don Hoak made a throwing error on an easy ground ball. Eddie Mathews bunted Mantilla into scoring position. Haddix was then forced to intentionally pass Hank Aaron to set up the double play for the slow-running Joe Adcock. But Adcock crossed up the strategy by hitting a three-run homer to right center.

Yet the final score was only 1–0. And Haddix got credit for another out. Technically, he could have been credited with an additional out. If he had, he might have gotten out of the inning without a run being scored.

Can you unravel that strange sequence of circumstances?
(*Answer appears on page 321.*)

Chapter Four

MULTIPLE CHOICE

33. FOUR BASES TO SCORE

1. _____ Who were the Dodger runners when Cookie Lavagetto's game-winning double with two outs in the bottom of the ninth inning broke up Bill Bevens' no-hitter in the 1947 World Series?
   a. Jackie Robinson and Eddie Stanky b. Eddie Miksis and Pete Reiser c. Jackie Robinson and Spider Jorgensen d. Al Gionfriddo and Eddie Miksis

2. _____ Whom did Don Larsen strike out for the final out in his perfect game in the 1956 World Series?
   a. Gil Hodges b. Roy Campanella c. Dale Mitchell d. Carl Furillo

3. _____ Against whom did Willie Mays hit his first major league home run?
   a. Bob Buhl b. Warren Spahn c. Larry Jansen d. Robin Roberts

4. _____ Against whom did Hank Aaron hit his first major league home run?
   a. Curt Simmons b. Vic Raschi c. Lew Burdette d. Don Newcombe

5. _____ Who hit the last home run in the initial Yankee Stadium?
   a. Duke Sims b. Norm Cash c. Carl Yastrzemski d. Bobby Murcer

6. _____ Who hit the first home run in Shea Stadium?
   a. Willie Stargell b. Frank Thomas c. Stan Musial d. Frank Howard

7. _____ Who were the Giant runners when Bobby Thomson hit the playoff home run against the Dodgers in 1951 to decide the pennant?
   a. Don Mueller and Whitey Lockman b. Al Dark and

Don Mueller c. Whitey Lockman and Al Dark d. Clint Hartung and Whitey Lockman

8. _____ Which team was the last all-white club that won the American League pennant?

    a. 1947 Yankees b. 1953 Yankees c. 1959 White Sox d. 1965 Twins

9. _____ Who hit .400 in World Series play a record three times?

    a. Ty Cobb b. Babe Ruth c. Lou Gehrig d. Eddie Collins

10. _____ Who was the only Yankee who has won two batting titles?

    a. Joe DiMaggio b. Mickey Mantle c. Lou Gehrig d. Babe Ruth

11. _____ Who was doubled off first when Sandy Amoros made the game-saving catch on Yogi Berra's fly ball in the seventh inning of the seventh game of the 1955 World Series between the Dodgers and the Yankees?

    a. Billy Martin b. Elston Howard c. Gil McDougald d. Hank Bauer

12. _____ Which team holds the American League record of 111 wins in one season?

    a. 1946 Red Sox b. 1927 Yankees c. 1959 White Sox d. 1954 Indians

13. _____ Who was the National League player who moved into third place on the all-time pinch-hit list in 1987?

    a. Lee Mazzilli b. Greg Gross c. Manny Sanguillen d. Graig Nettles

14. _____ Who was the American League rookie in 1987 who hit five home runs in two consecutive games?

    a. Mickey Brantley b. Bob Jackson c. Mark McGwire d. Ellis Burks

15. _____ Which National League team holds the major league record of 116 wins in one season?

    a. 1906 Cubs b. 1930 Cardinals c. 1952 Dodgers d. 1976 Reds

16. _____ Which of the following players has not recorded 500 putouts in one season?

    a. Joe DiMaggio b. Dom DiMaggio c. Vince DiMaggio d. Richie Ashburn

17. _____ Who is the only player who has won home run titles in both leagues?

    a. Frank Robinson b. Sam Crawford c. Hank Greenberg d. Johnny Mize

18. _____ Who is the only player who has won batting titles in both leagues?

a. Lefty O'Doul b. Dixie Walker c. Rogers Hornsby
d. Ed Delahanty

19. _____ Who was the last player who hit more than 50 home runs in one season?

a. Mickey Mantle b. Roger Maris c. George Foster
d. Willie McCovey

20. _____ Which of these former Yankees did not play in a World Series with a National League club?

a. Roger Maris b. Bill Skowron c. Hank Borowy d. Vic Raschi

21. _____ Which of the following players did not win the RBI title with two teams in the same league?

a. Orlando Cepeda b. Vern Stephens c. Johnny Mize
d. Ralph Kiner

22. _____ Which of the following pitchers did not lose more games than he won?

a. Bobo Newsom b. Murry Dickson c. Bob Friend
d. Dizzy Trout

23. _____ Whose line drive, which almost provided the margin of victory, did Bobby Richardson catch for the final out of the 1962 World Series?

a. Willie McCovey b. Jim Davenport c. Jose Pagan
d. Orlando Cepeda

24. _____ Which of the following pitchers won the first playoff game in American League history?

a. Denny Galehouse b. Bob Feller c. Gene Bearden
d. Mel Parnell

25. _____ Who was the losing pitcher for the Dodgers on the day that Don Larsen threw his perfect game in the 1956 World Series?

a. Clem Labine b. Johnny Podres c. Don Newcombe
d. Sal Maglie

26. _____ Which of the following umpires worked his last game behind the plate on the day that Don Larsen pitched his perfect game?

a. Jocko Conlan b. Augie Donatelli c. Babe Pinelli
d. George Magerkurth

27. _____ Which one of the following players won back-to-back American League batting titles in the 1950s?

a. Al Rosen b. Bobby Avila c. Ferris Fain d. Al Kaline

28. _____ Which one of the following players won back-to-back National League batting titles in the 1960s?

a. Matty Alou b. Dick Groat c. Tommy Davis d. Richie Ashburn

29. _____ Which one of the following shortstops did not win a batting title?

a. Dick Groat b. Lou Boudreau c. Luke Appling d. Luis Aparicio

30. _____ What was the name of the midget whom Bill Veeck sent up to the plate to pinch-hit for the Browns?

a. Frank Gabler b. Ed Gallagher c. Dick Kokos d. Eddie Gaedel

31. _____ Which one of the following first basemen was the only right-handed hitter?

a. Gordy Coleman b. Dick Gernert c. Norm Cash d. Luke Easter

32. _____ Which one of the following catchers never won an MVP Award?

a. Yogi Berra b. Bill Dickey c. Roy Campanella d. Johnny Bench

33. _____ Which one of the following players did not win the MVP Award three times?

a. Joe DiMaggio b. Stan Musial c. Willie Mays d. Roy Campanella

34. _____ Which runner stole home a record two times in World Series play?

a. Bob Meusel b. Ty Cobb c. Lou Brock d. Jackie Robinson

35. _____ Which one of the following teams did not win four world's championships in one decade?

a. 1910 Red Sox b. 1920 Giants c. 1930 Yankees d. 1940 Yankees

36. _____ Who was the last National League batter who hit .400?

a. Rogers Hornsby b. Lefty O'Doul c. Bill Terry d. Arky Vaughan

37. _____ Against whom did Babe Ruth "call his shot" in the 1932 World Series?

a. Lon Warneke b. Guy Bush c. Burleigh Grimes d. Charlie Root

38. _____ Who hit the "homer in the dark" for the Cubs in 1938?

a. Gabby Hartnett b. Billy Herman c. Stan Hack d. Phil Cavarretta

39. _____ Who misplayed two outfield fly balls for the Cubs when the Athletics rallied with ten runs in the seventh inning of the fourth game of the 1929 World Series to win, 10–8?

a. Kiki Cuyler b. Riggs Stephenson c. Cliff Heathcote d. Hack Wilson

40. _____ Which one of the following teams won the most recent pennant?

a. White Sox b. Phillies c. Indians d. Cubs

41. _____ Who has been the only American League player, in addition to Ty Cobb, who twice hit over .400?

a. Joe Jackson b. Nap Lajoie c. George Sisler d. Harry Heilmann

42. _____ Who was the last National League pitcher who won 30 games in a season?

a. Carl Hubbell b. Dizzy Dean c. Robin Roberts d. Sandy Koufax

43. _____ Who compiled the highest career batting average for left-handers in the history of the National League?

a. Lefty O'Doul b. Bill Terry c. Stan Musial d. Paul Waner

44. _____ Who holds the National League record for playing in the most consecutive games (1,209)?

a. Gus Suhr b. Stan Musial c. Billy Williams d. Steve Garvey

45. _____ Whose modern-day mark did Joe DiMaggio surpass when he batted safely in 56 consecutive games?

a. George Sisler b. Heinie Manush c. Ty Cobb d. Al Simmons

46. _____ Which one of Babe Ruth's following teammates was the only Yankee to hit more home runs in one season than the "Sultan of Swat" during the 1920s?

a. Bob Meusel b. Lou Gehrig c. Tony Lazzeri d. Bill Dickey

47. _____ Which pitcher came the closest to duplicating Johnny Vander Meer's feat of hurling consecutive no-hitters?

a. Nolan Ryan b. Sandy Koufax c. Virgil Trucks d. Ewell Blackwell

48. _____ Which one of the following players did not conclude his career with the Mets?

a. Richie Ashburn b. Gil Hodges c. Gene Woodling d. Eddie Yost

49. _____ Which one of the following catchers did not make an error in 117 games during the 1946 season?

a. Buddy Rosar b. Frank Hayes c. Del Rice d. Mickey Owens

50. _____ Which one of the following teams didn't Bucky Harris manage?

a. Phillies b. Tigers c. Senators d. Braves

51. _____ Who has been the only left-handed batter in National League history to hit 50 home runs in a season?

a. Roger Maris b. Johnny Mize c. Mel Ott d. Lou Gehrig

52. _____ Who holds the American League record for shutouts in one season by a left-handed pitcher?

a. Babe Ruth and Ron Guidry b. Lefty Grove c. Whitey Ford d. Mel Parnell

53. _____ Who was the youngest player ever elected to the Hall of Fame?

a. Ted Williams b. Roberto Clemente c. Sandy Koufax d. Dizzy Dean

54. _____ Which one of the following players did not hit two grand slams in one game?

a. Frank Robinson b. Frank Howard c. Tony Cloninger d. Jim Northrup

55. _____ Which one of the following Yankees stole home the most times (10) in the club's history?

a. Lou Gehrig b. Ben Chapman c. Phil Rizzuto d. George Stirnweiss

56. _____ Who holds the American League record for stealing home the most times (7) in one season?

a. Ty Cobb b. Eddie Collins c. Rod Carew d. Bert Campaneris

57. _____ Who holds the National League record for stealing home the most times (7) in one season?

a. Jackie Robinson b. Pete Reiser c. Lou Brock d. Maury Wills

58. _____ Who were the three players on the same team who hit more than 40 home runs each in the same season?

a. Babe Ruth, Lou Gehrig, Bob Meusel b. Hank Aaron, Davy Johnson, Darrell Evans c. Hank Aaron, Eddie Mathews, Wes Covington d. Johnny Mize, Willard Marshall, Walker Cooper

59. _____ Who was the first black coach in the American League?

a. Larry Doby b. Elston Howard c. Minnie Minoso d. Satchel Paige

60. _____ Who was the first black coach in the National League?

a. Ernie Banks b. Joe Black c. Buck O'Neil d. Willie Mays

61. _____ Who started the double play that ended Joe DiMaggio's 56-game hitting streak?

a. Ken Keltner b. Lou Boudreau c. Ray Mack d. Hal Trosky

62. _____ What was the most money that the Yankees ever paid Babe Ruth for a season?

a. $100,000 b. $125,000 c. $75,000 d. $80,000

63. _____ Which pair of players did not tie for a National League home run title?

a. Ralph Kiner–Johnny Mize b. Ralph Kiner–Hank Sauer c. Willie McCovey–Hank Aaron d. Willie Mays–Hank Aaron

64. _____ Which pair of players did not tie for an American League home run title?

a. Hank Greenberg–Jimmy Foxx b. Carl Yastrzemski–Harmon Killebrew c. Babe Ruth–Lou Gehrig d. Reggie Jackson–Dick Allen

65. _____ Who hit the first home run in the initial Yankee Stadium?

a. Babe Ruth b. Wally Pipp c. Bob Meusel d. Joe Dugan

66. _____ Who hit the first home run in the renovated Yankee Stadium?

a. Dan Ford b. Tony Oliva c. Graig Nettles d. Chris Chambliss

67. _____ Who led the National League in home runs for the most consecutive years (7)?

a. Chuck Klein b. Mel Ott c. Ralph Kiner d. Hank Aaron

68. _____ Who were the two players who hit five grand slams in one season?

a. Jim Northrup–Ralph Kiner b. Willie McCovey–Frank Robinson c. Ernie Banks–Jim Gentile d. Harmon Killebrew–Eddie Mathews

69. _____ Who has pitched the most consecutive shutouts (6) in one season?

a. Bob Gibson b. Sal Maglie c. Walter Johnson d. Don Drysdale

70. _____ Which one of the following pitchers did not strike out 19 batters in one game?

a. Bob Feller b. Steve Carlton c. Nolan Ryan d. Tom Seaver

71. _____ Who was the first major leaguer who hit .400 in a season?

a. Ty Cobb b. Nap Lajoie c. Joe Jackson d. George Sisler

72. _____ Who broke Ty Cobb's run of nine straight batting titles in 1916?

a. Tris Speaker b. George Sisler c. Hal Chase d. Harry Heilmann

73. _____ Who was the only non-Yankee who won a home run title in the 1920s?

a. Al Simmons b. Goose Goslin c. Ken Williams d. Jimmie Foxx

74. _____ Which one of the following American Leaguers did not win back-to-back batting titles?

  a. Ted Williams b. Pete Runnels c. Joe DiMaggio d. Carl Yastrzemski

75. _____ Which one of the following National Leaguers did not win back-to-back batting titles?

  a. Pete Rose b. Roberto Clemente c. Stan Musial d. Jackie Robinson

76. _____ Which one of the following pitchers lost a ground ball "in the sun" in a World Series game?

  a. Lefty Gomez b. Billy Loes c. Dave Koslo d. Vida Blue

77. _____ With what team did Red Ruffing conclude his career?

  a. Red Sox b. Yankees c. Athletics d. White Sox

78. _____ Against whom did Mickey Mantle hit his last World Series home run?

  a. Curt Simmons b. Barney Schultz c. Harvey Haddix d. Bob Gibson

79. _____ Which one of the following Cub players was called "Swish"?

  a. Stan Hack b. Phil Cavarretta c. Billy Jurges d. Bill Nicholson

80. _____ Which one of the following players had a career which did not span four decades?

  a. Stan Musial b. Ted Williams c. Mickey Vernon d. Early Wynn

81. _____ Which one of the following managers did not win a pennant in both leagues?

  a. Joe McCarthy b. Bill McKechnie c. Yogi Berra d. Al Dark

82. _____ Which one of the following Red pitchers played more than 200 games at third base?

  a. Paul Derringer b. Jim Maloney c. Bob Purkey d. Bucky Walters

83. _____ Which pitcher who won three games in the 1912 World Series later starred in the outfield for another American League team that played in the 1920 autumn classic?

  a. Babe Ruth b. Joe Wood c. Duffy Lewis d. Harry Hooper

84. _____ Which former Yankee pitcher switched to the outfield and compiled a .349 lifetime average?

  a. Rube Bressler b. Dixie Walker c. Lefty O'Doul d. Babe Ruth

85. _____ Which of the following Yankee players came up to the majors as a pitcher, switched to the outfield, and ended his big league career on the mound?

a. Johnny Lindell b. Cliff Mapes c. Marius Russo d. Ernie Bonham

86. _____ Which pair of the following players comprised a major league battery?

a. Ted Lyons–Buddy Rosar b. Ellis Kinder–Ernie Lombardi c. Allie Reynolds–Bill Dickey d. Rex Barney–Bruce Edwards

87. _____ Which one of the following players had the nickname of "Lucky"?

a. Whitey Lockman b. Jack Lohrke c. Jim Lemon d. Ted Lepcio

88. _____ Who was the player who once hit three home runs in one game off Whitey Ford?

a. Clyde Vollmer b. Dick Gernert c. Pat Seerey d. Jim Lemon

89. _____ Which one of the following one-two punches had the most home runs on the same team?

a. Babe Ruth–Lou Gehrig b. Mickey Mantle–Roger Maris c. Hank Aaron–Eddie Mathews d. Ernie Banks–Ron Santo

90. _____ Which one of the following pitchers took a timeout in World Series play to watch a plane fly overhead?

a. Daffy Dean b. Dizzy Trout c. Lefty Gomez d. Dazzy Vance

91. _____ Which pair of the following brothers competed against each other in World Series play?

a. Dizzy and Daffy Dean b. Jim and Gaylord Perry c. Ken and Clete Boyer d. Matty and Felipe Alou

92. _____ Which one of the following players was not a member of the "Whiz Kids"?

a. Andy Seminick b. Russ Meyer c. Mike Goliat d. Harry Walker

93. _____ Which one of the following pitchers was the only one to lose a World Series game?

a. Jack Coombs b. Herb Pennock c. Lefty Gomez d. Catfish Hunter

94. _____ Who was the only Phillie pitcher before 1980 who won a World Series game?

a. Grover Cleveland Alexander b. Robin Roberts c. Eppa Rixey d. Jim Konstanty

95. _____ Which one of the following players did not "jump" to the Mexican League?

a. Mickey Owen b. Luis Olmo c. Johnny Hopp d. Max Lanier

96. _____ Who made a shoestring catch of an infield fly to save a World Series?

a. Billy Herman b. Billy Johnson c. Billy Martin d. Bobby Avila

97. _____ Which one of the Indians' "Big Four" won a World Series game with another American League team?

a. Bob Feller b. Bob Lemon c. Mike Garcia d. Early Wynn

98. _____ Which one of the following players did not win an American League home run title with a total below 30?

a. Babe Ruth b. Nick Etten c. Vern Stephens d. Reggie Jackson

99. _____ Which one of the following players did not win a National League home run crown with a total below 30?

a. Hack Wilson b. Johnny Mize c. Ralph Kiner d. Mike Schmidt

100. _____ Which one of the following players once hit 54 home runs in a season but did not win the league's home run title?

a. Ralph Kiner b. Willie Mays c. Mickey Mantle d. Hank Greenberg

Exceptions to the Rule

Most umpires know the rule book from cover to cover. But occasionally a situation that is not covered by the rule book takes place. Then the umpires are in trouble.

Take, for example, the uproar that Herman "Germany" Schaefer created with his zany base running in a game between the Senators and the White Sox in 1911. With the score tied and two outs in the ninth inning, the Senators put runners on the corners, Clyde Milan on third and Schaefer on first. That's the moment when Schaefer decided to create confusion.

On the first pitch to a weak batter, Schaefer promptly stole second without a throw from the catcher. On the next pitch he proceeded to steal first, once again without a throw, but this time with a storm of protest from the White Sox bench. What base was Schaefer entitled to? the Sox wanted to know. The umpires thumbed through the rule book, but they failed to find any clause that prevented a runner from stealing any base that he had previously occupied. So, on the following pitch, Schaefer did the predictable: he stole second again. The frustrated catcher finally relented and threw the ball to second base. But Schaefer beat the throw and Milan raced home with the winning run.

Shortly thereafter, an amendment to the rule book was made: no base runner could steal a base out of sequence. The rules makers decided that Schaefer had tried to make a travesty of the game.

Another bizarre base running feat took place in 1963. This time it involved a Met runner, Jimmy Piersall, who was coming to the end of a celebrated—and clownish—career. In the game in which he hit his 100th career homer, he did something which indelibly impressed the event in the minds of all the people who saw it: he ran around the bases backwards.

Once again the umpires pored through the fine print of the rule book. But it was of no avail: there was no rule which prevented a runner from circling the bases backwards after he had hit a home run. Shortly thereafter, however, there was. The rules makers once again concluded that the runner (Piersall) had tried to make a mockery of the game.

So today, batters who hit home runs have to touch the bases in their proper order.

One more ludicrous baseball situation took place in St. Louis in 1951. In a game between the hometown Browns and the Tigers, the always innovative owner of St. Louis, Bill Veeck, staged a scene that baseball fans still laugh about. In the first inning of the second game of a double-header, Zack Taylor, the manager of St. Louis, sent a midget up to the plate to pinch-hit for the leadoff batter, Frank Saucier. The umpires demanded that Taylor put an end to the farce. But Taylor was ready for them, rule book in hand: there was no provision in the baseball guide that prevented the batter with the number ⅛ on his back from taking his turn at the plate. The next day, you can feel safe to assume, there was.

But before the amendment was made, the batter walked on four consecutive pitches before giving way to a pinch-runner. What most probably comes readily to mind is the name of the midget, Eddie Gaedel. He is the subject of an often-asked trivia question. But what might not come so quickly to mind is the name of the pitcher who threw to the smallest target in baseball history, the name of the catcher who gave the lowest target in the history of the game, and the umpire who had the smallest strike zone in the annals of the sport.

Consider yourself to be in the ranks of a select few if you can name two of the three individuals who figured prominently in one of the most bizarre pitcher-batter confrontations that has ever taken place.

(Answer appears on page 321.)

Chapter Five

FROM RUTH TO REGGIE

34. FROM RUTH TO REGGIE

1. _____ Which slugger (1933–47) missed almost six years of playing time because of the Second World War and injuries and still managed to hit 331 career home runs?

2. _____ Which Indian pitcher, who was 15–0 at the time, lost his only game of the year in his last start?

3. _____ Whose line drive in the 1937 All-Star Game broke Dizzy Dean's toe?

4. _____ Which White Sox pitcher lost one of his legs in a hunting accident?

5. _____ Who was the Indian manager whom the players petitioned the Cleveland owners to fire in 1940?

6. _____ Who pitched a no-hitter on the opening day of the 1940 season?

7. _____ Who was the only player to win the Rookie of the Year Award, the Most Valuable Player Award, and the Triple Crown?

8. _____ Whose home run on the final day of the 1945 season won the pennant for the Tigers?

9. _____ Whose home run on the final night of the 1976 season won the pennant for the Yankees?

10. _____ Which pitcher, who was acquired from the Yankees, led the Cubs to the pennant in 1945?

11. _____ Who scored the only run in the first game of the 1948 World Series after Bob Feller "almost" picked him off second base?

12. _____Who was the manager of the Red Sox in 1948–49 when they lost the pennants on the last day of the season?

13. _____ Who was the last playing manager?

14. _____ Who was the last playing manager who led his team to a pennant?

15. _____ Who was the name star that the Yankees traded to the Indians for Allie Reynolds in 1948?

16. _____ Who was the American League home run king of 1959 who was traded after the season for batting champ Harvey Kuenn?

17. _____ Which former Giant relief specialist, then with the Orioles, threw the pitch that Mickey Mantle hit for his 500th home run?

18. _____ Who invented the "Williams's Shift"?

19. _____ Which slugging American League outfielder broke his elbow in the 1950 All-Star Game?

20. _____ Which Dodger outfielder did Richie Ashburn throw out at the plate in the ninth inning of the last game of the 1950 season to send the Phillies into extra innings and subsequently the World Series?

21. _____ Who threw a no-hitter in his first major league start?

22. _____ Who threw the pitch that Mickey Mantle hit for his 565-foot home run?

23. _____ Which manager did Walter O'Malley fire for demanding a three-year contract?

24. _____ Who was the 20-game season winner and the two-game World Series winner for the Giants in 1954 whom they acquired from the Braves for Bobby Thomson?

25. _____ Who took Bobby Thomson's center-field position for the Giants?

26. _____ Who took Bobby Thomson's left-field position—when he broke his ankle—for the Milwaukee Braves?

27. _____ Which Indian slugging outfielder–first baseman was afflicted with polio in 1955?

28. _____ Which pitcher did Joe Adcock literally run off the mound in the early 1950s?

29. _____, Dave McNally, Jim Palmer, and Mike Cuellar were 20-game winners for the Orioles in 1971.

30. _____ Who was the one-time "Wildman" for the Yankees who lost the final game of the 1955 World Series to the Dodgers' Johnny Podres, 2–0?

31. _____ Which versatile infielder hit the line drive which struck Herb Score in the eye?

32. _____ Which pitcher, picked up on waivers from the Indians, won 13 games down the stretch, including

a no-hitter against the Phillies, to pitch the Dodgers to the 1956 pennant?

33. _____ Who hit two two-run homers against Don Newcombe in the 1956 World Series finale to lead the Yankees to a 9–0 victory over the Dodgers?

34. _____ Which Yankee infielder was hit in the throat by Bill Virdon's bad-hop ground ball in the 1960 World Series?

35. _____ Which team was the first in history to come back from a 3–1 World Series deficit in games and win the autumn classic?

36. _____ Which team was the most recent to perform the same feat?

37. _____ Who, in addition to Rogers Hornsby and Nap Lajoie, was the only right-handed batter to hit .400?

38. _____ Which Dodger catcher's throwing arm stopped the "Go-Go Sox" in the 1959 World Series?

39. _____ Who lost his job as a result of Bill Mazeroski's seventh-game home run in the 1960 World Series?

40. _____ Who threw the 60th home run ball to Babe Ruth in 1927?

41. _____ Who threw the 61st home run pitch to Roger Maris in 1961?

42. _____ Who was Whitey Ford's "save-ior" in 1961?

43. _____ Which of the Yankee reserve catchers hit four consecutive home runs in 1961?

44. _____ Who was the pitcher who was known as the "Yankee Killer" in the early 1960s?

45. _____ Which Hall of Famer wore the uniforms of all four New York teams: Giants, Dodgers, Yankees, and Mets?

46. _____ Which Yankee infielder was known for his "harmonica playing"?

47. _____ Which Giant pitcher once hit Johnny Roseboro with a bat?

48. _____ Whom did Sandy Koufax team up with in a joint holdout in 1966?

49. _____ Which Dodger outfielder committed three errors in one inning in the 1966 World Series?

50. _____ For whom did the Reds trade Frank Robinson?

51. _____ Who was known as "Bullet Bob"?

52. _____ What position did Jackie Robinson play when he first came up with the Dodgers?

53. _____ Who was the Commissioner of Baseball when Jackie Robinson broke the color barrier?

54. _____ Who was the first black manager?

55. _____ Who lost three fly balls in the sun, in the same World Series game for the Yankees, in 1957?

56. _____ Which Indian third baseman drove home better than 100 runs per season for five consecutive years in the early 1950s?

57. _____ Which Phillie outfielder didn't make an error during a record 266 consecutive games?

58. _____ Who was Babe Ruth's manager during his final major league season with the Boston Braves?

59. _____ Which free agent (Charley Finley style) did the Red Sox pick up in 1967 to help them win the pennant?

60. _____ Who was the last pitcher to win 30 or more games?

61. _____ Which Brave batter was awarded first base in the 1957 World Series when the black polish on the ball proved that he had been hit with the preceding pitch?

62. _____ Which Met batter was awarded first base in the same manner in the 1969 World Series?

63. _____ Which Senator outfielder filed suit against baseball's reserve system in the early 1970s?

64. _____ Who was the most recent player who won the batting title without hitting a home run?

65. _____ Which second-string catcher, at the time, hit four home runs in a World Series?

66. _____ Which manager resigned after leading his team to two world's championships in the 1970s?

67. _____ With what team did Leo Durocher break into the majors in 1928?

68. _____ Which 35-year-old pitcher, who had appeared in only 11 games all season long, surprised the baseball world by striking out a record 13 batters in the A's opening-game win over the Cubs in the 1929 World Series?

69. _____ Which National League team once posted a .315 team batting average but finished last in the standings?

70. _____ Who won seven games and saved four others in World Series play?

71. _____ Whose home run won the first All-Star Game in 1933?

72. _____ What city was the only one to produce two Triple Crown winners in the same year (1933)?

73. _____ Who succeeded John McGraw as manager of the Giants?

74. _____ Which pitching brothers won 49 games in 1934?

75. _____ Whom did Commissioner Kenesaw Mountain Landis remove from the last game of the 1934 World Series in order to insure the player's safety?

76. _____ Who had a career average of .439 for four World Series?

77. _____ Who got the most hits in one season in the National League?

78. _____ Who stole the most bases in one season in the American League?

79. _____ Which pitcher chalked up the best winning percentages for hurlers with less than 200 but more than 100 wins?

80. _____ Who lost more games than any other pitcher in World Series play?

81. _____ Who was the last Yankee player before Don Mattingly to amass 200 hits in a season?

82. _____ Who was the last Dodger player to win a home run title?

83. _____ Who was the last Yankee player to win a home run title?

84. _____ Who was the only American League player who won a batting title while splitting his time with two teams?

85. _____ Who was the only National League player who won a batting title while performing for two different teams?

86. _____ Who made nine hits in an 18-inning game?

87. _____ Which Yankee pitcher ended Mickey Cochrane's career when he felled the Tigers' playing manager with a high, hard one?

88. _____ Who was the last playing manager in the National League who led his team to a pennant?

89. _____ Which slugging Brave outfielder missed the 1948 World Series—he never played in one—because of a broken ankle he sustained in a collision at home plate during the last week of the season?

90. _____ Whom did the Dodgers trade to the Pirates because he "jumped" the team on its tour of Japan after the 1966 world Series?

91. _____ Which famous pitcher had to retire prematurely because of the potentially dire effects which could have been produced by his arthritic elbow?

92. _____ Who was the Commissioner of Baseball who was fired in 1968?

93. _____ Which National League manager, who was a former first baseman, was fired in August of 1938 when his team, the Cubs, was in third place? The Cubs then went on to win the pennant under Gabby Hartnett.

94. _____ Which Yankee catcher holds the major league record of handling 950 consecutive chances without making an error?

95. _____ Which Astro catcher set a major league record when he played 138 consecutive games without making an error?

96. _____ Who recorded the highest lifetime average (.358) in the history of the National League?

97. _____ Who holds the American League mark of 184 RBIs in a season?

98. _____ Which two players walked 148 times in one season to tie for the National League high in that department?

99. _____ Who recorded the most shutouts in one season in the American League?

100. _____ Whose base hit drove home the winning run for the Reds in the 1975 World Series against the Red Sox?

The Mystery Death

Going into the 1940 season, baseball experts would never have believed that the hero of the upcoming World Series would be Jimmie Wilson, for the .284 lifetime hitter had recently settled down to life as a full-time coach with the Reds after donning the "tools of ignorance" for 17 seasons. But fate has been known to throw tricky pitches to a baseball team.

Ernie Lombardi, the team's regular catcher, had won the batting title two years before; he would also win it two years later. Behind him was a .316 lifetime hitter. So there didn't seem to be any need for Wilson's services.

But on August 2 the second-string catcher took his own life in Boston, and in mid-September Lombardi sprained his ankle. So Wilson was rushed back into action.

Down the stretch, "Ace" batted only .234, but he was primed up by World Series time. He handled the serves of two-game winners Bucky Walters and Paul Derringer faultlessly, and he swung a torrid bat, hitting .353 in the six games he played. In addition, the 40-year-old catcher stole the only base of the entire series.

The following season, Wilson went into permanent retirement, Lombardi took over the regular catching chores once again, and the reasons for the substitute catcher's suicide remained a mystery.

The identity of that .316 lifetime hitter is pretty much a mystery, too. Can you solve it?

(Answer appears on page 321.)

Chapter Six

BASEBALL'S DID YOU KNOW

The PHILLIES of 1961 lost a record 23 straight games.

The METS of 1962 lost 120 games, a single-season record.

GAYLORD PERRY was the only pitcher to win the Cy Young Award in both leagues. He won it with the Indians in 1972 and the Padres in 1978.

SATCHEL PAIGE, who was 59 years old when he pitched for Kansas City in 1965, has been the oldest player to perform in the major leagues.

DIOMEDES OLIVO was 41 when he broke in with the 1960 Pirates. Two years later, at 43, he appeared in 62 games and was 5–1.

FRED ODWELL hit only one home run before his nine four-base blows won the title in 1905; afterward, the Red outfielder never hit another major league home run.

STAN MUSIAL, of the top 15 players to ground into career double plays, was the only left-handed batter.

THURMAN MUNSON was the only Yankee to win both the Rookie of the Year Award (1970) and the MVP Award (1976).

DAVE McNALLY and Mike Cuellar of the 1970 Orioles were the last two pitchers from the same team to tie for the league lead in victories with 24.

WILLIE MAYS has been the only player to hit four home runs in one game and three triples in another.

DAL MAXVILL of the 1968 Cards had the most official at-bats (22) without collecting a hit in a World Series.

J. C. MARTIN of the 1965 White Sox committed a record 33 passed balls in one season. Tom Egan of the 1970 Angels and Mike Stanley of the 1987 Rangers let five pitches get by them in one game; Ray Kaat of the 1954 Giants couldn't handle four serves in one inning.

ROGER MARIS, who hit a record 61 home runs in 1961, won only one home run title.

MARTY MARION, the stellar shortstop of the Cards, was the last manager (1953) of the Browns.

MICKEY MANTLE was the first player to hit a home run in the Astrodome. He did it in an exhibition game between the Yankees and the Astros in 1962.

BILL MADLOCK was the last player to win a batting title one year and be traded away the next season. In 1976 Madlock batted .339 to cop the crown while he was a member of the Cubs. The following year, he was traded to the Giants.

ERNIE LOMBARDI set a major league mark by grounding into the most double plays in the National League in five different seasons.

TED LYONS of the 1935 White Sox and Hank Borowy of the 1946 Cubs, both of whom were pitchers, doubled twice in the same inning.

LEFTY O'DOUL, a pitcher with the pennant-winning Yankees in 1922, and Rube Bressler, a pitcher with the pennant-winning Athletics of 1914, both gained fame as outfielders: O'Doul won two batting titles in the National League and hit .349 lifetime; Bressler hit .302 for his career.

SANDY KOUFAX, the youngest player ever to be elected to the Hall of Fame, received the most votes of any electee—344—in the 1972 balloting.

SANDY KOUFAX (1963 and 1965–66), Tom Seaver (1969, 1973, and 1975), and Jim Palmer (1973 and 1975–76) have won the Cy Young Award three times. Steve Carlton, of course, has won it a record four times.

DAVE KOSLO broke the Yankees' nine-game opening-game World Series winning streak in 1951 when he bested Allie Reynolds, 5–1. The last time that the Bronx Bombers had lost the lead game of the fall classic had been in 1936 when Carl Hubbell, also of the Giants, defeated them, 6–1.

GEORGE KELL of the 1945 Athletics went 0-for-10 in a 24-inning game. His lifetime average, though, was .306.

BOB KEEGAN, a 33-year-old rookie with the 1953 White Sox, won 16 games; at age 37 he pitched a no-hitter.

ADDIE JOSS of the 1908 Indians, on the next-to-last day of the season, pitched a perfect game, besting Ed Walsh of the White Sox, 1–0. Walsh pitched a two-hitter.

"SAD" SAM JONES of the Indians, Red Sox, Yankees, Browns, Senators, and White Sox hurled in the American League for a record 22 *consecutive* years.

WALTER JOHNSON of the 1912–19 Senators set a major league record by copping eight consecutive strikeout titles.

JACKIE JENSEN was the only person to be both an MVP in baseball and an All-American in football.

JOE JACKSON, Buck Weaver, Fred McMullin, Claude Williams, Swede Risberg, Happy Felsch, Eddie Cicotte, and Chick Gandil were the eight White Sox players who allegedly were bribed to throw the 1919 World Series.

The INDIANS of 1948 had an infield that averaged 108 RBIs: first baseman Eddie Robinson, 83; second baseman Joe Gordon, 124; shortstop Lou Boudreau, 106; and third baseman Kenny Keltner, 119.

RON HUNT and Joe Christopher of the 1964 Mets became the first regulars for the "Amazin' Ones" to bat .300.

TOM HUGHES, who threw nine-inning no-hitters for the Yankees and the Browns, racked up a 20–3 lifetime record in relief.

FRANK HOWARD of the 1968 Senators was the last player to lead the majors in homers (44) while playing for a last-place club.

ELSTON HOWARD of the Yankees played in the World Series his first four years in the majors. The Yanks won in 1956 and 1958; they lost in 1955 and 1957.

STAN MUSIAL of the 1954 Cards and Nate Colbert of the 1972 Padres each hit a record five home runs in a doubleheader.

ROGERS HORNSBY of the 1922 Cardinals became the first National Leaguer to hit 40 home runs in a season when he hit 42 base-clearing blows.

FRANK HAYES, catcher for the 1945 Indians and Athletics, took part in a record 29 double plays for a backstop.

BURLEIGH GRIMES, winding up his career in 1934 with the Yankees, Pirates, and Cards, was the last of the legal spitball pitchers;* Red Faber of the 1933 White Sox was the last of the legal spitball pitchers in the American League.

BILL GRAY of the 1909 Senators gave up eight walks in one inning.

HANK GOWDY of the Giants and the Braves was the only major leaguer to serve in both World War I and World War II.

FLOYD GIEBELL shut out Bob Feller and the Indians to win the 1940 pennant for the Tigers, but he never won another big-league game. In fact, he won a total of only three.

BOB GIBSON of the Cardinals didn't steal too often, but when he did, he was usually successful: he stole 13 career bases in 17 attempts.

BOB GIBSON lost his first and last World Series games; in between, he won seven straight, a record.

The GIANTS were the first team to use a public address announcer. They did so at the Polo Grounds on August 25, 1929.

LOU GEHRIG began his consecutive game streak by batting for Pee Wee Wanninger the day before he subbed for ailing first baseman Wally Pipp.

FRANK BAUMHOLTZ of the 1952 Cubs was the only batter that Stan Musial of the Cards pitched to in the majors.

STEVE BARBER and Stu Miller of the 1967 Orioles combined to lose a 2–1 no-hitter to the Tigers.

NEAL BALL, shortstop for the 1904 Indians, pulled off the first unassisted triple play in modern major league history.

The ATHLETICS of 1949 executed a record 217 double plays.

The A's and Dodgers of 1974 played in the only All-California World Series. The A's won four of the five games.

* Commissioner Kenesaw Mountain Landis decreed in 1920 that only existing spitball pitchers could continue to wet the ball. Red Faber of the 1933 White Sox was the last American League pitcher to legally dampen the ball; Burleigh Grimes of the 1934 Giants was the last major league pitcher to legally lubricate the ball.

BOB ASPROMONTE was the last Brooklyn Dodger to remain active in the major leagues. He faded from the scene with the Mets in 1971.

CAP ANSON, Al Kaline, Stan Musial, and Mel Ott played a record 22 years with the same teams. Anson spent his entire major league career with the Cubs; Kaline, the Tigers; Musial, the Cardinals; and Ott, the Giants. Ted Lyons played a 21-year career with the White Sox while Luke Appling and Red Faber donned Pale Hose uniforms for 20 years.

MIKE ANDREWS of the 1973 A's was fired by owner Charlie Finley because he made two errors in the twelfth inning of a World Series loss to the Mets. Commissioner Bowie Kuhn forced Finley to reinstate his second baseman.

MERLE ADKINS, pitcher for the 1902 Red Sox, got roughed up for 12 hits in one inning; Reggie Grabowski, chucker for the 1934 Phils, didn't retire the side in the ninth until he had yielded 11 hits.

BABE ADAMS of the 1909 Pirates, Frank Shea of the 1947 Yankees, Joe Black of the 1952 Dodgers, and Bob Walk of the 1980 Phillies were the only rookies who started—and won—the first game of a World Series.

CY YOUNG of the Red Sox, who was 41 when he no-hit the Yankees (Highlanders) in 1908, was the oldest pitcher to throw a no-hit game.

GEORGE SISLER of the 1920 Browns collected a record 257 hits. From 1920–22 he averaged 240 safeties per season.

TRIS SPEAKER was involved in a career-record 135 double plays in his 22-year career as an outfielder for the Red Sox, Indians, Senators, and Athletics.

JIM THORPE, Ernie Nevers, Paddy Driscoll, Ace Parker, and George Halas are football Hall of Famers who once played in the majors.

JIM BUNNING won 19 games a record four times.

MORDECAI "Three Finger" BROWN of the 1909–10 Cubs was the only pitcher to twice lead the league in saves and complete games in the same season.

WILLIE MAYS slammed more than 50 home runs in seasons ten years apart: in 1955, with New York, he ripped 51; in 1965, with San Francisco, he rocketed 52.

WALTER JOHNSON hit a record 206 batters during his 21-year career with the Senators.

ROGERS HORNSBY holds the club-high batting average for three different teams: .424 for the 1924 Cardinals, .387 for the 1928 Braves, and .380 for the 1929 Cubs.

The BRAVES of 1961 hit four home runs in a row in one inning. They were slugged by Eddie Mathews, Hank Aaron, Joe Adcock, and Frank Thomas, respectively.

The BRAVES of 1965 hit four home runs in a row in one inning. They were drilled by Joe Torre, Eddie Mathews, Hank Aaron, and Gene Oliver, respectively.

RON BLOMBERG of the 1973 Yankees became the first designated hitter in baseball history. He walked on five pitches against the Red Sox.

JACK BILLINGHAM of the Reds, in three World Series, turned in the lowest career ERA (0.36) in World Series history. Harry Brecheen of the Cardinals recorded the second lowest mark (0.83), and Babe Ruth of the Red Sox, the third lowest (0.87).

WALLY BERGER of the 1931 Braves was the last flychaser to chalk up four assists in one game.

AUGIE BERGAMO hit .316 for the 1945 Cards but wasn't invited back to the 1946 spring training camp.

AL BENTON, pitcher for the 1941 Tigers, laid down a record two sacrifice bunts in the same inning.

JIM COMMAND of the 1954 Phillies hit a grand slam off the Dodgers' Carl Erskine for his first major-league hit. He got only three more hits in the big time.

TY COBB (1907–15) won a record nine consecutive batting titles; Rogers Hornsby (1920–25) copped a record six consecutive National League crowns. Both Honus Wagner (1906–09) and Rod Carew (1972–75) dominated the batting averages in their respective leagues for four consecutive years.

TY COBB collected 200 or more hits in a season nine times, the American League mark.

EARL CLARK, flychaser for the 1929 Braves, made a league-record 12 putouts in one game.

TOM CHENEY of the 1962 Senators struck out 21 Orioles in a 16-inning game.

TOMMY BYRNE of the 1951 Browns walked 16 batters in a 13-inning game.

PHIL CAVARRETTA of the Cubs set the following records for a player before he reached his twentieth birthday: runs, 120; hits, 234; triples, 14; and runs batted in, 117.

BILL CAUDILL of the 1984 Blue Jays struck out the only three batters he has faced in All-Star competition: Tim Raines, Ryne Sandberg, and Keith Hernandez.

BILL CARRIGAN, manager of the Red Sox, retired after he had led Boston to back-to-back world titles in 1915–16; Dick Williams, skipper of the A's, resigned after he had guided Oakland to back-to-back world championships in 1972–73.

STEVE BUSBY of the 1973–74 Royals was the first and only pitcher to throw no-hitters in each of his first two seasons.

JIM BUNNING was the first pitcher to hurl for both leagues in the All-Star Game, first for the Tigers, later for the Phillies.

DON DRYSDALE of the 1959 Dodgers was the only pitcher to start two All-Star games in one year. He was not involved in the first decision, a 5–4 National League win, but he got tagged for the loss in the second decision, a 5–3 American League triumph.

PATSY DOUGHERTY of the 1903 Red Sox was the first player to homer twice in the same game of a World Series. He performed the feat in Game Two against the Pirates.

"WILD BILL" DONOVAN has been the only pitcher to post 25 or more win seasons in both leagues. He won 25 for the 1901 Dodgers and 25 for the 1907 Tigers.

VINCE DiMAGGIO led the National League in strikeouts four years in a row (1942–45). His total of 389 whiffs, however, pales in comparison to the 609 times that Reggie Jackson went down via the strikeout route during a four-year period.

JOE DiMAGGIO of the 1950 Yankees became the first player to get paid $100,000 for a season.

FRANK HOWARD of the 1968 Senators hit a record ten home runs in six games.

DOM DiMAGGIO, Joe DiMaggio, and Vince DiMaggio all have the same middle name—Paul.

BILL DICKEY, catcher for the 1931 Yankees, set an American League record by catching 125 consecutive games without committing a passed ball. Al Todd of the 1937 Pirates holds the major league record with 128 passed ball-free games.

BILL DAHLEN of the 1900 Dodgers, Curt Walker of the 1926 Reds, Al Zarilla of the 1946 browns, and Gil Coan of the 1951 Senators all hit two triples in the same inning.

The CUBS of 1906 won a record 116 games, but they lost the World Series to their intercity rivals, the White Sox, in six games.

GAVVY CRAVATH of the 1919 Phillies won the home run crown despite the fact that he had only 214 official at-bats. He hit 12 four-base blows.

DOC CRAMER of the Red Sox, Rip Radcliff of the Browns, and Barney McCosky of the Tigers each stroked 200 hits to tie for the major league lead in 1940.

JIM COONEY of the White Sox and Johnny Neun of the Tigers pulled off unassisted triple plays on successive days. Cooney, shortstop for the Cubs, recorded his on May 30, 1927; Neun, first baseman for the Tigers, executed his the following day.

JOE DiMAGGIO of the 1936 Yankees was the first rookie to play in an All-Star Game. He went hitless in five at-bats and made an error in the field.

ED COLEMAN of the 1936 Browns, who retired after the season, became the first player to pinch-hit safely 20 times in one season.

STEVE GARVEY of the Padres set the all-time errorless game streak at first base with 193 miscue-free games.

TITO FRANCONA hit .363 and slammed 20 home runs for the 1959 Indians, yet over a 13-year career he batted almost 100 points lower, .272, and parked 119 homers, an average of nine per season.

JIMMIE FOXX, Joe DiMaggio, Stan Musial, Roy Campanella, Yogi Berra, Mickey Mantle, and Mike Schmidt won MVP awards a record three times.

OSCAR FELSCH, outfielder for the 1919 White Sox, participated in a record 15 double plays in one season.

GAYLORD PERRY of the 1978 Padres was 40 years old when he won the Cy Young Award, making him the oldest player ever to win the coveted crown.

WILLIE MAYS has been the only player to amass 3,000 hits, 600 home runs, and 300 stolen bases.

BOB FELLER pitched a record 12 one-hitters.

DAN DRIESSEN of the 1976 Reds, in the first year that the DH was used in the World Series, hit .357 in his team's sweep of the Yankees.

DAZZY VANCE didn't win his first major league decision until he was 31, but by the time he hung up his spikes in 1935, he registered a career record of 197–140.

WILLIE MAYS and Stan Musial were the only players who appeared in all eight All-Star games—two per year—from 1959–62.

BABE RUTH was the only player to twice hit three home runs in a World Series game. He did it in 1926 and 1928, both times against the Cards.

MIKE RYBA of the Cards and the Red Sox was the only player to both pitch and catch in both leagues.

JOHNNY SAIN of the 1948 Braves was the only pitcher to lead the league in sacrifice hits—16.

HONUS WAGNER, who was 37 when he won the batting crown in 1911, was the oldest National League player to win the batting title.

RAY SCHALK of the 1914–22 White Sox caught four no-hitters.

WILLIARD SCHMIDT of the 1959 Reds and Frank Thomas of the 1962 Mets each got hit with two pitches in the same inning of a game.

RED SCHOENDIENST and Lou Brock have been the only players to collect 200 or more hits in a season which they split between two teams. Schoendienst played for the Giants and the Braves in 1957; Brock, the Cubs and the Cards in 1964.

FERDIE SCHUPP of the 1916 Giants posted an all-time low 0.90 ERA. He pitched in only 140 innings, though, so Bob Gibson of the 1968 Cardinals, who registered a 1.12 mark in 305 innings, is generally considered to own the lowest ERA for one season in the National League.

JIMMY SEBRING of the 1903 Pirates was the first player to hit a home run in the World Series! He homered in the first game of the initial fall classic and got 11 hits in the classic, two short of the all-time record.

ROY SIEVERS and Jimmie Foxx were the only players to hit pinch-hit grand-slam home runs in both leagues. Sievers did it for the 1961 White Sox and the 1963 Phillies; Foxx, for the 1931 Athletics and the 1945 Phillies.

The YANKEES of 1960 lost the World Series to the Pirates in seven games despite recording the highest team batting average (.338) ever.

The YANKEES, paced by Roger Maris's 61 home runs and Mickey Mantle's 54 circuit clouts, hit a record-setting 240 four-base blows in 1961. Maris and Mantle's combined total of 115 home runs by back-to-back sluggers in a lineup broke the former mark of 109, which had been set by Babe Ruth and Lou Gehrig in 1927.

The YANKEES defeated the Tigers, 9–7, in the American League's longest game (24 innings) on June 24, 1962. Jack Reed's home run, the only one that he hit in his career, broke up the game.

EARLY WYNN of the 1950 Indians led the American League with a 3.20 ERA, the highest earned run mark to lead either circuit.

JOE WOOD was the first player to appear in one World Series (1912) as a pitcher and another fall classic (1920) as an outfielder. Wood won three games for the Red Sox and batted .200 for the Indians.

RICK WISE of the 1971 Phils pitched a no-hitter and hit two home runs in a game against the Reds.

VIC WILLIS, who eight times won 20 or more games during a season, lost a major league record 29 games for the 1905 Braves.

The WHITE SOX of 1940 had the same batting average at the end of one game as they had before it. That's because Bob Feller no-hit them in the opening game of the season.

CARL WEILMAN (1913), Don Hoak (1956), Rich Reichardt (1966), Bill Cowan (1971), and Cecil Cooper (1974) all whiffed six times during extra-inning games.

BABE RUTH of the 1920 Yankees hit 54 home runs, 35 more than his runner-up, George Sisler (19), in the American League home run derby.

HAM HYATT (1909–18) of the Pirates, Cardinals, and Giants was the first player to amass 50 hits as a pinch-hitter. Career-wise, he batted safely 57 times in 240 pinch-hitting performances for a .238 average.

CHARLES HICKMAN, a second baseman for the 1905 Senators, Nap Lajoie, a second baseman for the 1915 Athletics, and Dave Brain, a third baseman for the 1906 Braves, all made five errors in a game.

HARRY STEINFELDT of the 1909 Cubs, Bob Meusel of the 1926 Yankees, Ernie Banks of the 1961 Cubs, and Russ Nixon of the 1965 Red Sox all hit three sacrifice flies in one game.

HONUS WAGNER led the National League in batting a record eight times. Rogers Hornsby and Stan Musial won National League batting titles seven times each.

RED ROLFE of the 1939 Yankees scored a record 30 runs in 18 consecutive games.

PIE TRAYNOR was the only regular named to the all-time team to play his entire career with one club. He played with the Pirates from 1920–37.

TRIS SPEAKER of the 1918 Red Sox executed two unassisted double plays in the month of April.

GEORGE UHLE of the Tigers and Indians, who pitched for 17 years, had a .288 lifetime batting average, the highest mark of any pitcher.

DAZZY VANCE of the 1922–28 Dodgers set a National League record when he won seven consecutive strikeout titles.

HONUS WAGNER, Christy Mathewson, Ty Cobb, Walter Johnson, and Babe Ruth, in 1936, became the first five players to be inducted into the Baseball Hall of Fame at Cooperstown, N.Y.

The PIRATES of 1925, Yankees of 1958, Tigers of 1968,

Pirates of 1979, and Royals of 1985 have won the World Series after trailing in games, three to one.

The PIRATES of 1917 hit nine home runs, the all-time low by a National League team.

The PIRATES of 1960 defeated the Yankees in the World Series despite having a pitching staff that recorded an ERA of 7.11.

The REDS of 1935, the host team, defeated the Phillies, 2–1, in the first night game played in the majors.

The RED SOX, who won four world championships in four tries in the same decade, defeated four different National League teams during a seven-year span: the Giants, 1912; the Phillies, 1915; the Dodgers, 1916; and the Cubs, 1918.

PEE WEE REESE of the 1952 Dodgers came to the plate three times in the same inning.

ROBIN ROBERTs' 28 wins for the 1952 Phillies has been the most wins by a National League pitcher since Dizzy Dean won 30 in 1934.

BROOKS ROBINSON hit into four triple plays in his career.

LYNWOOD "SCHOOLBOY" ROWE was the first major leaguer to play for each league in an All-Star Game. In 1936, when he was with the Tigers, he pitched for the American League; in 1947, when he was with the Phillies, he pinch-hit for the National League.

BABE RUTH reached first base safely a record 379 times in one season; Lefty O'Doul reached first base safely a record 334 times in the National League.

BABE RUTH in 1969 was chosen the greatest all-time player by that year's poll; Joe DiMaggio was voted the greatest living player.

JOE DiMAGGIO, who averaged 118 RBIs per season during his 13-year career, won only two titles in that department. In 13 years in the big leagues he averaged just under one RBI per game.

BABE RUTH walked an all-time-high 170 times in 1923.

A Checkered Career

The Giants of John McGraw had much good fortune—
they won ten pennants and three World Series—but they
had great misfortune also: they lost one pennant and three
World Series that they could have won.

In 1908 they were victimized by "Merkle's Boner." On
September 23, in a key game with the Cubs at the Polo
Grounds, Al Bridwell lined a ball to the outfield that chased
Moose McCormick home with the apparent winning run.
But Merkle, who was on first, did not run out the hit to
second. Instead he bolted straight to the clubhouse in center
field, a custom of the time when the winning hit was made
in the bottom of the ninth inning. Johnny Evers, the Cubs'
second baseman, alertly called for the ball; and Hank O'Day,
the umpire who saw the entire play, ruled that Merkle was
out. He also suspended the 1–1 contest because of darkness.
That necessitated a one-game playoff for the pennant. The
Cubs behind Mordecai Brown defeated Christy Mathewson
of the Giants, 4–2.

In 1912 the Giants muffed the World Series. Leading by
one run in the final inning of the eighth-and-decisive game—
the second game had ended in a 6–6 tie—they made two
costly errors, one of commission and one of omission. Fred
Snodgrass dropped Clyde Engle's routine fly ball for a two-
base error, and first baseman Merkle and catcher Chief
Meyers gave Tris Speaker a second life when they permitted
his easy foul pop to drop untouched. Speaker then singled
home the tying run and advanced what proved to be the
winning run to third. Larry Gardner's sacrifice fly clinched
the championship.

In 1917 the Giants made two physical errors and one
mental error in the fourth inning of the sixth-and-final game.
Heinie Zimmerman, the third baseman for the Giants, made
a bad throw on an easy grounder; Dave Robertson, the
right fielder, dropped an easy fly ball; and Bill Rariden, the
catcher, left home plate unattended in a rundown play that
led to the winning run.

In 1924, McGraw's last chance to win a World Series,
"Little Napoleon" saw fate intervene once again. In the
bottom of the 12th, with the score between the Giants and
the host Senators tied at three, Muddy Ruel lifted a high

foul behind the plate, but the Giant catcher tripped over his own mask, and Ruel, given another opportunity, doubled. Earl McNeely's hopper to third hit a pebble and bounced over Fred Lindstrom's head, scoring Ruel with the winning run.

The Giants' receiver was naturally distraught over his inability to handle Ruel's pop fly properly, for he was a veteran who was used to crisis situations. Up until that time he had been the only catcher to be on the winning side of a World Series sweep. When World War I erupted, he was the first major leaguer to volunteer for military service. Later, when World War II broke out, he became the only major leaguer to see service in both wars. And in the 1914 World Series he batted .545, the second highest average in the history of the Autumn Classic.

Who was this player with the checkered career?

(Answer appears on page 321.)

Chapter Seven

BASEBALL'S WHO'S WHO

35. BASEBALL'S WHO'S WHO

1. _____ Who pitched in 65 1–0 games, winning 38 of them and losing 27, even though in 20 of his losses he allowed four or fewer hits?

2. _____ Who batted for a .403 average over a five-year period of time?

3. _____ Who was the only manager before Dick Williams to win pennants with three different teams?

4. _____ Who was the youngest player to win a batting title?

5. _____ Who was the oldest player to win a batting title?

6. _____ Who was the first player to hit safely in 12 consecutive official at-bats?

7. _____ Who was the only other player to duplicate the feat?

8. _____ Who hit .382 in his last year (570 at-bats) in the majors?

9. _____ Who, in addition to Joe Jackson (.408), was the only player to bat .400 without winning the hitting crown?

10. _____ Who posted the most wins (12) in one season without losing a game?

11. _____ Who pitched three doubleheaders in one month and won all six games, none of which lasted more than one hour and fifty minutes?

12. _____ Who hit two game-winning home runs for the Giants against the Yankees in the 1923 series?

13. _____ Who was the only player to win the MVP Award for two teams in the same league?

14. _____ Who was the first infielder to wear glasses?

15. _____ Who was the first catcher to wear glasses?

16. _____ Who was the National League right-hander who led the circuit in strikeouts for four consecutive years (1932–35) but failed to whiff as many as 200 batters in a season?

17. _____ Who recorded the second-lowest career ERA in the World Series?

18. _____ Who won four batting titles in alternate years?

19. _____ Who won back-to-back batting titles three times?

20. _____ Who was the first baseman who teamed with Joe Gordon, Lou Boudreau, and Ken Keltner to give the Indians an infield that averaged 108 RBIs?

21. _____ Who was the one-time Yankee manager who neither hit a home run nor stole a base in eight major league seasons?

22. _____ Who was the one-time Yankee manager who never finished worse than fourth in 24 years as a major league skipper?

23. _____ Who was the pennant-winning manager who needed the most time—10 years—to win his first league title?

24. _____ Who hit a record six pinch-hit home runs in one year?

25. _____ Who hit five pinch-hit home runs in one year to set an American League record?

26. _____ Who was the only National League pitcher to lead his league in winning percentage for three consecutive years?

27. _____ Who was the only American League pitcher to lead his circuit in winning percentage for three consecutive years?

28. _____ Who shut out every team in the National League in three different years?

29. _____ Who was the left-handed slugger in the National League who tied for the home run title three times?

30. _____ Who was the right-handed slugger in the National League who tied for the home run crown three times?

31. _____ Who posted a 6–0 opening day record?

32. _____ Who pitched six opening day shutouts?

33. _____ Who was the only White Sox player to win a batting title?

34. _____ Who threw the pennant-winning home run to Chris Chambliss in 1976?

35. _____ Who was the only pitcher to win back-to-back MVP awards?

36. _____ Who was the pitcher for the 1914 pennant-winning Athletics who recorded a .302 lifetime mark as an outfielder?

37. _____ Who hit 40 or more home runs in the American League eight times, but never reached the 50 mark?

38. _____ Who hit 40 or more home runs in the National League eight times, but failed to hit the 50 mark?

39. _____ Who was the player who led the American League in batting in 1961 with an average of .361, but never before or after reached the .300 level?

40. _____ Who drove home 106 runs in 1969, at the age of 38, to become the oldest player to deliver that many ribbies?

41. _____ Who was the 273-game winner who hit over .300 eight times and pinch-hit safely 58 times?

42. _____ Who was the pitcher who pinch-hit safely 114 times?

43. _____ Who set a major league record by leading his league in ERA percentage nine times?

44. _____ Who was the only player to win the batting and home run titles with two teams in the same league?

45. _____ Who was the first switch-hitter to win a batting crown?

46. _____ Who was the National League relief pitcher from the 1950s and 1960s who recorded 193 career saves?

47. _____ Who was the player who three times won the batting crown and the home run title in the same year?

48. _____ Who finished 750 of 816 contests for a completion percentage of 92?

49. _____ Who was the only National League player to twice get six hits in six at-bats?

50. _____ Who was the only American League player to twice get six hits in six at-bats?

51. _____ Who was the only American League pitcher to win the Cy Young Award three times?

52. _____ Who, in addition to Sandy Koufax,

was the only National League pitcher to win the Cy Young Award three times?

53. _____ Who was the first National League relief pitcher to win the Cy Young Award?

54. _____ Who has won the Cy Young Award four times?

55. _____ Who was the only pitcher to win the Cy Young Award in both leagues?

56. _____ Who was the only American League pitcher to win the Rookie of the Year Award in the 1970s?

57. _____ Who was the only National League infielder who won the Rookie of the Year Award in the 1970s?

58. _____ Who was the last American League hitter to win consecutive batting crowns?

59. _____ Who has been the only player to win both the Rookie of the Year Award and the MVP Award in the same year?

60. _____ Who was the last National League player to win three consecutive batting titles?

61. _____ Who was the last American League player to win at least three consecutive batting titles?

62. _____ Who was the second, and most recent, National League relief pitcher to win the Cy Young Award?

63. _____ Who was the last National League player to win three consecutive home run crowns?

64. _____ Who was the last American League player to win back-to-back MVP awards?

65. _____ Who was the last National League player to win back-to-back MVP awards?

66. _____ Who is the other present-day player who won back-to-back MVP awards in 1980–81?

67. _____ Who has hit for the highest average in the National League since Stan Musial's .376 in 1948?

68. _____ Who strayed 200 or more hits in a record ten seasons?

69. _____ Who is the recent-day Cub pitcher who won 20 or more games in six consecutive seasons?

70. _____ Who was the recent-day pitcher who won 20 or more games with three different teams?

71. _____ Who was the recent-day pitcher who won 20 or more games eight times?

72. _____ Who is the only present-day left-handed pitcher to strike out 300 batters in a season?

73. _____ Who was the former Yankee relief pitcher who led the American League in saves in 1972 and 1976 with 35 and 23, respectively?

74. _____ Who was the most recent pitcher to both win and lose 20 games in the same season?

75. _____ Who was the player who holds the club batting mark lead with two different teams?

76. _____ Who is the recent-day pitcher who struck out more than 200 batters in nine consecutive seasons?

Classic Comebacks

They say that good things come in twos. That goes for no-hitters, too.

There have been four pitchers in the modern era to throw two no-hitters in one season: Johnny Vander Meer (1938), Allie Reynolds (1951), Virgil Trucks (1952), and Nolan Ryan (1973). One of them (Vander Meer) was the only pitcher to throw two no-hitters in successive starts.

Up until 1968, however, no two teams had exchanged no-hitters on successive days. Now it's been accomplished twice. The first time, on September 23, 1968, a Giant pitcher performed the feat against the visiting Cardinals. The following day, a St. Louis right-hander duplicated the feat against San Francisco.

One year later, two teams traded no-hitters on successive days for the second time. On April 30 a strong-armed Cincinnati right-hander set back the Astros. The next day an Astro flamethrower returned the favor.

If you could name just two of the four pitchers who were involved in these classic comebacks, you would be pitching in coveted company, too. Can you?

(Answer appears on page 321.)

Chapter Eight

BASEBALL'S NUMBER GAME

Just how trivial is baseball "trivia"?

Baseball fans, the most record-conscious of all sports followers, feel very strongly that names and numbers are a vital part of the national pastime. So do the players.

The numbers 56, 60, 61, 367, 511, 755, and 2,130 instantaneously draw to the minds of astute baseball fans and players the names of great diamond stars of the past: Joe DiMaggio, Babe Ruth, Roger Maris, Ty Cobb, Cy Young, Hank Aaron, and Lou Gehrig.

Numbers 300 and 3,000 probably hold the most lure for the baseball fan and player. Three hundred represents a batter's season's average and his career mark. It also signifies a pitcher's season's strikeouts and career wins. Three thousand can stand for either career hits by a batter or career strikeouts by a pitcher.

There are other magical numberes in baseball, too. Quite often they affect the longevity of a player's career.

Mickey Mantle, the great Yankee switch-hitter, lengthened his career two years because of the numbers game. In 1966, when he should have retired, Mantle's RBI total dipped to 56. But his batting average of .288 and his home run total of 23 were still respectable. It would have been a good time to bow out, while he was still on top. But he was just four home runs shy of 500. The temptation was simply too great. So he played another year. In 1967 he hit 22 home runs to up his total to 518, just three short of Ted Williams's 521 and 16 light of Jimmy Foxx's 534. So, of course, he played one more year, and he ended up with 536 home runs. Willie Mays's four-base total, the next rung on the home run ladder, was high above Mantle's. So, with no more numbers to catch, he retired.

The numbers game was costly to Mantle, though. His .245 and .237 batting averages during his last two years dragged his lifetime average down from .302 to .298. In Mantle's case a higher home run total was preferable to a higher lifetime batting average.

"It really bothers me that I didn't end up my career with a .300 lifetime average," Mantle says when he is asked about his decision to play those last two years. "I'd like to be remembered as a good hitter. At the time I fooled myself into thinking that I could hit the extra home runs and keep the .300 average. But it didn't work out."

Al Kaline got caught up in the numbers game, too. His situation was similar to Mantle's. He played two extra years in order to wind up in the select 3,000 Hit Club. He made it with a herculean effort in 1974, when he got 146 hits to finish up his career with 3,007. But, in those last two years, he slipped four points, from .301 to .297, in his lifetime average.

Once Kaline reached 3,000 hits, he was faced with another dilemma. He had 399 home runs. Should he play another year in order to end up in another select circle of hitters: the 400 Home Run Club?

"No, I decided not to," Kaline said shortly after his retirement. "It would have been nice to hit 400 home runs. But the toll that would have been exacted from my body by playing another season would have been too much. I had a good career. I'm satisfied with it."

Unlike Mantle, home runs were less important to him than base hits. Yet he is one of only three members of the 3,000 Hit Club who did not finish his career with a .300 lifetime average.

The numbers game was not always as important to the baseball player as it is today, though.

Take the case of Sam Rice, who played the outfield for the Washington Senators from 1915 to 1934. He ended up his career with a lifetime average of .322 and a total of 2,987 hits, just 13 short of the magic 3,000. But Rice, who had hit .293 and collected 98 hits in his final season, elected to retire. Had he been a modern-day performer, he undoubtedly would have played one more year in order to reach the prestigious milestone. Rice's decision to retire, though he didn't know it at the time, cost him baseball immortality. There are not too many modern-day fans who even recognize his name. A mere 13 additional hits would have added luster to his name. The present-day fans would then include him with the greatest hitters of all time.

"We didn't pay too much attention to records in those days," Rice said shortly before his death. "There wasn't so much emphasis put on them at the time. If I had it to do all over again, though, I think I would have hung around for a while. With all of this stress on records today, history has sort of cheated me, you know."

Sam Crawford was another player who looked back and rued the day that he retired. Today he is mostly remembered as an outfielder who played alongside Ty Cobb. But "Wahoo" Sam turned in a .309 lifetime average, led the major leagues in triples with 309, and proved to be the only player who has led both the National and American leagues in home runs.

But he finished his career with 2,964 hits. He also could have played an extra year, as so many modern baseball players will do, and made the 3,000 Hit Club. Then perhaps he would have moved out of Cobb's shadow. But one hit shy of 3,000 is as distant as 1,000 short of the mark. Most baseball buffs know that Roberto Clemente ended up his career with 3,000 hits on the nose. But few people realize that Rice and Crawford missed the mark by a whisker and could have hit it, if they had elected to do so.

Crawford legally deserves the 3,000 Hit Club recognition anyway. In 1899 he got 87 hits with Grand Rapids in the Western League. When the American League was formed in 1900, the National Commission ruled that any player from the Western League who entered either the National or American leagues would be credited with all the hits that he had made in the Western League. But the statistician who compiled Crawford's lifetime average inadvertently overlooked those hits. So he finished his career with 2,964 hits instead of 3,051, to which he is entitled.

Crawford, it seems, was dealt a double twist of fate: he was victimized by the numbers game and the record book.

Lefty O'Doul was also cheated by the numbers game. The two-time batting champ in the National League finished his career with a .349 average. Yet he is not ranked with the top hitters of all time because the baseball rules makers say that he did not play the required ten years in order to qualify for such exalted distinction. Actually, O'Doul played 11 years in the big leagues. But the first four were spent as a pitcher. The record compilers don't count those years.

But the late, irrepressible Irishman did. "I spent 11 years in the big leagues and ended up with a .349 average," he often said to the surprise of unknowing listeners. "That's lifetime average, not a single season's mark. Only Cobb,

Hornsby, and Jackson ever did better. That's pretty good company."

O'Doul was also denied entrance into another elite club—the .400 Hitters—by a single base hit. In 1929 he batted .398, the closest that anyone has come to .400 without hitting it. (Harry Heilmann also hit .398. But in another season, he batted .401.)

"Only eight hitters in the history of baseball ever hit .400," O'Doul said regretfully. "If an official scorer had ruled one of many plays a hit rather than an error, I would have been the ninth."

Babe Ruth didn't miss .400 by too much, either. In 1923 he hit .393 and didn't even win the batting title. (Heilmann did.) When people think of the Babe, they envision the legendary long-ball hitter. But they sometimes forget that he was a .342 lifetime hitter, too. If the Babe had been able to get three more hits in 1923, they would never be able to forget it.

Ten players in the history of the game have hit 50 or more home runs in one season. You can probably name all of them. But can you recall the six players who did not hit 50, but did smack 49? Well, they are Lou Gehrig, Ted Kluszewski, Frank Robinson, Harmon Killebrew, Mark McGwire, and Andre Dawson.

"Close only counts in horseshoes," they say. So these six sluggers have been relegated to a lower echelon of long-ball hitters.

Billy Goodman wound up his major league career with a lifetime average of .300. Minnie Minoso hit .299. Is there a difference? Well, Minoso prevailed upon Chicago White Sox owner Bill Veeck to reactivate him, at the age of 57, in the final month of the 1976 season. In 1980 he returned for two more at-bats. (His lifetime average dropped a point to .298.) You might say that Minoso thought there was a difference.

Thirteen pitchers have won 30 or more games in one season. "Three-Finger" Brown, George Mullin, Ed Cicotte, and Hal Newhouser did not. They won 29. In the record book that looms as one very important win.

Spud Chandler, like Lefty O'Doul, has been footnoted out of the record book. The Yankees' right-hander won 109 games and lost only 43 for a phenomenal winning percentage of .717. That's the best mark of all time for any pitcher who has won 100 or more games. But the rules makers say that a pitcher has to have recorded 200 victories in order to rank with the all-time best. So Whitey Ford (236–106) tops the list with a mark of .690.

Jim Bunning pitched no-hitters in both leagues. He won over 100 games in each league, too. And he also struck out more than 1,000 batters in each league. Overall, he struck out 2,855 batters. Another 145 would have guaranteed him a bust in Cooperstown. He'll probably never make it, though.

Tom Seaver struck out 200 or more batters in nine consecutive years. That's a record. But his personal high of 289 is still far from the top. Eleven pitchers have gone over 300 strikeouts in a season.

Roy Face still thinks about the one decision in 19 which he dropped in 1959. Nineteen and oh? Wouldn't that be something!

Vic Willis of the old Boston Braves might have welcomed one more loss, though. In 1905 he dropped 29 decisions. No one else has ever done that. But 30 losses? That would really single him out!

Early Wynn and Robin Roberts typify the modern-day players' conflict with the numbers game.

Wynn won only one game in 1963. That was his last major league victory. It was also his 300th career win. He got it in relief. That's struggling. With satisfaction, though.

Roberts struggled, too. In vain, though. Eleven years after his last 20-game season, he called it quits, 14 victories short of the coveted 300 Win Club.

Why did those Hall of Famers put so much time and toil into so few victories at the tail end of their careers? They did so because, competitive as baseball players are prone to be, they played the game to the hilt, until their number(s) were up.

To them, it wasn't any trivial matter!

Speaking of trivia, though, I've got a question for you: who were those two players, in addition to Al Kaline, who collected more than 3,000 lifetime hits but failed to finish their careers with an average of .300?

(Answer appears on page 321.)

98

The Fateful Farewell

In the 1947 World Series, three players—Bill Bevens, Cookie Lavagetto, and Al Gionfriddo—came out of relative obscurity to figure prominently in the seven-game set between the Yankees and the Dodgers. Afterward they slipped back into obscurity. But they are still remembered today for the pivotal parts they played in the 1947 Fall Classic, one of the most dramatic series of all time.

In Game Four, with the Yankees holding a one-contest lead, Bevens, a pitcher with a less than enviable 7–13 record during the regular season, made World Series history.

With one out remaining in the game, Bevens held tenuously to a 2–1 lead. Up to that point, Bevens had neutralized the Dodgers' big bats; he had not allowed a single base hit. That is not to say, however, that he hadn't allowed any base runners. As a matter of fact, he yielded ten of them, all via the base-on-balls route. (And that's a record!) Two of them, plus a sacrifice and an infield out, cost him a run in the fifth inning. But it was the last two walks he granted that cost him World Series immortality.

In the ninth inning he walked Carl Furillo for pass number nine. Furillo gave way to a pinch-runner, who proceeded to steal second base off rookie catcher Yogi Berra. Then with two outs and a base open, Yankee manager Bucky Harris decided to walk pinch-hitter Pete Reiser, who also gave way to a pinch-runner. That set the stage for pinch-hitter Harry Lavagetto, who responded with a double off the right-field wall to break up the no-hitter and, more important, to win the game for the Dodgers.

In Game Six, Al Gionfriddo, who played the role of a super-sub in the Series, prevented the tying run from scoring with one of the most memorable defensive plays in World Series history.

The Yankees, who had won Game Five on Joe DiMaggio's home run off Rex Barney, had high hopes of wrapping up the classic in Game Six. Once again, it was DiMaggio who almost provided them with the impetus. But with the Dodgers leading 8–5 in the sixth inning, Dodger manager Burt Shotton once again went to his bench. He called on Gionfriddo, whom he inserted in left field as a defensive precaution.

Immediately, Gionfriddo justified the move. DiMaggio boomed a 415-foot shot to the bull pen in deep left center field. But Gionfriddo, who had broken with the crack of the bat, made a circus catch to prevent the homer that would have tied the game. The Dodgers then hung on to win, 8–6. But the Yankees came back to win the seventh game (5–2) and the Series (4–3).

One might think that Bevens, Lavagetto, and Gionfriddo got raises the following year. But in fact none of the three ever played another regular-season major league game.

You can earn a bonus, however, if you can identify the pinch-runner for Furillo, the pinch-runner for Reiser, and the left-fielder whom Gionfriddo replaced in the Dodger lineup.

(Answer appears on page 321.)

Chapter Nine

NICKNAMES

36. MATCHING NAMES

Match the following players with their nicknames.

Tommy Henrich	Walter Johnson
Carl Hubbell	Dom DiMaggio
Frankie Frisch	Tris Speaker
Honus Wagner	Ted Williams
Luke Appling	Casey Stengel
Johnny Mize	Vernon Law
Bobby Thomson	Ty Cobb
Allie Reynolds	Babe Ruth
Joe DiMaggio	Lou Gehrig
Paul Waner	Mickey Mantle

1. "Staten Island Scot" _____
2. "Super Chief" _____
3. "Splendid Splinter" _____
4. "Big Cat" _____
5. "Little Professor" _____
6. "Old Professor" _____
7. "Old Reliable" _____
8. "Deacon" _____
9. "Yankee Clipper" _____
10. "Georgia Peach" _____
11. "Flying Dutchman" _____
12. "Grey Eagle" _____
13. "Sultan of Swat" _____
14. "Big Train" _____
15. "Iron Horse" _____
16. "Meal Ticket" _____
17. "Commerce Comet" _____
18. "Old Aches and Pains" _____
19. "Big Poison" _____
20. "Fordham Flash" _____

37. FIRST NAMES

Substitute the players' first names for their nicknames.

Edwin	Elwin
George	Jerome
Harry	Charles
Edward	Joe
James	Johnny
Leon	Leroy
Fred	Enos
Larry	Robert
Paul	Lynwood
Bill	Charles Dillon

1. "Moose" Skowron　　　　_____
2. "Daffy" Dean　　　　　　_____
3. "Dizzy" Dean　　　　　　_____
4. "Yogi" Berra　　　　　　_____
5. "Preacher" Roe　　　　　_____
6. "Snuffy" Stirnweiss　　　_____
7. "Flash" Gordon　　　　　_____
8. "Pepper" Martin　　　　　_____
9. "Schoolboy" Rowe　　　　_____
10. "Duke" Snider　　　　　_____
11. "Casey" Stengel　　　　　_____
12. "Dixie" Walker　　　　　_____
13. "Peanuts" Lowrey　　　　_____
14. "Satchel" Paige　　　　　_____
15. "Country" Slaughter　　　_____
16. "Chuck" Dressen　　　　_____
17. "Whitey" Ford　　　　　_____
18. "Goose" Goslin　　　　　_____
19. "Lefty" Grove　　　　　_____
20. "Dusty" Rhodes　　　　　_____

38. MIDDLE NAMES

Place the following nicknames between the players' first and last names.

"The Whip"	"The Kid"
"Poosh 'Em Up"	"Birdie"
"Pee Wee"	"The Crow"
"Bobo"	"The Barber"
"Three Finger"	"Home Run"
"Puddin' Head"	"The Lip"
"The Dutch Master"	"King Kong"
"The Man"	"Pie"
"The Hat"	"Twinkletoes"
"The Cat"	"Louisiana Lightning"

1. Harry _____ Walker
2. Stan _____ Musial
3. Harry _____ Brecheen
4. Johnny _____ Vander Meer
5. Sal _____ Maglie
6. Ron _____ Guidry
7. Leo _____ Durocher
8. Ewell _____ Blackwell
9. Charlie _____ Keller
10. Willie _____ Jones
11. Frank _____ Crosetti
12. Frank _____ Baker
13. Tony _____ Lazzeri
14. Billy _____ Martin
15. Harold _____ Traynor
16. Louis _____ Newsom
17. George _____ Tebbetts
18. George _____ Selkirk
19. Mordecai _____ Brown
20. Harold _____ Reese

39. LAST NAMES

Match the players' last names with their nicknames and their first names.

Doby	Reiser
Keeler	Murphy
Jones	Hubbell
Feller	Crawford
Jackson	Dugan
Piniella	Cochrane
Houk	Grimm
Medwick	Bottomley
Wood	Turner
Greenberg	Newhouser

1. "Ducky" Joe _____
2. "Wahoo" Sam _____
3. "Shoeless" Joe _____
4. "Smokey" Joe _____
5. "Jumping" Joe _____
6. "Sweet" Lou _____
7. "Hammerin' " Hank _____
8. "Blackjack" Mickey _____
9. "Rapid" Robert _____
10. "Jolly Cholly" _____
11. "Pistol" Pete _____
12. "Sunny" Jim _____
13. "Larrupin' " Larry _____
14. "Prince" Hal _____
15. "Major" Ralph _____
16. "Wee" Willie _____
17. "Fireman" Johnny _____
18. "Milkman" Jim _____
19. "Sad" Sam _____
20. "King" Carl _____

40. MULTIPLE NAMES

Supply the whole name.

1. "Dr. Strangeglove" _____
2. "Daddy Wags" _____
3. "The Say Hey Kid" _____
4. "Charlie Hustle" _____
5. "The Vacuum Cleaner" _____

Supply the first name.

1. "Hondo" Howard _____
2. "Stretch" McCovey _____
3. "Tug" McGraw _____
4. "Killer" Killebrew _____
5. "Hawk" Harrelson _____

Supply the nickname.

1. Walter Williams _____
2. Jim Hunter _____
3. John Powell _____
4. John Odom _____
5. Jim Grant _____

Supply the last name.

1. "Sudden" Sam _____
2. "Gettysburg" Eddie _____
3. "Shake and Bake" _____
4. "Stonewall" Travis _____
5. "Vinegar Bend" _____

The Iron Horse

There is a touch of irony in respect to the manner in which Lou Gehrig broke into the Yankees' lineup and the way in which he departed from it.

When the 1925 season started, Gehrig was the back-up first baseman. The first-string first sacker was a veteran of 12 years, a two-time home run champion, and the American League's leader in triples (19) the previous year. About one-third of the way through the season, though, the first stringer got hit in the head with a pitch, and he suffered from headaches for the remainder of the season. One day he asked manager Joe McCarthy for a game's rest. Lou Gehrig substituted for him and the rest of the story is history: the "Iron Horse" remained in the lineup for a record 2,130 consecutive games. But he died a short two years after he hung up his cleats.

The player whom he replaced lived for 40 years after he departed from the Yankee lineup. Can you name him?

(Answer appears on page 321.)

Chapter Ten

BREAKING THE BARRIERS

41. DID THEY OR DIDN'T THEY?

Mark "T" or "F" for "True" or "False" before each statement.

1. _____ Don Newcombe hit more home runs (7) in one season than any other pitcher in the history of the National League.

2. _____ Roy Campanella hit more home runs (242) than any other catcher in National League history.

3. _____ Elston Howard hit a home run in his first World Series at-bat.

4. _____ Bob Gibson was the first black pitcher to win the Cy Young Award.

5. _____ Two black pitchers have won the Cy Young Award in the same season.

6. _____ Richie Allen has been the only black third baseman to be named Rookie of the Year.

7. _____ Willie Mays has been the only black player to twice hit more than 50 home runs in a season.

8. _____ Bob Gibson once played for the Harlem Globetrotters.

9. _____ Elston Howard was the last Yankee to win the MVP Award.

10. _____ Ralph Garr's nickname is "The Road Runner."

11. _____ Roy Campanella won a record-tying three MVP awards.

12. _____ Willie Mays was the first player to collect more than 3,000 hits and 500 home runs.

13. _____ Frank Robinson was a unanimous choice as the American League's MVP in 1966.

14. _____ Matty and Felipe Alou have been the only brothers to finish one-two in a batting race.

15. _____ Jackie Robinson was the only black player to appear in the 1947 World Series.

16. _____ Bobby Bonds has four times hit more than 30 home runs and stolen more than 40 bases in a season.

17. _____ Reggie Jackson has hit .300 in a season.

18. _____ Don Newcombe was the first black pitcher to win a series game.

19. _____ Larry Doby was the first black player to win the American League's MVP Award.

20. _____ Jackie Robinson was the first black player to win the National League's MVP Award.

21. _____ Hank Aaron, Roberto Clemente, and Lou Brock won the MVP Award.

22. _____ Reggie Jackson, when he hit three home runs in the final game of the 1977 series, delivered the four-base blows against three different pitchers.

23. _____ Willie Mays never won an RBI crown.

24. _____ No black player has ever won the Triple Crown.

25. _____ Don Newcombe lost all four of his pitching decisions in series play.

26. _____ Roy Campanella was the first black to hit a home run in series play.

27. _____ Larry Doby was the first black to hit two home runs in the same series.

28. _____ Hank Aaron was the first black to hit three home runs in a series.

29. _____ Jim Rice hit more home runs in one season than any other Red Sox player.

30. _____ Al Downing was the first black to appear in a World Series game for the Yankees.

31. _____ Willie Mays never batted .300 or hit a home run in series play.

32. _____ J. R. Richard has been the only black to strike out more than 300 batters in a season.

33. _____ Bob Gibson won more consecutive World Series games than any other pitcher.

34. _____ Al Downing was the first black pitcher to win a series game for an American League team.

35. _____ The Dodgers opened the 1966 World Series against the Orioles with six black players in their starting lineup.

36. _____ Bob Gibson was the last pitcher to win three games in a series.

37. _____ Dave Cash has had more at-bats in one season than any other major leaguer.

38. _____ Ferguson Jenkins has won more games than any other black pitcher.

39. _____ Willie McCovey played in four decades of major league ball.

40. _____ Jackie Robinson recorded the highest lifetime average (.311) of any black or hispanic player who finished his career with at least ten years of active service.

41. _____ Curt Flood handled 538 consecutive chances without making an error.

42. _____ Maury Wills ranks number two to Lou Brock in the number of career steals by a National Leaguer.

43. _____ Willie Mays scored the run in the 1962 Series which snapped Whitey Ford's scoreless inning skein at 33⅔ innings.

44. _____ Zoilo Versalles, Rod Carew, and Reggie Jackson have won the MVP Award in the American League.

45. _____ Willie Mays has a higher lifetime batting average than Mickey Mantle.

46. _____ Before Bill Madlock won back-to-back batting titles (1975–76), the last black or hispanic player in the National League to perform the feat was Tommy Davis (1962–63).

47. _____ Jackie Robinson was the last player in the series to execute a steal of home that was not on the front end of a double theft.

48. _____ Dick Allen won home run titles in both leagues.

42. THE TRAILBLAZERS

The following black or hispanic players were the first ones to perform for teams that previously were exclusively white: Larry Doby, Hank Thompson–Willard Brown, Sam Hairston, Bob Trice, Carlos Paula, Valmy Thomas, Jackie Robinson, Curt Roberts, Elston Howard, Hank Thompson–Monte Irvin, Ozzie Virgil, Sam Jethroe, Pumpsie Green, Ernie Banks–Gene Baker, Joe Black, and Tom Alston–Brooks Lawrence. Match the players with their respective teams.

1. _____ Browns
2. _____ Pirates
3. _____ Phillies
4. _____ Yankees
5. _____ Athletics
6. _____ Indians
7. _____ Cubs
8. _____ Reds
9. _____ Red Sox
10. _____ Senators
11. _____ Dodgers
12. _____ Braves
13. _____ Cardinals
14. _____ Giants
15. _____ Tigers
16. _____ White Sox

43. BLACK CLOUTERS

Fifteen black players have won a total of 33 league home run titles (ties count as wins). Match the following players with the number of times they have won the crown: George Foster, Ben Oglivie, Jim Rice, Larry Doby, Hank Aaron, Dick Allen, Jesse Barfield, Willie Mays, Frank Robinson, Reggie Jackson, Willie McCovey, Willie Stargell, Ernie Banks, George Scott, and Andre Dawson.

1. _____ (4)
2. _____ (4)
3. _____ (4)
4. _____ (3)
5. _____ (3)
6. _____ (2)
7. _____ (2)
8. _____ (2)
9. _____ (2)
10. _____ (2)
11. _____ (1)
12. _____ (1)
13. _____ (1)
14. _____ (1)
15. _____ (1)

44. SINGLE-SEASON SLUGGERS

Ten black players hold the single-season high in home runs for their respective club(s). (Three of them are co-holders of a club's mark.) The numbers of home runs and the clubs are provided. The players are not. One of the players holds the top position for two different teams.

1. _____ (52) San Francisco Giants
2. _____ (52) Cincinnati Reds
3. _____ (51) New York Giants *
4. _____ (49) Baltimore Orioles
5. _____ (47) Atlanta Braves **
6. _____ (47) Toronto Blue Jays
7. _____ (39) California Angels
8. _____ (38) San Diego Padres
9. _____ (37) Chicago White Sox ***
10. _____ (37) Houston Astros
11. _____ (32) Montreal Expos

   * Johnny Mize is the co-holder of this record.
  ** Eddie Mathews is the co-holder of this record.
*** Carlton Fisk is the co-holder of this record.

45. NATIONAL LEAGUE
BATTING CHAMPS

Fifteen black or hispanic players have won the National League batting title a total of 25 times: Bill Madlock, Ralph Garr, Al Oliver, Matty Alou, Roberto Clemente, Willie McGee, Jackie Robinson, Billy Williams, Tony Gwynn, Willie Mays, Rico Carty, Tim Raines, Tommy Davis, Dave Parker, and Hank Aaron. Match the players with the years in which they copped the crowns. Two of the players won the title four times. Five of them won it twice.

1. _____ (1949)
2. _____ (1954)
3. _____ (1956)
4. _____ (1959)
5. _____ (1961)
6. _____ (1962)
7. _____ (1963)
8. _____ (1964)
9. _____ (1965)
10. _____ (1966)
11. _____ (1967)
12. _____ (1970)
13. _____ (1972)
14. _____ (1974)
15. _____ (1975)
16. _____ (1976)
17. _____ (1977)
18. _____ (1978)
19. _____ (1981)
20. _____ (1982)
21. _____ (1983)
22. _____ (1984)
23. _____ (1985)
24. _____ (1986)
25. _____ (1987)

46. AMERICAN LEAGUE
BATTING CHAMPS

Six black or hispanic players—Alex Johnson, Frank Robinson, Tony Oliva, Rod Carew, Willie Wilson, and Bobby Avila—have won the American League batting title a total of 13 times. Match the players with the years in which they copped the crown(s). One of them did it seven times, one of them did it three times, and three of them did it once.

1. _____ (1954)
2. _____ (1964)
3. _____ (1965)
4. _____ (1966)
5. _____ (1969)
6. _____ (1970)
7. _____ (1971)
8. _____ (1972)
9. _____ (1973)
10. _____ (1974)
11. _____ (1975)
12. _____ (1977)
13. _____ (1978)
14. _____ (1982)

47. ROOKIES OF THE YEAR

Six of the first seven Rookie of the Year awards in the National League went to black players: Sam Jethroe, Jim Gilliam, Don Newcombe, Willie Mays, Joe Black, and Jackie Robinson. Can you place them in their proper order?

1. _____ (1947)
2. _____ (1949)
3. _____ (1950)
4. _____ (1951)
5. _____ (1952)
6. _____ (1953).

48. THE HALL OF FAME

Twenty-two black or hispanic players have been elected to the Hall of Fame. You should be able to name at least ten of them. If you can name 15, though, you're entitled to a little bit of fame for yourself.

1. _____
2. _____
3. _____
4. _____
5. _____
6. _____
7. _____
8. _____
9. _____
10. _____
11. _____
12. _____
13. _____
14. _____
15. _____
16. _____
17. _____
18. _____
19. _____
20. _____
21. _____
22. _____

To Catch a Thief

The final game of the 1926 World Series has gone down in baseball history as one of the most exciting finishes in the annals of the fall classic.

It certainly did not lack drama.

With the visiting Cardinals leading the Yankees 3–2 in the bottom of the sixth, Jesse Haines developed a finger blister while the Yankees loaded the bases with two out. Rogers Hornsby, the manager of St. Louis, decided to replace Haines with Grover Alexander, who had already won two games in the series. Alexander, one of the all-time greats of the hill, had to face Tony Lazzeri, a long-ball-hitting rookie. On the second pitch of the confrontation, Lazzeri almost decisively won the duel: he hit a long line drive to left that tailed a few feet left of the foul pole. Three pitches later, Alexander struck Lazzeri out on a sweeping curveball.

In a groove, Alexander mowed the Yankees down in order in both the seventh and the eighth innings. He had retired nine consecutive batters before he faced Babe Ruth, with two outs, in the ninth. Working cautiously, he proceeded to walk the Babe. But Alex was still not out of danger. He had to face Bob Meusel, who had won the home run crown the year before. On the first pitch to Meusel, however, Ruth pulled the unexpected: he tried to steal second base. But the Cardinals' catcher threw a strike to Hornsby to nail Ruth, who became the first and only base runner to make the last out of a World Series on an attempted steal.

After the series ended, owner Sam Breadon traded manager Hornsby to the Giants and named his catcher the team's manager. Maybe the backstop's final throw of the 1926 World Series had something to do with the owner's decision.

Who was that veteran of 21 seasons who stopped the Yankees in 1926 and led the Cardinals in 1927?

(Answer appears on page 321.)

Chapter Eleven

THE HOT CORNER

49. WHAT'S THE RETIREMENT AGE?

Fifteen familiar names are listed with the dates on which they broke into the majors. You provide the dates, within two years, when they bowed out of the big leagues.

1. _____ (1930) Luke Appling
2. _____ (1953) Ernie Banks
3. _____ (1948) Roy Campanella
4. _____ (1936) Bob Feller
5. _____ (1952) Harvey Haddix
6. _____ (1949) Monte Irvin
7. _____ (1947) Willie Jones
8. _____ (1946) Ralph Kiner
9. _____ (1941) Stan Musial
10. _____ (1926) Mel Ott
11. _____ (1940) Pee Wee Reese
12. _____ (1942) Johnny Sain
13. _____ (1946) Bobby Thomson
14. _____ (1939) Mickey Vernon
15. _____ (1944) Eddie Yost

50. ONE-TOWN MEN

Which ten of the following 20 players performed for the same club throughout their major league careers: Luke Appling, Brooks Robinson, Bill Terry, Stan Hack, Ralph Kiner, Lefty Grove, Joe Cronin, Walter Johnson, Grover Alexander, Mel Ott, Gil Hodges, Johnny Podres, Lew Burdette, Al Kaline, Ted Kluszewski, Ernie Banks, Cecil Travis, Pee Wee Reese, Eddie Mathews, and Dallas Green.

1. _____
2. _____
3. _____
4. _____
5. _____
6. _____
7. _____
8. _____
9. _____
10. _____

51. THE FIRST INNING

There have been 20 new major league franchises since 1953. Can you recall their first respective managers? The following list may give you a clue: Darrell Johnson, Ted Williams, Gene Mauch, Bob Kennedy, Harry Craft, Harry Lavagetto, Roy Hartsfield, Lou Boudreau, Charlie Grimm, Bill Rigney, Mickey Vernon, Casey Stengel, Joe Gordon, Preston Gomez, Dave Bristol, Joe Schultz, Bobby Bragan, Walt Alston, and Jimmy Dykes.

1. _____ (1953) Milwaukee Braves
2. _____ (1954) Baltimore Orioles
3. _____ (1955) Kansas City Athletics
4. _____ (1958) San Francisco Giants
5. _____ (1958) Los Angeles Dodgers
6. _____ (1961) Minnesota Twins
7. _____ (1961) Washington Senators
8. _____ (1961) Los Angeles Angels
9. _____ (1962) Houston Astros
10. _____ (1962) New York Mets
11. _____ (1966) Atlanta Braves
12. _____ (1968) Oakland A's
13. _____ (1969) Kansas City Royals
14. _____ (1969) Seattle Pilots
15. _____ (1969) Montreal Expos
16. _____ (1969) San Diego Padres
17. _____ (1970) Milwaukee Brewers
18. _____ (1972) Texas Rangers
19. _____ (1977) Seattle Mariners
20. _____ (1977) Toronto Blue Jays

52. THE LAST INNING

There have been ten major league franchises that have switched cities. Can you name the last respective managers of the original franchises? The following ten names should give you a start: Walt Alston, Harry Lavagetto, Charlie Grimm, Ted Williams, Joe Schultz, Marty Marion, Luke Appling, Eddie Joost, Bobby Bragan, and Bill Rigney.

1. _____ (1952) Boston Braves
2. _____ (1953) St. Louis Browns
3. _____ (1954) Philadelphia Athletics
4. _____ (1957) New York Giants
5. _____ (1957) Brooklyn Dodgers
6. _____ (1960) Washington Senators
7. _____ (1965) Milwaukee Braves
8. _____ (1967) Kansas City A's
9. _____ (1969) Seattle Pilots
10. _____ (1971) Washington Senators

53. SECONDARY PURSUITS

Match the following former players with the corresponding pursuits that they took up in their post-playing days.

1. _____ Vinegar Bend Mizell
2. _____ Joe Cronin
3. _____ Moe Berg
4. _____ Bobby Brown
5. _____ Billy Sunday
6. _____ George Moriarty
7. _____ Ralph Terry
8. _____ Johnny Berardino
9. _____ Al Schacht
10. _____ Red Rolfe
11. _____ Jim Brosnan
12. _____ Charlie Keller
13. _____ Greasy Neale
14. _____ Jim Thorpe
15. _____ Clark Griffith

a. Umpire
b. Actor
c. Congressman
d. Horse breeder
e. Secret agent
f. Pro football player
g. American League executive
h. Author
i. Pro football coach
j. Heart specialist
k. Golfer
l. Baseball club owner
m. Comedian ("Clown Prince of Baseball")
n. Athletic director of Dartmouth
o. Evangelist

54. MAJOR LEAGUE OWNERS

Some names of major league owners (past and present) are synonymous with the franchises they direct(ed). See how many of the following you can associate.

1. _____ Connie Mack
2. _____ Horace Stoneham
3. _____ Dan Topping
4. _____ Walter O'Malley
5. _____ Charles Comiskey
6. _____ Sam Breadon
7. _____ Tom Yawkey
8. _____ Lou Perini
9. _____ Bob Carpenter
10. _____ Bill Veeck
11. _____ Walter O. Briggs
12. _____ Clark Griffith
13. _____ Bob Short
14. _____ William Crosley
15. _____ Charles Finley
16. _____ Phillip K. Wrigley
17. _____ Mrs. Joan Payson
18. _____ Arthur Krock
19. _____ Calvin Griffith
20. _____ Gene Autry

a. Reds
b. Indians
c. Dodgers
d. Twins
e. Athletics
   (Philadelphia)
f. Tigers
g. Cubs
h. Giants
i. Padres
j. Yankees
k. Braves
l. Mets
m. Rangers
n. Phillies
o. Cardinals
p. White Sox
q. Athletics (Oakland)
r. Angels
s. Senators
t. Red Sox

55. THE MISSING LINK

Can you supply the third starting outfielder for the respective teams from the list of players that follow: Carl Furillo, Dick Sisler, Yogi Berra, Frank Robinson, Terry Moore, Roy White, Joe Rudi, Sid Gordon, Jackie Jensen, Al Simmons, Earle Combs, Vic Wertz, Don Mueller, Ted Williams, Jimmy Wynn, Reggie Smith, Roger Maris, Al Kaline, Charlie Keller, Cesar Cedeno, Harry Heilmann, Duffy Lewis, Casey Stengel, Lou Piniella, Matty Alou, and Pete Reiser.

1. Mickey Mantle, Roger Maris, and _____ (Yankees, 1961)
2. Joe DiMaggio, Tommy Henrich, and _____ (Yankees, 1941)
3. Stan Musial, Enos Slaughter, and _____ (Cardinals, 1942)
4. Tris Speaker, Harry Hooper, and _____ (Red Sox, 1916)
5. Babe Ruth, Bob Meusel, and _____ (Yankees, 1927)
6. Andy Pafko, Duke Snider, and _____ (Dodgers, 1952)
7. Dom DiMaggio, Al Zarilla, and _____ (Red Sox, 1950)
8. Bobby Bonds, Elliott Maddox, and _____ (Yankees, 1975)
9. Whitey Lockman, Willie Mays, and _____ (Giants, 1954)
10. Roberto Clemente, Willie Stargell, and _____ (Pirates, 1966)
11. Richie Ashburn, Del Ennis, and _____ (Phillies, 1950)
12. Lou Brock, Curt Flood, and _____ (Cardinals, 1968)
13. Ted Williams, Jimmy Piersall, and _____ (Red Sox, 1954)
14. Hoot Evers, Johnny Groth, and _____ (Tigers, 1950)
15. Willard Marshall, Bobby Thomson, and _____ (Giants, 1947)

16. Dixie Walker, Joe Medwick, and _____ (Dodgers, 1941)

17. Mule Haas, Bing Miller, and _____ (Athletics, 1931)

18. Ty Cobb, Heinie Manush, and _____ (Tigers, 1923)

19. Ross Youngs, Irish Meusel, and _____ (Giants, 1922)

20. Paul Blair, Don Buford, and _____ (Orioles, 1970)

21. Carl Yastrzemski, Tony Conigliaro, and _____ (Red Sox, 1970)

22. Willie Norton, Jim Northrup, and _____ (Tigers, 1969)

23. Jim North, Reggie Jackson, and _____ (Athletics, 1973)

24. Bob Watson, Jimmy Wynn, and _____ (Astros, 1973)

25. Bill Buckner, Willie Crawford, and _____ (Dodgers, 1974)

56. WHO PLAYED THIRD?

There have been many outstanding double-play combinations in the history of the major leagues. Twenty-five of the more recognizable ones, since 1940, are listed. Can you recall the third baseman who played in the same infield with them?

1. _____ Mark Belanger to Davy Johnson to Boog Powell (Orioles, 1970)
2. _____ Bert Campaneris to Dick Green to Gene Tenace (A's, 1974)
3. _____ Larry Bowa to Dave Cash to Willie Montanez (Phillies, 1974)
4. _____ Bill Russell to Dave Lopes to Steve Garvey (Dodgers, 1974)
5. _____ Phil Rizzuto to Joe Gordon to Johnny Sturm (Yankees, 1941)
6. _____ Joe Cronin to Bobby Doerr to Jimmie Foxx (Red Sox, 1941)
7. _____ Pee Wee Reese to Billy Herman to Dolph Camilli (Dodgers, 1941)
8. _____ Marty Marion to Red Schoendienst to Stan Musial (Cardinals, 1946)
9. _____ Lou Boudreau to Joe Gordon to Eddie Robinson (Indians, 1948)
10. _____ Eddie Joost to Pete Suder to Ferris Fain (A's, 1949)
11. _____ Vern Stephens to Bobby Doerr to Billy Goodman (Red Sox, 1949)
12. _____ Pee Wee Reese to Jackie Robinson to Gil Hodges (Dodgers, 1952)
13. _____ Granny Hamner to Mike Goliat to Eddie Waitkus (Phillies, 1950)
14. _____ Al Dark to Ed Stanky to Whitey Lockman (Giants, 1951)
15. _____ Phil Rizzuto to Billy Martin to Joe Collins (Yankees, 1952)
16. _____ Ray Boone to Bob Avila to Luke Easter (Indians, 1952)
17. _____ Roy McMillan to Johnny Temple to Ted Kluszewski (Reds, 1954)

18. _____ Johnny Logan to Red Schoendienst to Joe Adcock (Braves, 1958)

19. _____ Dick Groat to Bill Mazeroski to Dick Stuart (Pirates, 1960)

20. _____ Tony Kubek to Bobby Richardson to Bill Skowron (Yankees, 1961)

21. _____ Luis Aparicio to Nellie Fox to Roy Sievers (White Sox, 1961)

22. _____ Dick Groat to Julian Javier to Bill White (Cardinals, 1964)

23. _____ Don Kessinger to Gene Beckert to Ernie Banks (Cubs, 1965)

24. _____ Billy Myers to Lonny Frey to Frank McCormick (Reds, 1940)

25. _____ Pete Runnels to Cass Michaels to Mickey Vernon (Senators, 1951)

57. BROTHER COMBINATIONS

Provide the first name of the other brother who played in the major leagues.

1. _____, Joe, Dom DiMaggio
2. _____, Rick Ferrell
3. _____, Walker Cooper
4. _____, Larry Sherry
5. _____, Jesse Barnes
6. _____, Jerome Dean
7. _____, Gaylord Perry
8. _____, Phil Niekro
9. _____, Stan Coveleski
10. _____, Henry Mathewson
11. _____, Matty, Felipe Alou
12. _____, Johnny O'Brien
13. _____, Joe Torre
14. _____, Tony Conigliaro
15. _____, Clete, Cloyd Boyer
16. _____, Bob Meusel
17. _____, George Dickey
18. _____, Henry Aaron
19. _____, Paul Waner
20. _____, Jose, Tommy Cruz
21. _____, Harry Walker
22. _____, Dick Sisler
23. _____, Marv Throneberry
24. _____, Tom, Tim, Joe, Frank Delahanty
25. _____, Hal Keller

58. NO HANDICAP

During the annals of major league baseball, there have been many players who had to overcome adversity in order to fulfill their lifelong ambitions. Five of them follow: Mordecai Brown, Pete Gray, Red Ruffing, John Hiller, and William Hoy. Match them with the physical impairments that they had.

1. _____ Missing toes
2. _____ Deaf and dumb
3. _____ Missing fingers
4. _____ Missing arm
5. _____ Heart condition

59. BASEBALL TRAGEDIES

Match the following players who died tragically—either during or shortly after their playing careers—with the year in which they passed away: Roberto Clemente, Kenny Hubbs, Harry Agganis, Lou Gehrig, Thurman Munson, Ray Chapman, and Ed Delahanty.

1. _____ (1903)
2. _____ (1920)
3. _____ (1941)
4. _____ (1955)
5. _____ (1964)
6. _____ (1972)
7. _____ (1979)

60. NO UNTOUCHABLES

It's pretty hard to believe that the top three hitters who ever lived—Ty Cobb, Rogers Hornsby, and Joe Jackson— were traded from one team to another. That's been the case of many great players, though. Twenty-five players who ended up their careers with .300 or better lifetime averages are listed with the team with which they first made their name. Name the team to which they were either traded or sold.

1. _____ Ty Cobb (Tigers)
2. _____ Rogers Hornsby (Cardinals)
3. _____ Joe Jackson (Indians)
4. _____ Tris Speaker (Red Sox)
5. _____ Babe Ruth (Red Sox)
6. _____ George Sisler (Browns)
7. _____ Al Simmons (A's)
8. _____ Paul Waner (Pirates)
9. _____ Eddie Collins (A's)
10. _____ Jimmie Foxx (A's))
11. _____ Joe Medwick (Cardinals)
12. _____ Chuck Klein (Phillies)
13. _____ Frank Frisch (Giants)
14. _____ Hank Greenberg (Tigers)
15. _____ Johnny Mize (Cardinals)
16. _____ Mickey Cochrane (A's)
17. _____ Richie Ashburn (Phillies)
18. _____ George Kell (Tigers)
19. _____ Dixie Walker (Dodgers)
20. _____ Ernie Lombardi (Reds)
21. _____ Harvey Kuenn (Tigers)
22. _____ Hank Aaron (Braves)
23. _____ Willie Mays (Giants)
24. _____ Joe Cronin (Senators)
25. _____ Enos Slaughter (Cardinals)

61. WHEN DID THEY COME UP?

1930s—1940s

See if you can match the players that follow with the year in which they first broke into the majors (if you are within one year of the actual season, before or after, count it as a correct answer): Tom Henrich, Warren Spahn, Red Schoendienst, Joe DiMaggio, Eddie Yost, George Kell, Joe Gordon, Stan Musial, Ted Williams, and Dom DiMaggio.

1. _____ (1936)   6. _____ (1941)
2. _____ (1937)   7. _____ (1942)
3. _____ (1938)   8. _____ (1943)
4. _____ (1939)   9. _____ (1944)
5. _____ (1940)   10. _____ (1945)

1940s—1950s

We're in the post-war era now. See how you do with the following ten players (if you are within one year of the actual season, before or after, count it as a correct answer): Whitey Ford, Willie Mays, Yogi Berra, Rocky Colavito, Jackie Robinson, Hank Aaron, Al Kaline, Richie Ashburn, Jerry Coleman, and Eddie Mathews.

1. _____ (1946)   6. _____ (1951)
2. _____ (1947)   7. _____ (1952)
3. _____ (1948)   8. _____ (1953)
4. _____ (1949)   9. _____ (1954)
5. _____ (1950)   10. _____ (1955)

1950s—1960s

We're moving into your wheelhouse now. Take a good cut at the following players (if you are within one year of the actual season, before or after, count it as a correct answer): Mel Stottlemyre, Roger Maris, Ed Kranepool, Frank Robinson, Maury Wills, Pete Rose, Catfish Hunter, Carl Yastrzemski, Juan Marichal, and Ron Fairly.

1. _____ (1956)	6. _____ (1961)
2. _____ (1957)	7. _____ (1962)
3. _____ (1958)	8. _____ (1963)
4. _____ (1959)	9. _____ (1964)
5. _____ (1960)	10. _____ (1965)

1960s—1970s

We're now in the present era. It's a home run contest. The pitches are coming right down the middle. See how you can do with the following offerings (if you are within one year of the actual season, before or after, count it as a correct answer): Fred Lynn, Cesar Cedeno, George Scott, Jim Rice, Rod Carew, Mike Schmidt, Dave Parker, Bobby Bonds, Chris Speier, and Thurman Munson.

1. _____ (1966)	6. _____ (1971)
2. _____ (1967)	7. _____ (1972)
3. _____ (1968)	8. _____ (1973)
4. _____ (1969)	9. _____ (1974)
5. _____ (1970)	10. _____ (1975)

Two Strikes Against Him

Ray Chapman, had he not been hit by an errant pitch by the Yankees' Carl Mays, might have ended up in the Hall of Fame.

A .278 lifetime hitter, the 29-year-old shortstop was just coming into his own right as a batsman, averaging over .300 in three of his last four years. And he was an accomplished base runner, stealing 233 career bases, including 52 in 1917, the most bases that any Indian had ever pilfered in one season until Miguel Dilone swiped 61 in 1980.

But the deuces were stacked against him on August 16, 1920. The number-two batter in the lineup that day, he stroked two hits—both of them doubles—scored two runs and stole two bases. Defensively, he made two assists, two putouts, and two errors. In fact, he was hit with two pitches by Mays. The second one killed him.

His replacement in the lineup, had Chapman not been killed by that ill-fated pitch, might not have ended up in the Hall of Fame. For he very well could have been relegated to years on the bench behind a blossoming star. But Chapman's back-up did go on to play 14 years in the big leagues. He averaged .312 lifetime and batted .300 ten times, including nine times in his first ten years in the majors. The one time that he failed to bat .300, he missed by just one point. But perhaps the most incredible story about this Hall of Famer was his ability to make contact. He averaged only eight strikeouts per season for 14 years. In his last nine seasons he whiffed just five times per year. And in both 1930 and 1932 he fanned only three times, the all-time low for a full-time player.

Who was this one-time Indian–Yankee star who got his best break on the day that Chapman got the worst break of any major league player?

(Answer appears on page 322.)

Chapter Twelve

TOUCHING ALL THE BASES

62. WHOM DID THEY PRECEDE?

See if you can determine whom the following players preceded at their positions in the field.

1. _____ Bill White (Giants)
   a. Nippy Jones b. Steve Bilko c. Joe Torre d. Orlando Cepeda
2. _____ Tony Lazzeri (Yankees)
   a. George Stirnweiss b. Frankie Crosetti c. Joe Gordon d. Jerry Priddy
3. _____ Leo Durocher (Dodgers)
   a. Arky Vaughan b. Pee Wee Reese c. Billy Herman d. Frenchy Bordagaray
4. _____ Eddie Mathews (Braves)
   a. Clete Boyer b. Dennis Menke c. Frank Bolling d. Roy McMillan
5. _____ Bobby Thomson (Giants)
   a. Clint Hartung b. Whitey Lockman c. Willie Mays d. Monte Irvin*
6. _____ Harry Walker (Phillies)
   a. Richie Ashburn b. Del Ennis c. Dick Sisler d. Bill Nicholson
7. _____ Joe DiMaggio (Yankees)
   a. Cliff Mapes b. Mickey Mantle c. Johnny Lindell d. Irv Noren
8. _____ Dom DiMaggio (Red Sox)
   a. Jackie Jensen b. Gene Stephens c. Tommy Umphlett d. Jimmy Piersall

* Position: Center field.

9. _____ Yogi Berra (Yankees)
   a. Elston Howard b. John Blanchard c. Jake Gibbs
   d. Jesse Gonder
10. _____ Del Crandall (Braves)
    a. Joe Torre b. Del Rice c. Stan Lopata d. Bob Uecker

63. WHOM DID THEY SUCCEED?

See if you can figure out whom the following players succeeded at their positions on the field.

1. _____ Babe Dahlgren (Yankees)
   a. Nick Etten b. George McQuinn c. Wally Pipp d. Lou Gehrig
2. _____ Jackie Robinson (Dodgers)
   a. Eddie Miksis b. Eddie Stanky c. Cookie Lavagetto d. Don Zimmer*
3. _____ Chico Carrasquel (White Sox)
   a. Luke Appling b. Cass Michaels c. Don Kolloway d. Willie Miranda
4. _____ Brooks Robinson (Orioles)
   a. Vern Stephens b. Billy Hunter c. George Kell d. Billy Goodman
5. _____ George Selkirk (Yankees)
   a. Ben Chapman b. Earle Combs c. Bob Meusel d. Babe Ruth
6. _____ Carl Yastrzemski (Red Sox)
   a. Ted Williams b. Clyde Vollmer c. Sam Mele d. Al Zarilla
7. _____ Lou Brock (Cardinals)
   a. Enos Slaughter b. Wally Moon c. Stan Musial d. Joe Cunningham
8. _____ Roger Maris (Yankees)
   a. Tommy Henrich b. Hank Bauer c. Norm Siebern d. Harry Simpson
9. _____ John Roseboro (Dodgers)
   a. Roy Campanella b. Bruce Edwards c. Joe Pignatano d. Rube Walker
10. _____ Wes Westrum (Giants)
    a. Ernie Lombardi b. Sal Yvars c. Walker Cooper d. Ray Mueller

* Position: Second base.

64. CHIPS OFF THE OLD BLOCK

The players who are listed below had fathers who preceded them to the major leagues. Name the source of the
offspring.

1. _____ Dick Sisler
2. _____ Tom Tresh
3. _____ Mike Hegan
4. _____ Buddy Bell
5. _____ Doug Camilli
6. _____ Hal Lanier
7. _____ Bob Boone
8. _____ Bump Wills
9. _____ Roy Smalley
10. _____ Steve Trout

65. THE GAS HOUSE GANG

In the 1930s the St. Louis Cardinals had a colorful group
of players who were known as the Gas House Gang. Match
the Gas Housers with the nicknames that they acquired.

1. _____ James Collins   a. Ducky
2. _____ Frankie Frisch   b. Spud
3. _____ Leo Durocher   c. Wild
4. _____ Johnny Martin   d. Rip
5. _____ Joe Medwick   e. Dizzy
6. _____ Enos Slaughter   f. The Fordham Flash
7. _____ Virgil Davis   g. Daffy
8. _____ Jerome Dean   h. The Lip
9. _____ Paul Dean   i. Pepper
10. ____ Bill Hallahan   j. Country

66. THE YEAR OF _____

Fit the phrases listed below to the years to which they apply.

The Whiz Kids
The Amazin' Ones
The Hitless Wonders
Gionfriddo's Gem
Feller's Pick-off (?)
Sandy's Snatch
Maz's Sudden Shot
The Gas House Gang
Larsen's Perfect Game
The M&M Boys
Pesky's Pause
Home Run Baker
Murderers' Row

The Babe Calls His Shot
The Go-Go Sox
The Black Sox
The Wild Hoss of the Osage
Merkle's Boner
Mays's Miracle Catch
Ernie's Snooze
Billy the Kid
Alex's Biggest Strikeout
The Miracle Braves
Mickey's Passed Ball
The Miracle of Coogan's
Bluff

1. _____ (1906)
2. _____ (1908)
3. _____ (1911)
4. _____ (1914)
5. _____ (1919)
6. _____ (1926)
7. _____ (1927)
8. _____ (1931)
9. _____ (1932)
10. _____ (1934)
11. _____ (1939)
12. _____ (1941)
13. _____ (1946)
14. _____ (1947)
15. _____ (1948)
16. _____ (1950)
17. _____ (1951)
18. _____ (1953)
19. _____ (1954)
20. _____ (1955)
21. _____ (1956)
22. _____ (1959)
23. _____ (1960)
24. _____ (1961)
25. _____ (1969)

67. THE MEN AT THE MIKE

Most teams have an announcer who becomes known in his bailiwick as the "voice" of the club. Some of the announcers who are listed in the left-hand column have called the play-by-play with more than one team. But they have made their reputations as the "voice" of one particular club. Match the "voice" with the respective team.

1. _____ Mel Allen		a.	Pirates
2. _____ Red Barber		b.	Browns
3. _____ Russ Hodges		c.	White Sox
4. _____ Lindsey Nelson		d.	A's (Oakland)
5. _____ Curt Gowdy		e.	Reds
6. _____ By Saam		f.	Giants
7. _____ Bob Prince		g.	Yankees
8. _____ Vince Scully		h.	Tigers
9. _____ Waite Hoyt		i.	Dodgers (Brooklyn)
10. _____ Chuck Thompson		j.	Red Sox
11. _____ Dizzy Dean		k.	Cardinals
12. _____ Jack Brickhouse		l.	Orioles
13. _____ Ernie Harwell		m.	Dodgers (Los Angeles)
14. _____ Harry Carey		n.	Mets
15. _____ Monte Clark		o.	Phillies

68. INFIELD INFLATION

The infield of the 1911 Philadelphia Athletics is said to have been worth $100,000; the infield of the 1948 A's is reported to have been valued at $1,000,000. Take the following ten players and place them at their respective positions: Stuffy McInnis, Hank Majeski, Frank Baker, Ferris Fain, Pete Suder, Jack Barry, Eddie Collins, Eddie Joost, Ira Thomas, and Buddy Rosar.

1911 Athletics
1B _____
2B _____
SS _____
3B _____
 C _____

1948 Athletics
1B _____
2B _____
SS _____
3B _____
 C _____

69. PEN NAMES

In the following pairs of names, see if you can distinguish the major league player from the major league writer. Which one was the artist on the diamond?

1. Grantland Rice–Del Rice
2. Dan Parker–Wes Parker
3. Fred Winchell–Walter Winchell
4. Woody Woodward–Stanley Woodward
5. Frank Sullivan–Ed Sullivan
6. Gary Schumacher–Hal Schumacher
7. Dick Williams–Joe Williams
8. Tom Meany–Pat Meany
9. Art Fowler–Gene Fowler
10. Frank Graham–Jack Graham
11. Quentin Reynolds–Carl Reynolds
12. Frank Adams–Babe Adams
13. Bill Dailey–Arthur Dailey
14. Don Gross–Milton Gross
15. Babe Young–Dick Young
16. Red Smith–Hal Smith
17. Babe Twombly–Wells Twombly
18. Earl Lawson–Roxie Lawson
19. Ray Murray–Jim Murray
20. Johnny Powers–Jimmy Powers

70. MATCHING MOGULS

Match the present-day major league moguls in the left-hand column with the big-league teams that they own in the right-hand column.

1. _____ Peter O'Malley	a. Atlanta
2. _____ Bill Giles	b. Baltimore
3. _____ Eddie Chiles	c. Boston
4. _____ Tom Monaghan	d. California
5. _____ Tribune Co.	e. Chicago Cubs
6. _____ Bud Selig	f. Chicago
7. _____ August Busch, Jr.	White Sox
8. _____ Charles Bronfman	g. Cincinnati
9. _____ Edward Bennett Williams	h. Cleveland
10. _____ John Labatt Ltd.	i. Detroit
11. _____ Nelson Doubleday,	j. Houston
Fred Wilpon	k. Kansas City
12. _____ Joan Kroc	l. Los Angeles
13. _____ Carl Pohlad	m. Milwaukee
14. _____ Jerry Reinsdorf	n. Minnesota
15. _____ Haywood Sullivan	o. Montreal
16. _____ Robert Lurie	p. New York
17. _____ Richard Jacobs,	Mets
David Jacobs	q. New York
18. _____ Gene Autry	Yankees
19. _____ Robert Haas	r. Oakland
20. _____ Mac Prine	s. Philadelphia
21. _____ John McMullen	t. Pittsburgh
22. _____ Ted Turner	u. St. Louis
23. _____ Ewing Kauffman	v. San Diego
24. _____ George Argyros	w. San Francisco
25. _____ Marge Schott	x. Seattle
26. _____ George Steinbrenner	y. Texas
	z. Toronto

71. A STAR IS BORN

Match the players listed with the cities in which they were born.

1. _____ Hank Aaron   a. Omaha, Neb.
2. _____ Johnny Bench   b. Martinez, Calif.
3. _____ Tommy Davis   c. Hertford, N.C.
4. _____ Al Kaline   d. Mobile, Ala.
5. _____ Brooks Robinson   e. Beaumont, Tex.
6. _____ Frank Robinson   f. Oklahoma City,
7. _____ Pete Rose   Oklahoma
8. _____ Bob Gibson   g. Little Rock, Ark.
9. _____ Jim Hunter   h. Cincinnati, Ohio
10. _____ Frank McGraw   i. Brookyn, N.Y.
                                      j. Baltimore, Md.

72. THE NATIONAL PASTIME

Baseball truly is the national pastime. Today's players come from every state in the United States except one. They come from large cities, small hamlets, and rural intersects. In the following five quizzes, they come to you in groups of ten. One of the quizzes contains one state that has not produced a present-day major-league player. See how well you can match up the players in the left-hand columns with their places of birth.

Alabama to Georgia

1. _____ Brian Dayett
2. _____ Tim Raines
3. _____ Eddie Murray
4. _____ Don Sutton
5. _____ Jody Davis
6. _____ Don Martin
7. _____ Ron Hassey
8. _____ Kevin McReynolds
9. _____ Goose Gossage
10. _____ Scott Loucks

a. Clio, Ala.
b. Anchorage, Alaska
c. Tuscon, Ariz.
d. Little Rock, Ark.
e. Los Angeles, Calif.
f. Colorado Springs, Colo.
g. New London, Conn.
h. Dover, Del.
i. Sanford, Fla.
j. Gainesville, Ga.

Hawaii to Maryland

1. _____ Rickey Henderson
2. _____ John Shelby
3. _____ Charlie Hough
4. _____ Bob Horner
5. _____ Cal Ripken
6. _____ Don Mattingly
7. _____ Vance Law
8. _____ Bob Stanley
9. _____ Tim Laudner
10. _____ Ron Guidry

a. Honolulu, Hawaii
b. Boise, Idaho
c. Chicago, Ill.
d. Evansville, Ind.
e. Mason City, Iowa
f. Junction City, Kans.
g. Lexington, Ky.
h. Lafayette, La.
i. Portland, Maine
j. Havre de Grace, Md.

Massachusetts to New Jersey

1. _____	Dave Winfield	a. Brockton, Mass.
2. _____	Rick Sutcliffe	b. Detroit, Mich.
3. _____	Wade Boggs	c. St. Paul, Minn.
4. _____	John Lowenstein	d. Jackson, Miss.
5. _____	Rick Cerone	e. Independence, Mo.
6. _____	Frank Tanana	f. Wolf Point, Mont.
7. _____	Charlie Kerfeld	g. Omaha, Neb.
8. _____	Mike Flanagan	h. Carson City, Nev.
9. _____	Steve Balboni	i. Manchester, N. H.
10. _____	Dave Parker	j. Newark, N. J.

New Mexico to South Carolina

1. _____	Willie Randolph	a. Tularosa, N. M.
2. _____	Johnny Ray	b. Brooklyn, N. Y.
3. _____	Steve Ontiveros	c. Goldsboro, N. C.
4. _____	Bruce Sutter	d. Fargo, N. D.
5. _____	Lou Whitaker	e. Dayton, Ohio
6. _____	Davey Lopes	f. Chouteau, Okla.
7. _____	Jerry Narron	g. Pendleton, Ore.
8. _____	Dave Kingman	h. Lancaster, Pa.
9. _____	Mike Schmidt	i. East Providence, R. I.
		j. Holly Hill, S. C.

South Dakota to Wyoming

1. _____	Ron Cey	a. Rapid City, S. D.
2. _____	Dave Collins	b. Memphis, Tenn.
3. _____	Dan Spillner	c. Refugio, Tex.
4. _____	Pat Putnam	d. Bellows Falls, Utah
5. _____	Shane Rawley	e. Bethel, Vt.
6. _____	George Brett	f. Richmond, Va.
7. _____	Bill Madlock	g. Tacoma, Wash.
8. _____	Carlton Fisk	h. Moundsville, W. Va.
9. _____	Johnny Grubb	i. Racine, Wis.
10. _____	Nolan Ryan	j. Casper, Wyo.

73. THE INTERNATIONAL PASTIME

Not all of the major leaguers in the history of baseball have been born on the mainland of the United States. Many of them have come from foreign states, countries, islands, territories, and provinces. See if you can match the players with their place of birth.

1. _____ Sandy Alomar
2. _____ Cesar Cedeno
3. _____ Bert Campaneris
4. _____ Rod Carew
5. _____ Dave Concepcion
6. _____ Irish McIlveen
7. _____ Jorge Orta
8. _____ Ferguson Jenkins
9. _____ Bobby Thomson
10. _____ Moe Drabowsky
11. _____ Elmer Valo
12. _____ Masanori Murakami
13. _____ Reno Bertoia
14. _____ Elrod Hendricks
15. _____ Andre Rodgers
16. _____ Mike Lum
17. _____ Al Campanis
18. _____ Jimmy Austin

a. Otsuki, Japan
b. Swansea, Wales
c. Gatun, Panama
d. Salinas, Puerto Rico
e. Chartham, (Ontario) Canada
f. Ozanna, Poland
g. Mantanzas, Cuba
h. Honolulu, Hawaii
i. Mazatian, Mexico
j. Santo Domingo, Dominican Republic
k. Nassau, Bahamas
l. Kos, Greece
m. Glasgow, Scotland
n. Ribnik, Czechoslovakia
o. St. Vito, Udine, Italy
p. Aragua, Venezuela
q. St. Thomas, Virgin Islands
r. Belfast, Ireland

Where Are The Iron Men?

What's happened to the complete game in World Series play?

Why, in the first World Series (1903) that was ever played, a Pirate strongman pitched five complete games. That's right, it's still a record. But, in that same series, a rubber arm for the Red Sox pitched four complete games. That's the second highest number of complete games that has ever been pitched in one series.

As recently as 1956, though, five different Yankee pitchers threw complete games in consecutive contests. They were Whitey Ford, Tom Sturdivant, Don Larsen, Bob Turley, and Johnny Kucks, respectively. That's a record, too.

They must not make them the way they used to, though. Take the National League, for example. In the 1970s, 61 World Series games were played. But National League pitchers threw only five complete games. (And one of the pitchers hurled full games twice.) That's a complete-game average of 8.2 percent.

During the 1970s, 29 different pitchers in the National League started a game. Some of them did it a number of times. But only four of those 29 pitchers managed to complete a game. That's a pitcher-completion average of 13.8 percent.

National League pitchers began the decade by failing to get a complete game out of the first seven starters. In 1971 two different pitchers completed three games. But from 1972 to Game Two of the 1977 series, Senior Circuit hurlers failed to complete a game in 31 attempts. Two different pitchers completed games for the National League representative in 1977, but Chub Feeney's league got on another streak: in the next 18 games the National League did not get a route-going performance from one of its starters.

If you can name two of the four complete-game pitchers, you're already doing better than the National League hurlers of the 1970s did. If you can name three of them, you can take your turn with Ford, Kucks, *et al*. If you can come up with four of the pitchers, Bill Dinneen of the 1903 Red Sox will have to move over in order to make room for you. And if you can spiel off all four pitchers, including the one pitcher who did it twice, you and Deacon Phillippe of the 1903 Pirates are in a class by yourselves.

(Answer appears on page 322.)

Chapter Thirteen

THE MANAGERS

74. QUICK QUIZZING
THE MANAGERS

I.

From the names listed in the right-hand column, list in order: 1.) the youngest manager ever to begin a season, 2.) the youngest manager ever to finish a season, 3.) the youngest manager ever to win a pennant, 4.) the oldest manager ever to debut as manager, and 5.) the oldest manager ever to win a pennant for the first time.

1. _____ Roger Peckinpaugh
2. _____ Tom Sheehan
3. _____ Burt Shotton
4. _____ Joe Cronin
5. _____ Lou Boudreau

II.

Match the successful managers listed on the right-hand side with the number of pennants and World Series (combined total) they won. The total is contained in parentheses on the left-hand side.

1. _____ (17)   Walter Alston
2. _____ (16)   Casey Stengel
3. _____ (14)   John McGraw
4. _____ (13)   Joe McCarthy
5. _____ (11)   Connie Mack

III.

The men listed on the left-hand side were all playing managers who won at least one pennant. Yet each was traded—while still a player on that team—to another one which, in every case but one, the player continued to manage. Match the playing manager with the trade in which he was connected.

1. _____ Joe Cronin   a. Indians–Red Sox
2. _____ Rogers Hornsby   b. Senators–Tigers
3. _____ Lou Boudreau   c. Cardinals–Giants
4. _____ Bucky Harris   d. Cubs–Yankees
5. _____ Frank Chance   e. Senators–Red Sox

IV.

Match the managers in the right-hand column with their respective all-time winning percentages in the left-hand column.

1. _____ (.614)   Billy Southworth
2. _____ (.593)   Frank Chance
3. _____ (.593)   John McGraw
4. _____ (.589)   Joe McCarthy
5. _____ (.582)   Al Lopez

75. DID THEY OR DIDN'T THEY . . . MANAGE?

When we look back, we sometimes find it hard to sort out fact from fiction in baseball. See if you can zero in on the 20 players who became managers from the following list of 40.

Joe Adcock	Red Rolfe
Bobby Brown	Roy Smalley
Joe Gordon	Duke Snider
Ken Keltner	Ben Chapman
Enos Slaughter	Jim Landis
Kerby Farrell	Jim Lemon
Bill Dickey	Jerry Lynch
Bucky Walters	Freddie Fitzsimmons
Bobby Wine	Irv Noren
Eddie Pellagrini	Wally Post
Walker Cooper	Bob Elliott
Nippy Jones	Eddie Lopat
Phil Cavarretta	Jerry Priddy
Christy Mathewson	Gene Hermanski
Sid Hudson	Babe Ruth
Bob Friend	Johnny Pesky
Bobby Thomson	Jim Hegan
Luke Appling	Dick Sisler
Eddie Joost	Mel McGaha
Mickey Vernon	Eddie Stanky

1. _____	11. _____
2. _____	12. _____
3. _____	13. _____
4. _____	14. _____
5. _____	15. _____
6. _____	16. _____
7. _____	17. _____
8. _____	18. _____
9. _____	19. _____
10. _____	20. _____

76. POST-WAR WORLD SERIES WINNERS

There have been 29 managers who have led their teams to World Series victories in the post-World War II era. Fourteen of them have been National League managers; fifteen of them have been American League skippers. One of them has won titles in both leagues. See how many of them you can name.

National League	American League
1. _____	1. _____
2. _____	2. _____
3. _____	3. _____
4. _____	4. _____
5. _____	5. _____
6. _____	6. _____
7. _____	7. _____
8. _____	8. _____
9. _____	9. _____
10. _____	10. _____
11. _____	11. _____
12. _____	12. _____
13. _____	13. _____
14. _____	14. _____
	15. _____

77. BACK-TO-BACK PENNANT
WINNERS

There have been 11 major league managers in the post-World War II era who have led their teams to consecutive pennants. Two of them have done it twice. See if you can place the name with the period.

1. _____ (1949–53)
2. _____ (1952–53)
3. _____ (1955–56)
4. _____ (1955–58)*
5. _____ (1957–58)
6. _____ (1961–63)
7. _____ (1965–66)*
8. _____ (1967–68)
9. _____ (1969–71)
10. _____ (1972–73)
11. _____ (1975–76)
12. _____ (1976–77)
13. _____ (1977–78)

* The second time.

78. MANAGERS IN SEARCH OF A PENNANT

Name the ten managers from the following 20 who never led a team to the pennant: Red Rolfe, Steve O'Neill, Eddie Stanky, Bill Rigney, Al Dark, Birdie Tebbetts, Fred Hutchinson, Al Lopez, Mike Higgins, Bobby Bragan, Danny Murtaugh, Harry Walker, Mel Ott, Sam Mele, Hank Bauer, Fred Haney, Johnny Keane, Gene Mauch, Dick Williams, and Paul Richards.

1. _____
2. _____
3. _____
4. _____
5. _____
6. _____
7. _____
8. _____
9. _____
10. _____

79. YOU'RE HIRED TO BE FIRED

In the left-hand column are listed men who managed 16 different major league clubs. To their right is noted the team that they managed (many of them guided more than one) and the year in which they were succeeded by a manager who started the season with his team. This eliminates interim managers who finished up a season while their owners were looking for full-time field leaders. Some of the managers who are listed were fired, some resigned, and one died. Match them with their successors who are listed in the right-hand column.

1. _____ Joe McCarthy   a. Burt Shotton
     (Yanks, 1947)   b. Bill Terry
2. _____ Yogi Berra   c. Leo Durocher
     (Yanks, 1965)   d. Dick Sisler
3. _____ John McGraw   e. Bucky Harris
     (Giants, 1933)   f. Bobby Bragan
4. _____ Mel Ott   g. Johnny Keane
     (Giants, 1949)*   h. Eddie Dyer
5. _____ Leo Durocher   i. Walt Alston
     (Dodgers, 1949)*   j. Gene Mauch
6. _____ Charlie Dressen   k. Whitey Lockman
     (Dodgers, 1954)   l. Harry Walker
7. _____ Billy Southworth   m. Red Schoendienst
     (Cards, 1946)   n. Earl Weaver
8. _____ Johnny Keane   o. Al Lopez
     (Cards, 1965)   p. Al Dark
9. _____ Eddie Sawyer   q. Kerby Farrell
     (Phils, 1961)   r. Joe McCarthy
10. _____ Danny Murtaugh   s. Rogers Hornsby
     (Pirates, 1965)   t. Billy Martin
11. _____ Fred Hutchinson
     (Reds, 1965)
12. _____ Leo Durocher
     (Cubs, 1973)
13. _____ Birdie Tebbetts
     (Braves, 1963)

* These managers were involved in two shake-ups by team organizations shortly into the season.

14. _____ Al Lopez
    (Indians, 1957)
15. _____ Mayo Smith
    (Tigers, 1971)
16. _____ Dick Williams
    (A's, 1974)
17. _____ Zack Taylor
    (Browns, 1952)
18. _____ Marty Marion
    (White Sox, 1957)
19. _____ Joe Cronin
    (Red Sox, 1948)
20. _____ Hank Bauer
    (Orioles, 1969)

80. MANAGERIAL HALF TRUTHS

Mark "T" or "F" for "True" or "False" before each statement.

1. _____ Joe Cronin was the last Red Sox manager to direct the Bosox to a World Series victory.

2. _____ Joe Cronin was the last Senator manager to win a pennant.

3. _____ Lou Boudreau was the last Indian manager to win a World Series.

4. _____ Bill Carrigan (1915–16) has been the only Red Sox manager to direct Boston to back-to-back world championships.

5. _____ Del Baker was the first bench manager to guide the Tigers to a pennant (1940).

6. _____ Mickey Cochrane has been the only Tiger manager to guide the Bengals to back-to-back pennants.

7. _____ Bill Rigney was the last Giant manager to lead his charges to a pennant.

8. _____ Bill Dickey never managed the Yankees.

9. _____ Chuck Dressen was the last manager to win back-to-back pennants (1952–53) with the Dodgers.

10. _____ Walter Alston has been the only manager to lead the Dodgers to the world championship.

11. _____ Leo Durocher's tenure as manager of the Dodgers was longer than his reign as boss of the Giants.

12. _____ Charlie Grimm never managed a World Series winner.

13. _____ Frank Chance was the only manager of the Cubs who has won a world championship.

14. _____ Eddie Dyer, Johnny Keane, and Red Schoendienst have led the Cardinals to world titles in the post-World War II era.

15. _____ Frankie Frisch was a retired player when the Cardinals won the pennant and World Series in 1934.

16. _____ Al Lopez won pennants with two different clubs.

17. _____ Fred Haney directed the Braves to their first world title in 1957.

18. _____ Bucky Harris was the only Senator manager to lead his team to two pennants.

19. _____ Bucky Harris was the youngest manager to lead his team to a world title.

20. _____ Gil Hodges had a losing record as a major league manager.

21. _____ Rogers Hornsby never managed in the American League.

22. _____ Ralph Houk won pennants in his first three years as manager of the Yankees.

23. _____ Miller Huggins won more World Series than he lost.

24. _____ Fred Hutchinson never managed a pennant winner.

25. _____ Hughie Jennings of the Tigers (1907–09) was the only manager to lose three consecutive World Series.

26. _____ Fielder Jones of the White Sox was the winning manager in the only intercity World Series in Chicago.

27. _____ Johnny Keane was the last Cardinal manager to lead the Redbirds to the world title.

28. _____ Al Lopez, in his first nine years of managing (1951–59), never brought his teams home worse than second.

29. _____ Connie Mack's teams won nine pennants, but they appeared in only eight World Series.

30. _____ Gene Mauch managed the last pennant winner for the Phillies.

31. _____ Joe McCarthy had a better World Series winning percentage with the Yankees than Casey Stengel.

32. _____ John McGraw lost more World Series than any other team leader.

33. _____ Bill McKechnie was the only Red manager to lead his team to two consecutive pennants.

34. _____ Walter Alston was the only National League manager to lead his team to more than one pennant in the 1960s.

35. _____ Walter Alston's managerial opponent in the 1965 World Series was Sam Mele.

36. _____ Danny Murtaugh was the only Pirate manager to lead his team to the world title.

37. _____ Steve O'Neill was the last Tiger manager to lead the Bengals to the world championship.

38. _____ Wilbert Robinson won more pennants with the Dodgers than Leo Durocher.

39. _____ Billy Martin led two different teams to pennants.

40. _____ Red Schoendienst won more consecutive pennants as manager of the Cardinals than any other Redbird leader.

158

41. _____ Luke Sewell was the only Brown manager to lead his team to a pennant.

42. _____ Bill Virdon managed the Yankees.

43. _____ Mayo Smith's 1968 Tigers were the first team to defeat the Cardinals in the World Series since Joe McCarthy's 1943 Yankees.

44. _____ Billy Southworth won pennants with two different National League teams.

45. _____ Tris Speaker never managed a World Series winner.

46. _____ Earl Weaver has a winning record in World Series play.

47. _____ Bill Terry's managerial opponent in the 1933 Series (Giants–Senators) was Bucky Harris.

48. _____ Hank Bauer led a team to a World Series sweep.

49. _____ Rogers Hornsby won more games than he lost in World Series play.

50. _____ Luke Appling, Ted Lyons, and Jimmy Dykes all managed the White Sox.

The Trivia Tandem

Sometimes we have a tendency to remember events which happened long ago better than those which occurred "only yesterday."

Take the case of Joe DiMaggio and Pete Rose, for example. Both of them manufactured the longest batting streaks in the history of their respective leagues. In 1941 DiMaggio hit safely in 56 consecutive games, which is the major league record; in 1978 Rose batted cleanly in 44 consecutive games, which is the modern-day National League record.

On the nights on which their respective streaks came to a close, they were handcuffed by a starting and a relieving pitcher. Much has been written about the duo of Indian pitchers who halted DiMaggio's streak. Jim Bagby, the son of a former 31-game season winner for the Indians, was the starter; Al Smith, who won 12 of 25 decisions that year, came on in relief.

So far little has been written about the two Brave pitchers who helped to stop Rose's streak. Undoubtedly, in time, they will become a more important trivia tandem. One of them was a rookie at the time; the other one was a journeyman relief pitcher.

I'll be surprised if you can name both of them. Can you?
(Answer appears on page 322.)

Chapter Fourteen

THE ALL-STAR GAME

81. ALL-STAR GAME STANDOUTS

Match the players who are listed below with the All-Star Game records that they set.

Phil Cavarretta	Tommy Bridges
Roberto Clemente	Terry Moore
Whitey Ford	Ted Williams
Yogi Berra	Stan Musial
Willie Mays	Pete Rose
Satchel Paige	Dave Winfield
Nelson Fox	Rod Carew
Charlie Gehringer	Brooks Robinson
Joe DiMaggio	Pie Traynor
Tony Oliva	Goose Gossage
Willie Jones	Atlee Hammaker
Hank Aaron	Joe Morgan
Luis Aparicio	George Brett
Tommy Bridges	Jim Palmer
Dwight Gooden	Steve Garvey
Mickey Mantle	Don Drysdale
Lefty Gomez	

1. _____ He, like Willie Mays, played on 17 winning teams.
2. _____ He played on 15 losing teams.
3. _____ He pinch-hit ten times.
4. _____ He has been the youngest player.
5. _____ He was the oldest participant.
6. _____ He played five different positions in total games.
7. _____ He batted .500 in total games.

8. _____ He had the most total at-bats (10) without a hit.

9. _____ He had the most at bats in a game (7) without a hit.

10. _____ He scored four runs in one game.

11. _____ He was the American Leaguer who hit in seven consecutive games.

12. _____ He was the National Leaguer who hit in seven consecutive games.

13. _____ He, like Ted Williams, reached base safely five times in one game.

14. _____ He has hit four doubles in total games.

15. _____ He hit two triples in one game.

16. _____ He struck out four times in one game.

17. _____ He's hit three sacrifice flies in total games.

18. _____ He, like Pete Rose, hit into three double plays.

19. _____ He was the only player to steal home.

20. _____ He got caught stealing twice in one game.

21. _____ He finished six games.

22. _____ He pitched 19 ⅓ innings in total games.

23. _____ He pitched six innings in one game.

24. _____ He allowed 13 runs in total games.

25. _____ He allowed seven runs in one inning.

26. _____ He allowed seven hits in one game.

27. _____ He granted three home runs in one game.

28. _____ He played ten games at first base.

29. _____ He played 13 games at second base.

30. _____ He played ten games at shortstop.

31. _____ He played 14 games at catcher.

32. _____ He stole six bases in total games.

82. WHO'S WHO?

Identify the player who starred in a particular year.

1. _____ (1933) Who hit the event's first home run?

2. _____ (1934) Who struck out Babe Ruth, Lou Gehrig, Jimmie Foxx, Al Simmons, and Joe Cronin consecutively?

3. _____ (1934) Who was the National Leaguer who homered for the second consecutive year? (In World Series play he didn't hit a home run in 197 official at-bats.)

4. _____ (1935) Who three-hit the National League over a record six innings?

5. _____ (1937) Who was the American League pitcher who won his third decision in five years?

6. _____ (1937) Who was the National Leaguer, the Triple Crown winner that year, who paced the Senior Circuit to victory with four hits?

7. _____ (1937) Who was the Hall of Famer whose injury in this year's game abruptly short-circuited a great career?

8. _____ (1937) Who was the Hall of Famer whose line drive broke the preceding pitcher's toe?

9. _____ (1941) Who was the player whose three-run homer with two outs in the bottom of the ninth lifted the American League to a 7–5 victory?

10. _____ (1941) Who was the first player to hit two home runs in one game?

11. _____ (1942) Who was the National Leaguer who hit the game's first pinch-hit home run?

12. _____ (1943) Who was the National League pitcher who tied Carl Hubbell's mark of six strikeouts in one game?

13. _____ (1943) Who was the DiMaggio who hit a single, a triple, and a home run?

14. _____ (1944) Who was the National League first baseman who became the first player to reach base five times in one game?

15. _____ (1946) Who was the player whose

four hits, including two home runs, and five RBIs led the American League to a 12–0 win?

16. _____ (1946) Who was the pitcher who gave up his first and only eephus ball home run?

17. _____ (1948) Who was the pitcher whose two-run single turned the game in the American League's favor?

18. _____ (1949) Who were the first four blacks to play in the All-Star Game?

19. _____

20. _____

21. _____

22. _____ (1950) Who was the National League second baseman whose 14th-inning home run gave the Senior Circuit a 2–1 victory?

23. _____ (1950) Who was the Hall of Famer who broke his elbow making a great catch off the left-field wall?

24. _____ (1952) Who was the Cub outfielder whose two-run home run gave the National League a 3–2 win in a five-inning game that was shortened by rain?

25. _____ (1953) Who was the great black pitcher who appeared in his only All-Star Game?

26. _____ (1954) Who was the American League third baseman whose two home runs and five RBIs tied a record?

27. _____ (1955) Who was the Hall of Famer whose home run in the bottom of the 12th gave the National League a sudden-death victory?

28. _____ (1956) Who was the third baseman whose great fielding plays and three hits sparked the National League?

29. _____ (1959) Who was the four-time home run champ whose run-tying single got the National League even in the eighth inning?

30. _____ (1959) Who was the four-time home run champ who followed the above with a game-winning triple?

31. _____ (1960) Who was the famous center fielder who got three hits in each of that year's two games?

32. _____ (1963) Who was the player whose 24th All-Star appearance set a record?

33. _____ (1964) Who was the player whose three-run homer in the bottom of the ninth gave the National League a dramatic come-from-behind 7–4 win?

34. _____ (1966) Who was the infield speedster whose tenth-inning single gave the National League a 2–1 win?

35. _____ (1967) Who was the big first baseman whose 15th-inning homer gave the National League a victory in the All-Star Game's longest contest?

36. _____ (1967) Who was the Cub pitcher whose six strikeouts tied the mark set by Hubbell and equaled by Vander Meer?

37. _____ (1969) Who was the National League first baseman who became the fourth player to hit two home runs in one game?

38. _____ (1971) Who hit the tape-measure home run on top of the roof at Tigers Stadium?

39. _____ (1971) Who became the first player to homer for both leagues?

40. _____ (1974) Who was the player, not even listed on the All-Star ballot, who was the game's star?

41. _____ (1975) Who was the long-ball-hitting left-fielder who hit a three-run pinch-hit homer?

42. _____ (1978) Who was the National League first baseman whose single tied the score in the third and whose triple proved to be the game-winner?

43. _____ (1979) Who was the Met outfielder who hit a pinch-hit home run in the eighth to tie the game, and walked with the bases loaded in the ninth to win the game?

44. _____ (1981) Who was the eight-time home run champ whose two-run homer in the eighth inning gave the National League a one-run victory?

45. _____ Who was the National League hurler who pitched in six consecutive games?

46. _____ Who was the American League moundsman who pitched in six consecutive games?

The Black Sox

The 1919–20 Chicago White Sox, referred to in history books as the infamous Black Sox, had a staggering array of talent.

In the season before they were declared ineligible to play professional baseball—for allegedly conspiring to fix the 1919 World Series—Joe Jackson batted .382, Happy Felsch hit .338, and Buck Weaver averaged .333. Moundsmen Claude "Lefty" Williams and Ed Cicotte won 22 and 21 games, respectively. Chick Gandil and Swede Risberg were solid starters, and Fred McMullin was a valuable utility man. It's little wonder that the White Sox, who were the best team in baseball at the time, did not win another pennant, after 1919, for another 40 years. Their roster was razed.

If it were not for the scandal, Jackson, Weaver, and Cicotte would be comfortably enshrined at the Baseball Hall of Fame in Cooperstown, N. Y. Felsch and Williams might be, too.

The notoriety of the trial of the disqualified players, however, detracted from the honorable records of the Sox stalwarts who transcended the alleged temptation and remained unsullied by the scandal.

History books have paid more attention to the barred players than they have to the untainted stars who managed to win their niche in Cooperstown. There were three such players. If you can name two of them, you deserve a special niche of your own.

(Answer appears on page 322.)

Chapter Fifteen

THE CHAMPIONSHIP SERIES

83. FROM BANDO TO WASHINGTON

Match the following players with the Championship Series records that they set: Richie Hebner, Pete Rose, Jay Johnstone, Reggie Jackson, Claudell Washington, George Brett, Jim Palmer, Mickey Rivers, Phil Niekro, Fred Lynn, Paul Blair, Mike Cuellar, Jerry Martin, Chris Chambliss, Paul Popovich, Steve Garvey, Bob Robertson, Bill North, Chet Lemon, and Sal Bando.

1. _____ He was the youngest non-pitcher to play in the Championship Series.
2. _____ He got 11 hits in one series.
3. _____ He went hitless in 31 consecutive at-bats.
4. _____ He appeared in ten series.
5. _____ He was the pinch-hitter who batted for six total bases in one series.
6. _____ He played on seven losing teams.
7. _____ He played in seven series with one team.
8. _____ He was the oldest non-pitcher to play.
9. _____ He hit .386 in total series.
10. _____ He hit .778 in a three-game series.
11. _____ He hit .611 in a five-game series.
12. _____ He went hitless in 13 total series at-bats.
13. _____ He has a .728 total series slugging average.
14. _____ He slugged the ball for a 1.250 average in one series.
15. _____ He had five hits in one game.

167

16. _____ He got three consecutive pinch-hit base hits.

17. _____ He got six consecutive hits.

18. _____ He was the only pitcher to hit a grand slam.

19. _____ He had the biggest time span (1969–82) between series appearances.

20. _____ He was the only player to decide a 1–0 game with a home run in the American League's favor.

84. FROM BAYLOR TO WYNN

Match the following players with the Championship Series records that they set: Pete Rose, Rusty Staub, Bob Robertson, Don Baylor, Joe Morgan, Jimmy Wynn, Steve Balboni, Cesar Geronimo, Pedro Guerrero, Tony Taylor, Davey Lopes, Reggie Jackson, Hal McRae, Tug McGraw, Bert Blyleven, Phil Niekro, Jim Hunter, Dave Giusti, Jim Palmer, and Bruce Kison.

1. _____ He sports a 4–0 record.
2. _____ He started ten games.
3. _____ He finished nine games.
4. _____ He pitched five complete games.
5. _____ He has been the youngest pitcher to appear.
6. _____ He has been the oldest pitcher to appear.
7. _____ He went down swinging seven consecutive times.
8. _____ He hit two home runs in consecutive innings.
9. _____ He drove home 21 runs in total series.
10. _____ He collected ten RBIs in one series.
11. _____ He grounded into five double plays in total series.
12. _____ He grounded into three double plays in one game.
13. _____ He stole nine bases in total series.
14. _____ He struck out eight times in one series.
15. _____ He walked nine times in one series.
16. _____ He walked 23 times in total series.
17. _____ He was caught stealing six times in total series.
18. _____ He has been the only player to steal home.
19. _____ He played four positions in series play.
20. _____ He hit for 14 total bases in one game.

85. FROM ANDERSON TO WYNN

Match the following players with the Championship Series records that they set: Tug McGraw, Dave Giusti, Jerry Reuss, Ken Holtzman, Dave McNally, Jim Hunter, Eric Show, Steve Carlton, Mike Cuellar, Jim Palmer, Dave Stieb, Nolan Ryan, Tommy John, Earl Weaver, Sparky Anderson, Billy Martin, Steve Garvey, George Brett, Pete Rose, and Gaylord Perry.

1. _____ He managed four different clubs in series play.
2. _____ He managed in six American League series.
3. _____ He managed five winning teams.
4. _____ He allowed four walks in one inning, nine walks in one game, and 13 walks in one series.
5. _____ He struck out seven batters in relief.
6. _____ He struck out 46 batters in total series.
7. _____ He struck out 18 batters in one series.
8. _____ He hit three batsmen and threw four wild pitches in total series.
9. _____ He recorded five saves in total series.
10. _____ He issued 28 walks in total series.
11. _____ He recorded three saves in one series.
12. _____ He allowed five home runs in one series.
13. _____ He lost seven consecutive games.
14. _____ He got touched for 19 hits in one series.
15. _____ He allowed 12 home runs in total series.
16. _____ He pitched 11 consecutive hitless innings in one game.
17. _____ He pitched 19⅓ consecutive scoreless innings in total series.
18. _____ He scored 22 runs in total series.
19. _____ He sprayed 45 hits in total series.
20. _____ He banged six long hits in one series.

86. FROM BANDO TO YASTRZEMSKI

All of the players who are listed below hit .400 or better for an American League team in a Championship Series. Ten of them hit .500 or better. See if you can zero in on the ten .500 hitters. One of them did it twice.

Spike Owen
Bob Boone
Wally Joyner
Brooks Robinson
Eddie Murray
Kirk Gibson
Carl Yastrzemski
Fred Lynn
Reggie Jackson
Larry Milbourne
Rod Carew
Paul Blair
Sal Bando
Bob Watson
Cliff Johnson
Cecil Cooper
Cal Ripken

Frank White
Chris Chambliss
Carlton Fisk
Graig Nettles
Thurman Munson
Boog Powell
Amos Otis
Chris Chambliss*
Brooks Robinson*
Charlie Moore
Mickey Rivers
Tony Oliva
Jerry Mumphrey
Rick Burleson
George Brett
Hal McRae
Reggie Jackson*

* They hit .400 or better twice.

1. _____
2. _____
3. _____
4. _____
5. _____
6. _____
7. _____
8. _____
9. _____
10. _____

87. FROM BAKER TO ZISK

All of the players who are listed below hit .400 or better for a National League team in a Championship Series. Seven of them hit .500 or better. See if you can zero in on the seven .500 hitters.

Darrell Porter   Dave Concepcion*
Jose Cruz   Willie Stargell**
Bob Boone   Pete Rose
Dusty Baker   Derrel Thomas
Mike Schmidt   Bob Robertson
Jay Johnstone   Terry Puhl
Bill Russell   Gary Carter
Steve Garvey   Ozzie Smith*
Phil Garner   Pete Rose**
Bob Tolan   Willie Stargell**
Tony Perez   Richie Zisk
Art Shamsky   Cleon Jones
Orlando Cepeda   Willie McCovey
Dave Concepcion   Dave Cash
Willie Stargell   Terry Landrum
Pete Rose   Gary Matthews
Ozzie Smith

 * They hit .400 or better twice.
** They hit .400 or better three times.

1. _____
2. _____
3. _____
4. _____
5. _____
6. _____
7. _____

88. FROM AARON TO STAUB

Match the following players with the number of Championship Series home runs that they've hit: Greg Luzinski, Rich Hebner, Boog Powell, Pete Rose, Jim Rice, George Brett, Gary Matthews, Willie Stargell, Tony Perez, Steve Garvey, Reggie Jackson, Ron Cey, Graig Nettles, Johnny Bench, Al Oliver, Hank Aaron, Sal Bando, Bill Madlock, Rusty Staub, Bob Robertson, and George Foster.

1. _____ (9)
2. _____ (8)
3. _____ (6)
4. _____ (5)
5. _____ (5)
6. _____ (5)
7. _____ (5)
8. _____ (5)
9. _____ (4)
10. _____ (4)
11. _____ (4)
12. _____ (4)
13. _____ (4)
14. _____ (3)
15. _____ (3)
16. _____ (3)
17. _____ (3)
18. _____ (3)
19. _____ (3)
20. _____ (3)
21. _____ (2)

89. CHAMPIONSHIP SERIES GAME WINNERS

National League

There have been many dramatic hits in Championship Series play. Some of them are referred to below. See if you can identify the players who provided the drama.

1. _____ Who was the Red in Game One of 1970 whose 10th-inning single, which was followed by Lee May's two-run double, broke up a scoreless pitching duel between winner Gary Nolan and Doc Ellis?

2. _____ Who was the Red in Game Three of 1970 whose single in the eighth inning enabled Cincinnati to break a 2–2 tie and sweep the Bucs?

3. _____ Who was the Pirate in Game Three of 1971 whose eighth-inning homer off Juan Marichal snapped a 1–1 tie and gave Bob Johnson a 2–1 win?

4. _____ Who was the Pirate in Game Three of 1972 who homered for the first Pittsburgh run and drove in the tie-breaking counter in the eighth inning to give his team a 3–2 win?

5. _____ Who was the Red in Game One of 1973 whose ninth-inning homer off Tom Seaver gave Cincinnati a 2–1 come-from-behind victory?

6. _____ Who was the Red in Game Four of 1973 whose 12th-inning home run off Met pitcher Harry Parker gave Cincinnati a 2–1 win?

7. _____ Who was the Dodger in Game Three of 1977 whose ninth-inning single capped a three-run rally that lifted Los Angeles over the Phillies, 6–5?

8. _____ Who was the Dodger in Game Four of 1978 whose tenth-inning single, following Garry Maddox's muff of a fly ball, scored Ron Cey with the winning run to give the Dodgers the National League Championship?

9. _____ Who was the Pirate in Game One of 1979 whose three-run homer in the 11th gave Pittsburgh a 5–2 win over the Reds?

10. _____ Who was the Pirate in Game Two of 1979 whose tenth-inning single gave Pittsburgh a 3–2 win?

11. _____ Who was the Phillie in Game Five of

1980 whose tenth-inning double downed Houston, 8–7, and gave Philadelphia its first pennant since 1950?

12. _____ Who was the Expo in Game Three of 1981 whose three-run homer gave Montreal a 4–1 win over the Dodgers?

13. _____ Who was the Dodger in Game Five of 1981 whose homer with two outs in the ninth inning gave Los Angeles a 2–1 win over Montreal and the National League pennant?

14. _____ Who was the Cardinal in Game Two of 1982 whose ninth-inning single gave St. Louis a 4–3 win over Atlanta?

15. _____ Who was the Phillie in Game One of 1983 whose home run gave Steve Carlton a 1–0 win over Jerry Reuss and the Dodgers?

16. _____ Who was the Padre in Game Four of 1984 whose two-run homer in the bottom of the ninth inning gave San Diego a 7–5 win over the Cubs?

17. _____ Who was the Astro in Game One of 1986 whose home run gave Mike Scott a 1–0 victory over Dwight Gooden and the Mets?

18. _____ Who was the Met in Game Three of 1986 whose two-run homer in the ninth inning lifted New York over Houston, 6–5?

19. _____ Who was the Astro in Game Four of 1986 whose two-run homer made the difference in Houston's 3–1 win over the Mets?

20. _____ Who was the Met in Game Five of 1986 whose 12th-inning single gave New York a 2–1 win over Houston?

American League

1. _____ Who was the Oriole in Game One of 1969 whose two-out suicide squeeze bunt in the 12th inning gave Baltimore a 4–3 win over Minnesota?

2. _____ Who was the Oriole in Game Two of 1969 whose pinch-hit single in the bottom of the 11th inning gave Dave McNally a 1–0 win over Minnesota?

3. _____ Who was the Oriole in Game One of 1971 whose two-run double in the seventh inning ignited Baltimore to a 5–3 win over Oakland?

4. _____ Who was the A in Game Five of

1972 whose only hit of the series drove home George Hendrick with the winning run of the game, 2–1, and the series.

5. _____ Who was the A in Game Three of 1973 whose home run in the bottom of the 11th inning gave Ken Holtzman a 2–1 win over Mike Cuellar of the Orioles?

6. _____ Who was the Oriole in Game Four of 1973 whose eighth-inning homer gave Baltimore a come-from-behind 5–4 victory over the A's?

7. _____ Who was the A in Game Three of 1974 whose home run provided Vida Blue the edge in a 1–0 win over Jim Palmer of the Orioles?

8. _____ Who was the A in Game Four of 1974 whose double scored the deciding run in the game, 2–1, and the series, 3–1?

9. _____ Who was the Yankee in Game Five of 1976 whose sudden-death homer in the ninth gave the Yankees their first pennant since 1964?

10. _____ Who was the Yankee in Game Three of 1978 whose two-run homer in the eighth inning gave New York a 6–5 win over Kansas City?

11. _____ Who was the Yankee in Game Four of 1978 whose sixth-inning homer gave New York a 2–1 win and the American League pennant?

12. _____ Who was the Oriole in Game One of 1979 whose three-run pinch-hit home run gave Baltimore a 6–3 win over California?

13. _____ Who was the Angel whose looping double in the bottom of the ninth gave California a 4–3 win?

14. _____ Who was the Royal in Game Three of 1980 whose three-run homer powered Kansas City to its first pennant?

15. _____ Who was the Brewer in Game Three of 1982 whose two-run homer proved to be the margin of difference, 5–3, over the Angels?

16. _____ Who was the Brewer in Game Five of 1982 who singled in the tying and winning runs to give Milwaukee its first American League pennant?

17. _____ Who was the Oriole in Game Four of 1983 whose tenth-inning home run was the catalyst in Baltimore's pennant-winning game?

18. _____ Who was the Tiger in Game Two of 1984 whose two-run double in the eleventh inning sparked Detroit to a 5–3 victory?

19. _____ Who was the Angel in Game Four of

1986 whose ninth-inning hit into the left-field corner gave California a 4–3 victory and a 3–1 lead in games?

20. _____ Who was the Red Sox player in Game Five of 1986 whose two-run homer in the bottom of the ninth gave Boston a 6–5 victory and prevented California manager Gene Mauch from winning his first pennant?

The Shoe Polish Plays

Everything is not always black and white in baseball. But in the following two instances it was.

In the fourth game of the 1957 World Series, with the Yankees leading the host Braves by the score of 5–4 in the tenth inning, a pinch-hitter came to the plate for Warren Spahn. A pitch from Tommy Byrne to the pinch-hitter was called a ball. But the substitute batter, who claimed that the ball had hit him, retrieved it and showed the enlightened Augie Donatelli a smudge of black shoe polish on the spheroid. Bob Grim relieved Byrne and was greeted with a game-tying double by Johnny Logan and a game-winning homer by Eddie Mathews. So the shoe polish call was a pivotal one.

In the fifth-and-final game of the 1969 World Series, a similar play took place. In the sixth inning one of the host Mets was hit on the foot with a pitch by Dave McNally. Umpire Lou DiMuro called the pitch a ball. The batter protested. Upon inspection of the ball, DiMuro gave the hitter first base: he detected shoe polish on the ball. The shoe polish call once again proved to be pivotal. At the time the Mets were losing 3–0. But Donn Clendenon followed with a two-run homer, and the Mets were back in the game. Al Weis homered in the seventh to tie the game. The Mets went on to score the decisive two runs of a 5–3 series-clinching victory in the eighth on doubles by two Met outfielders and errors by two Oriole infielders.

Both of the players who figured prominently in the shoe polish plays had the same last name. That should give you a solid clue. Who are the two?

(Answer appears on page 322.)

Chapter Sixteen

THE WORLD SERIES

90. WORLD SERIES STANDOUTS

I.

Match the following players with the World Series records that they set: Lou Gehrig, Hank Bauer, Pee Wee Reese and Elston Howard, Yogi Berra, Willie Wilson, Casey Stengel, Pepper Martin, Babe Ruth, Bobby Richardson, and Mickey Mantle.

1. _____ He was on the winning club ten times.
2. _____ He was on the losing team six times.
3. _____ He was a series manager ten times.
4. _____ He hit .625, the all-time high, in one series.
5. _____ He had a career average of .418.
6. _____ He collected 12 RBI in one series.
7. _____ He hit safely in 17 consecutive games.
8. _____ He hit four home runs in four games.
9. _____ He struck out 12 times in one series.
10. _____ He struck out 54 times in series play.

II.

Match the following pitchers with the World Series records they set: Bill Bevens, Whitey Ford, Harry Brecheen, Babe Ruth, Darold Knowles, Don Larsen, Christy Mathewson, Carl Mays, Bob Gibson, and Jim Palmer.

1. _____ He pitched 33⅔ consecutive scoreless innings.
2. _____ He pitched seven games in one series.
3. _____ He pitched three shutouts in one series.

4. _____ He struck out 17 batters in one game.
5. _____ He issued 10 walks in one game.
6. _____ He did not allow a single walk in 26 innings of pitching in one series.
7. _____ He gave up a total of four hits in two consecutive games.
8. _____ He was the youngest pitcher who threw a shutout.
9. _____ He was the first post-World War II pitcher who won three games.
10. _____ He pitched the longest game, 14 innings, which he won.

III.

Match the following teams that have won consecutive World Series with the proper time spans (teams may be used more than once): Yankees, Cubs, Athletics, Giants, Red Sox, and Reds.

1. _____ (1907–08)
2. _____ (1910–11)
3. _____ (1915–16)
4. _____ (1921–22)
5. _____ (1927–28)
6. _____ (1929–30)
7. _____ (1936–39)
8. _____ (1949–53)
9. _____ (1961–62)
10. _____ (1972–74)
11. _____ (1975–76)
12. _____ (1977–78)

IV.

Match the following World Series defensive standouts with the years in which they excelled: Dick Green, Tommie Agee, Willie Mays, Al Gionfriddo, Brooks Robinson, Billy Cox, Bill Virdon, Mickey Mantle, Eddie Mathews, and Sandy Amoros.

1. _____ (1947)
2. _____ (1952)
3. _____ (1954)
4. _____ (1955)

180

5.   —————————————— (1956)
6.   —————————————— (1957)
7.   —————————————— (1960)
8.   —————————————— (1969)
9.   —————————————— (1970)
10. —————————————— (1974)

V.

Match the following World Series starting pitchers with the years in which they stood in the sun: Sandy Koufax, Lew Burdette, Mickey Lolich, Harry Brecheen, Johnny Podres, Bob Gibson, Whitey Ford, Bob Turley, Jim Hunter, and Don Larsen.

1.   —————————————— (1946)
2.   —————————————— (1955)
3.   —————————————— (1956)
4.   —————————————— (1957)
5.   —————————————— (1958)
6.   —————————————— (1960)
7.   —————————————— (1963)
8.   —————————————— (1967)
9.   —————————————— (1968)
10. —————————————— (1972)

91. WORLD SERIES PLAYERS

From the performers listed below, pick out the ones who played in the World Series. The key word is "played."

Richie Ashburn	Vada Pinson
Ernie Banks	Felipe Alou
Ted Williams	Jesus Alou
Al Kaline	Matty Alou
Luke Appling	Gus Bell
Mickey Vernon	Willard Marshall
Nelson Fox	Walker Cooper
Dean Chance	Ray Sadecki
Ralph Kiner	Bob Allison
Richie Allen	Vern Stephens
Harvey Kuenn	Eddie Yost
George Kell	Ferguson Jenkins
Herb Score	Satchel Paige
Hank Sauer	Johnny Callison
Johnny Logan	Buddy Kerr
Ted Kluszewski	Bill White
Ted Lyons	Jeff Heath
Gordy Coleman	Milt Pappas
Ferris Fain	Frank Torre
Gaylord Perry	Hank Majeski

1. _____   11. _____
2. _____   12. _____
3. _____   13. _____
4. _____   14. _____
5. _____   15. _____
6. _____   16. _____
7. _____   17. _____
8. _____   18. _____
9. _____   19. _____
10. _____ 20. _____

92. TWO-TEAM WORLD SERIES PLAYERS

From the performers listed below, pick out the ones who played in the World Series with two different teams.

Rocky Nelson

Juan Marichal

Denny McLain

Gino Cimoli

Rudy York

Tommy Holmes

Willie Horton

Bill Skowron

Roger Maris

Al Dark

George McQuinn

Mickey Cochrane

Julian Javier

Rusty Staub

Jim Lonborg

Reggie Smith

Joe Gordon

Curt Simmons

Tommy Davis

Johnny Sain

Enos Slaughter

Don Hoak

Ron Fairly

Orlando Cepeda

Maury Wills

Bob Tolan

Moe Drabowsky

Joe Cronin

Luis Aparicio

Don Gullett

Dick Groat

Ron Perranoski

Claude Osteen

Frank Robinson

Willie Davis

Camilo Pascual

Tony Oliva

Mike Garcia

Ken Boyer

Curt Flood

1. _____

2. _____

3. _____

4. _____

5. _____

6. _____

7. _____

8. _____

9. _____

10. _____

11. _____

12. _____

13. _____

14. _____

15. _____

16. _____

17. _____

18. _____

19. _____

20. _____

93. MOUND CLASSICS

Below you will find the matchups and years in which pitchers have engaged in 1–0 mound duels since 1946. Name the pitcher who won their duels.

1. _____ Bob Feller vs. Johnny Sain (1948)
2. _____ Don Newcombe vs. Allie Reynolds (1949)
3. _____ Preacher Roe vs. Vic Raschi (1949)
4. _____ Vic Raschi vs. Jim Konstanty (1950)
5. _____ Bob Turley vs. Clem Labine (1956)
6. _____ Whitey Ford vs. Lew Burdette (1957)
7. _____ Bob Shaw, Billy Pierce, and Dick Donovan vs. Sandy Koufax (1959)
8. _____ Ralph Terry vs. Jack Sanford (1962)
9. _____ Jim Bouton vs. Don Drysdale (1963)
10. _____ Claude Osteen vs. Wally Bunker (1966)
11. _____ Don Drysdale vs. Dave McNally (1966)
12. _____ Jack Billingham and Clay Carroll vs. John Odom (1972)
13. _____ Bruce Hurst vs. Ron Darling (1986)

94. SEVENTH-GAME WINNERS

From the following pairs of seventh-game starting pitchers since the end of World War II, pick the 12 moundsmen who have been credited with wins. One of the 12 pitchers picked up two victories.

1. _____ (1946) Boo Ferriss (Red Sox) vs. Murry Dickson (Cardinals)

2. _____ (1947) Hal Gregg (Dodgers) vs. Frank Shea (Yankees)

3. _____ (1952) Ed Lopat (Yankees) vs. Joe Black (Dodgers)

4. _____ (1953) Carl Erskine (Dodgers) vs. Whitey Ford (Yankees)

5. _____ (1955) Johnny Podres (Dodgers) vs. Tommy Byrne (Yankees)

6. _____ (1956) Johnny Kucks (Yankees) vs. Don Newcombe (Dodgers)

7. _____ (1957) Lew Burdette (Braves) vs. Don Larsen (Yankees)

8. _____ (1958) Don Larsen (Yankees) vs. Lew Burdette (Braves)

9. _____ (1960) Bob Turley (Yankees) vs. Vernon Law (Pirates)

10. _____ (1962) Ralph Terry (Yankees) vs. Jack Sanford (Giants)

11. _____ (1964) Mel Stottlemyre (Yankees) vs. Bob Gibson (Cards)

12. _____ (1967) Bob Gibson (Cards) vs. Jim Lonborg (Red Sox)

13. _____ (1968) Mickey Lolich (Tigers) vs. Bob Gibson (Cards)

14. _____ (1971) Steve Blass (Pirates) vs. Dave McNally (Orioles)

15. _____ (1972) John Odom (A's) vs. Jack Billingham (Reds)

16. _____ (1973) Jon Matlack (Mets) vs. Ken Holtzman (A's)

17. _____ (1975) Don Gullett (Reds) vs. Bill Lee (Red Sox)

18. _____ (1979) Jim Bibby (Pirates) vs. Scott McGregor (Orioles)

19. _____ (1982) Pete Vuckovich (Brewers) vs. Joaquin Andujar (Cards)

20. _____ (1985) John Tudor (Cards) vs. Bret Saberhagen (Royals)

21. _____ (1986) Bruce Hurst (Red Sox) vs. Ron Darling (Mets)

22. _____ (1987) Joe Magrane (Cards) vs. Frank Viola (Twins)

95. WORLD SERIES SHORTS

Three-Game Winners

The last five pitchers who won three games in a World Series were Lew Burdette, Stan Coveleski, Harry Brecheen, Mickey Lolich, and Bob Gibson. Put them in their proper order.

1. _____ (1920)
2. _____ (1946)
3. _____ (1957)
4. _____ (1967)
5. _____ (1968)

Home Run Hitters

Match the following players with the number of series homers they hit: Duke Snider, Mickey Mantle, Babe Ruth, Lou Gehrig, and Yogi Berra.

1. _____ (18)
2. _____ (15)
3. _____ (12)
4. _____ (11)
5. _____ (10)

Individual Records

Match the following players with the World Series records they set: Whitey Ford, Christy Mathewson, Lefty Gomez, Lefty Grove, and Bob Gibson.

1. _____ Fewest number of chances accepted (0), series (26 innings)
2. _____ Most career wins (10)
3. _____ Most strikeouts per nine innings (10.22)
4. _____ Most career shutouts (4)
5. _____ Best career-winning percentage (1.000), six decisions

Career Records

Match the following players with the career World Series records they set: Yogi Berra, Bobby Richardson, Frank Isbell, Dusty Rhodes, and Eddie Collins and Lou Brock.

1. _____ Tied for stolen base leadership (14)
2. _____ Most games (75)
3. _____ Most runs batted in (7) consecutive times at bat
4. _____ Most two-base hits (4), one game
5. _____ Most consecutive games played (30)

96. FOUR HOMERS IN ONE SERIES

Reggie Jackson, of course, hit five home runs in the 1977 World Series. But there have been six players who hit four home runs in a series. One of them did it twice. Out of the following players pick the ones who accomplished the feat: Mickey Mantle, Willie Mays, Lou Gehrig, Gene Tenace, Roy Campanella, Joe DiMaggio, Babe Ruth, Duke Snider, Johnny Bench, Hank Bauer, and Willie Aikens. Also, see if you can put them in their proper time spans. And remember, one of them did it twice.

1. _____ (1926)
2. _____ (1928)
3. _____ (1952)
4. _____ (1955)
5. _____ (1958)
6. _____ (1972)
7. _____ (1980)

97. WORLD SERIES CHRONOLOGY

There have been 84 World Series. The autumn classic began in 1903 and has been played every year with the exception of 1905, when the Giants refused to play the Red Sox, winners of the first series. I'm going to give you one question for each series, presented in sequence. Let's see how you know the World Series—from start to finish.

1. _____ Who hit the first home run?
2. _____ Who has been the only pitcher to spin three shutouts in the same series?
3. _____ Who struck out a record 12 batters in the intercity series between the White Sox and Cubs in 1906?
4. _____ Who was the other member of the Tinker to Evers to Chance infield who hit .471 in 1907?
5. _____ Who was the Cub pitcher, in addition to Three Finger Brown, who won two games in 1908?
6. _____ Who has been the only rookie pitcher to win three games in one series?
7. _____ Who managed to win all three of his decisions in 1910 despite the fact that he yielded 23 hits and 14 free passes?
8. _____ Who hit home runs in consecutive games for the Athletics in 1911?
9. _____ Who won three games for the Red Sox in 1912?
10. _____ Who was the only substitute whom the Athletics used in 1913?
11. _____ Who was the member of the Tinker to Evers to Chance infield who hit .438 for the winning Braves in 1914?
12. _____ Who was the Red Sox pitcher who won two games and batted .500 in 1915?
13. _____ Who strung together the most consecutive scoreless innings in one game?
14. _____ Who was the White Sox pitcher who won three games in 1917?
15. _____ Who was the Cub second baseman who became the last out of the third game in 1918 when he unsuccessfully tried to steal home?

16. _____ Who was the untainted member of the 1919 Black Sox who won both of his decisions?

17. _____ Who hit the first grand slam?

18. _____ Who did not allow an earned run in 27 innings of pitching, but lost the final game of 1921 on an error?

19. _____ Who was the first pitcher to win the final game of two consecutive series?

20. _____ Who was the first player to hit three home runs in the same series?

21. _____ Who hit the bad-hop single that gave the Senators their first and only world championship?

22. _____ Who was the first pitcher to win the seventh game of one world series (1924) and lose the seventh game of the following post-season get-together?

23. _____ Who, in addition to Grover Alexander, won two games for the Cardinals in 1926?

24. _____ Who hit the only two home runs of the 1927 classic?

25. _____ Who was deprived of a "quick-pitch" strikeout of Babe Ruth in 1928?

26. _____ Who was the Athletic outfielder who, in addition to Jimmie Foxx and Mule Haas, hit two home runs in 1929?

27. _____ Who was the 46-year-old pitcher who appeared in the 1930 series?

28. _____ Who "peppered" 12 hits and swiped five bases in 1931?

29. _____ Who was the Yankee player who, in addition to Babe Ruth and Lou Gehrig, hit two home runs in one game in 1932?

30. _____ Who hit the home run in the tenth inning that won the 1933 finale?

31. _____ Who, in 1934, played on his second world championship team with one club in the 1930s after performing on two world title clubs with another team in the 1920s?

32. _____ Who was the veteran outfielder whose single in 1935 gave the Tigers their first world championship?

33. _____ Who was the Giant pitcher who stopped the Yankees' 12-game win streak in 1936?

34. _____ Who was the 20-game winner for the Giants in 1937 who lost both of his series decisions?

35. _____ Who won two games during the Yankees' four-game sweep in 1938?

36. _____ Who won his fourth and final game (1939) without a defeat in series play?

37. _____ Who won both of his decisions, weaved a 1.50 ERA, and hit a home run in 1940?

38. _____ Who was the Dodger pitcher in 1941 who broke the Yankees' ten-game winning streak?

39. _____ Who hit a two-run homer in the final game of 1942 to give the Cardinals the world title?

40. _____ Who allowed only one run in 18 innings of pitching as the Yankees scored a turnabout five-game win over the Cardinals in 1943?

41. _____ Who was the Cardinal pitcher who lost a two-hitter to the Browns in 1944?

42. _____ Who was the starting pitcher who did not retire a single Tiger batter in Game Seven of 1945?

43. _____ Who scored the decisive run of 1946 by racing from first to home on a single?

44. _____ Who was the Dodger pitcher who finished a record six games against the Yankees in 1947?

45. _____ Who was the Indian pitcher who suffered both of his team's reversals in 1948?

46. _____ Who hit the ninth-inning home run that scored the only run in a classic duel between Allie Reynolds and Don Newcombe in the 1949 opener?

47. _____ Who was the 21-year-old rookie pitcher who won the final game in 1950?

48. _____ Who made the sliding catch that ended the 1951 series on a victorious note for the Yankees?

49. _____ Who was the Yankee part-time player who hit a record three home runs in three consecutive games in 1952?

50. _____ Who was the Dodger pitcher who struck out a record 14 batters in one game?

51. _____ Who was the Indian slugger who hit the 450-foot fly ball that Willie Mays ran down in Game One of 1954?

52. _____ Who was the Dodger slugger who drove home both runs in Johnny Podres' 2–0 win over Tommy Byrne in Game Seven of 1955?

53. _____ Who was the 40-year-old outfielder whose three-run game-winning homer (Game Three) turned the series around for the Yankees in 1956?

54. _____ Who was the Brave pitcher of 1957 who won three games?

55. _____ Who won two of the last three games—and saved the other one—in 1958?

56. _____ Who was the former Rose Bowl performer who set a record by hitting two pinch-hit homers for the Dodgers in 1959?

57. _____ Who was the Pirate pitcher who saved three games in a winning cause in 1960?

58. _____ Who was the Yankee pitcher who won two games for the second consecutive year in 1961?

59. _____ Who was the former Yankee celebrity who defeated the Pinstripers in his only decision in 1962?

60. _____ Who was the Yankee pinch-hitter whom Sandy Koufax fanned for his record 15th strikeout in 1963?

61. _____ Who was the last runner to steal home?

62. _____ Who (in addition to Sandy Koufax, who threw two shutouts) pitched a whitewash for the Dodgers in 1965?

63. _____ Who was the only Oriole pitcher who did not complete a game in 1966?

64. _____ Who was the only Cardinal pitcher to throw three consecutive complete-game wins in a series?

65. _____ Who picked two runners off first base in the sixth inning of the final game in 1968?

66. _____ Who was the light-hitting infielder for the Mets who batted .455 in 1969?

67. _____ Who was the Oriole player who excelled on offense and defense in 1970?

68. _____ Who was the Pirate player who extended his batting streak to 14 games in 1971?

69. _____ Who was the Oakland starter who picked up his second win of the series in relief in Game Seven of 1972?

70. _____ Who outpitched Jon Matlack in both the first and last game of 1973?

71. _____ Who, in addition to Catfish Hunter, won two games for the A's in 1974?

72. _____ Who was the Red slugger who hit three home runs in 1975?

73. _____ Who was the Red slugger who batted .533 during his team's sweep of the Yankees in 1976?

74. _____ Who was the Yankee batter who extended his consecutive-game hitting streak to ten in 1977?

75. _____ Who was the Yankee fill-in infielder who batted .438 in 1978?

76. _____ Who, in addition to Willie Stargell, collected 12 hits for the Pirates in 1979?

77. _____ Who was the Phillie pitcher who won Game Five and saved Game Six in 1980?

78. _____ Who, in addition to Pedro Guerrero, hit an eighth-inning home run in Game Five of 1981 to give Jerry Reuss and the Dodgers a 2–1 win?

79. _____ Who was the Brewer who got 12 hits in 1982?

80. _____ Who was the Oriole slugger who came out of a slump to hit two home runs in the series-clinching game of 1983?

81. _____ Who was the Tiger who hit two home runs in the series-clinching game of 1984?

82. _____ Who was the second-year Royal pitcher who was 2–0 in 1985?

83. _____ Who was the 1986 MVP whom the winning team didn't sign for 1987?

84. _____ Who was the pitcher who won the first and seventh games for the Twins in 1987?

98. WORLD SERIES MULTIPLE CHOICE

1. _____ Who was eligible to play in 37 games but appeared in only one?

    a. Gus Niarhos b. Jake Gibbs c. Charlie Silvera d. Stan Lopata

2. _____ Who was eligible to play in 23 games but didn't appear in one of them?

    a. Dick Williams b. Arndt Jorgens c. Bruce Edwards d. Mike Hegan

3. _____ Who played on four world championship teams his first four years in the majors?

    a. Jackie Robinson b. Reggie Jackson c. Charlie Keller d. Joe DiMaggio

4. _____ Who was the infielder who played in his first and in his second series 14 years apart?

    a. Billy Herman b. Stan Hack c. Rabbit Maranville d. Johnny Evers

5. _____ Who was the pitcher who played in his first and in his last series 17 years apart?

    a. Walter Johnson b. Jim Kaat c. Grover Alexander d. Eppa Rixey

6. _____ Who was the outfielder who played in his first and in his last series 22 years apart?

    a. Sam Crawford b. Al Kaline c. Willie Mays d. Mickey Mantle

7. _____ Who was the pitcher who played in his first and in his last series 18 years apart?

    a. Burleigh Grimes b. Christy Mathewson c. Joe Bush d. Herb Pennock

8. _____ Who was the pitcher who played the most years in the majors before appearing in his first series?

    a. Joe Niekro b. Steve Carlton c. Ted Lyons d. Early Wynn

9. _____ Who was the oldest regular-day player to appear in the series?

    a. Enos Slaughter b. Johnny Hopp c. Johnny Mize d. Pete Rose

10. _____ Who pinch-hit in ten games?

    a. Bobby Brown b. Johnny Blanchard c. Dusty Rhodes d. Gino Cimoli

11. _____ Who pinch-ran in nine games?
   a. Herb Washington b. Allan Lewis c. Bill North d. Sam Jethroe

12. _____ Who twice got four hits in a game?
   a. Pete Rose b. Lou Brock c. Robin Yount d. Paul Molitor

13. _____ Who went hitless in 31 consecutive at-bats?
   a. Mark Belanger b. Marv Owen c. Julian Javier d. Dal Maxvill

14. _____ Who hit ten doubles in total series?
   a. Mickey Mantle b. Joe Medwick c. Frank Frisch d. Pee Wee Reese

15. _____ Who hit six doubles in one series?
   a. Pete Fox b. Nellie Fox c. Frank Isbell d. Pete Rose

16. _____ Who was the rookie who hit three home runs in his first series?
   a. Tony Kubek b. Willie Aikens c. Amos Otis d. Charlie Keller

17. _____ Who twice hit four home runs in a series?
   a. Hank Bauer b. Duke Snider c. Gene Tenace d. Roberto Clemente

18. _____ Who hit seven home runs in two consecutive series?
   a. Babe Ruth b. Reggie Jackson c. Lou Gehrig d. Mickey Mantle

19. _____ Who hit nine home runs in three consecutive series?
   a. Mickey Mantle b. Roger Maris c. Reggie Jackson d. Babe Ruth

20. _____ Who got the most long hits in one game?
   a. Reggie Jackson b. Frank Isbell c. Yogi Berra d. Babe Ruth

21. _____ Who drove home six runs in one game?
   a. Bobby Richardson b. Monte Irvin c. Gil Hodges d. Hank Aaron

22. _____ Who was hit by pitches three times in one series?
   a. Minnie Minoso b. Ron Hunt c. Don Baylor d. Max Carey

23. _____ Who grounded into five double plays in one series?
   a. Willie Mays b. Irv Noren c. Joe DiMaggio d. Gil McDougald

24. _____ Who was caught stealing nine times in total series?
   a. Ty Cobb b. Pee Wee Reese c. Frank Schulte d. Willie Randolph

25. _____ Who pitched consecutive games in consecutive series?

a. Deacon Phillippe b. George Earnshaw c. Lefty Grove
d. Ed Reulbach

26. _____ Who was the relief pitcher who appeared in 16
games in total series?

a. Johnny Murphy b. Wilcy Moore c. Rollie Fingers
d. Hugh Casey

27. _____ Who was the relief pitcher who appeared in six
different series?

a. Joe Page b. Bob Kuzava c. Elroy Face d. Johnny
Murphy

28. _____ Who won seven consecutive games?

a. Bob Gibson b. Red Ruffing c. Lefty Gomez d. Herb
Pennock

29. _____ Who pitched four consecutive opening games?

a. Allie Reynolds b. Whitey Ford c. Red Ruffing d. Carl
Hubbell

30. _____ Who was the pitcher who was on the losing end
of three shutouts, including two 1–0 scores?

a. Vic Raschi b. Preacher Roe c. Bob Turley d. Eddie
Plank

31. _____ Who pitched a 12-inning game without issuing a
base on balls?

a. Whitey Ford b. Schoolboy Rowe c. Dizzy Dean
d. Tommy Bridges

32. _____ Who, in a nine-inning game, struck out 11 batters but lost, 1–0?

a. Don Newcombe b. Bob Turley c. Tom Seaver d. Bob
Feller

33. _____ Who, in a ten-inning game, struck out 11 batters
but lost, 1–0?

a. Carl Hubbell b. Bob Turley c. Ewell Blackwell d. Lefty
Grove

34. _____ Who, in a 12-inning game, struck out 12 batters
but lost?

a. Rube Waddell b. Christy Mathewson c. Chief Bender
d. Walter Johnson

35. _____ Who was the first baseman who didn't make an
error in 31 consecutive games?

a. Gil Hodges b. Bill Skowron c. Bill Terry d. Hank
Greenberg

36. _____ Who played in seven series at second base?

a. Frank Frisch b. Joe Gordon c. Jackie Robinson d.
Eddie Stanky

37. _____ Who was the second baseman who didn't make
an error in 23 consecutive games?

a. Junior Gilliam b. Red Schoendienst c. Tony Lazzeri d. Billy Martin

38. _____ Who played in six series at third base?

a. Pepper Martin b. Red Rolfe c. Billy Cox d. Sal Bando

39. _____ Who was the third baseman who didn't make an error in 22 consecutive games?

a. Graig Nettles b. Ron Cey c. Pete Rose d. Brooks Robinson

40. _____ Who was the shortstop who didn't make an error in 21 consecutive games?

a. Leo Durocher b. Marty Marion c. Pee Wee Reese d. Phil Rizzuto

41. _____ Who played in 12 series as an outfielder?

a. Casey Stengel b. Joe DiMaggio c. Babe Ruth d. Mickey Mantle

42. _____ Who was the catcher who didn't make an error in 30 consecutive games?

a. Roy Campanella b. Yogi Berra c. Walker Cooper d. Bill Dickey

43. _____ Who was the pitcher who didn't make an error in 18 consecutive games?

a. Carl Hubbell b. Sandy Koufax c. Don Drysdale d. Whitey Ford

44. _____ Who was the youngest manager of a series winner?

a. Lou Boudreau b. Bucky Harris c. Joe Cronin d. Mickey Cochrane

45. _____ Who was the youngest manager of a series club?

a. Joe Cronin b. Roger Peckinpaugh c. Frank Frisch d. Lou Boudreau

46. _____ Who was the manager who lost 28 series games?

a. Connie Mack b. Leo Durocher c. John McGraw d. Bill Terry

47. _____ Who was the manager who won 37 series games?

a. Casey Stengel b. Joe McCarthy c. Walter Alston d. Connie Mack

48. _____ Who managed in the series with three different teams from the same league?

a. Sparky Anderson b. Dick Williams c. Bill McKechnie d. Alvin Dark

49. _____ Who appeared in 15 series as a coach?

a. Jimmy Dykes b. Art Fletcher c. Frank Crosetti d. Chuck Dressen

50. _____ Who appeared in 18 series as an umpire?

a. Shag Crawford b. Bill Klem c. Tom Connolly d. Bill McKinley

99. WORLD SERIES CLUES
WHO'S WHO

1. _____ Who pitched a record ten complete games in World Series play?
   a. He won five and lost five.
   b. He pitched 27 consecutive scoreless innings in one series.

2. _____ Who was the Yankee pitcher from the 1930s and 1940s who won seven of nine decisions in series action?
   a. He twice led the American League in losses.
   b. He won 20 or more games four straight years.

3. _____ Who was the Yankee pitcher from the 1920s and 1930s who won five of five decisions in series play?
   a. He got three saves, too.
   b. He won 240 career games.

4. _____ Who was the Yankee pitcher from the 1940s and 1950s who won seven of nine decisions in World Series play?
   a. He picked up four saves, too.
   b. In 1953, his last series, he saved Game Six and he won Game Seven in relief.

5. _____ Who picked up a record six series saves?
   a. He picked them up in three consecutive series.
   b. In those three series he pitched in a total of 16 games.

6. _____ Who struck out a record 11 batters in relief in one series game?
   a. He did it for the Orioles . . .
   b. . . . against the Dodgers.

7. _____ Who was picked off base twice in the same series game?
   a. He played with the 1918 Cubs at the time.
   b. He once played with two different teams on the same day.

8. _____ Who was the pitcher who walked a record two times with the bases loaded in the same series game?
   a. Eight times he won 20 or more games.
   b. He won three Cy Young awards.

9. _____ Who hit a double and a triple in the same inning of a series game?

    a. He did it for the 1921 Giants.

    b. He hit .300 in nine of his ten seasons.

10. _____ Who was the player who ripped five consecutive extra-base hits in series action?

    a. He got 25 hits in two consecutive series.

    b. He stole seven bases in each of those series, too.

11. _____ Who was the player for the Giants who got all three of his team's hits in a 1923 series game against the Yankees?

    a. He batted .310 lifetime, one point higher than his brother.

    b. He and his brother played against each other in three World Series.

12. _____ Who allowed a record eight home runs in series play?

    a. He pitched in four series from 1920–32.

    b. He pitched for the Dodgers, Cards, and Cubs.

13. _____ Who got a record five hits in one series game?

    a. He got 11 hits in the entire series.

    b. He did it in 1982.

14. _____ Who was the pitcher who allowed three home runs in the same inning?

    a. He pitched for the 1967 Cards.

    b. Two years later he was out of baseball.

15. _____ Who was the outfielder who started two double plays in the same series game?

    a. He did it for the 1919 Reds.

    b. A Hall of Famer, he hit .323 lifetime.

16. _____ Who was the youngest player ever to appear in a series?

    a. He was 18.

    b. In that series he got four hits in one game against Walter Johnson.

17. _____ Who played in 50 games and never hit a homer?

    a. He appeared for the Giants and the Cards.

    b. He hit two home runs in All-Star games.

18. _____ Who, in addition to Bob Gibson, has been the only pitcher to hit two home runs in series play?

    a. He won four of six series decisions . . .

    b. . . . for the Orioles.

19. _____ Who hit three home runs in each of back-to-back series?
   a. He played for the 1924–25 Senators.
   b. He batted .316 lifetime and .287 in five series with the Senators and the Tigers.

20. _____ Who threw out ten runners in one series?
   a. He did it for the 1919 White Sox.
   b. He's in the Hall of Fame.

21. _____ Who pitched the longest complete-game loss in series history?
   a. In two series he had an 0.89 ERA.
   b. His initials are S.S.

22. _____ Who hit two home runs in one game and two triples in another?
   a. He did it in the first series for the winning Red Sox.
   b. Two years later he played with the winning White Sox.

23. _____ Who was the player who was fired after a series because he struck out nine times?
   a. The series took place in 1909.
   b. He played for the Pirates, who defeated the Tigers.

24. _____ Who was the three-game winner for the White Sox who tried to steal third with the base already occupied?
   a. He did it in 1917.
   b. He won 254 major league games.

25. _____ Who retired the last 21 batters of a game in order?
   a. He did it in 1926.
   b. He was 39 at the time.

26. _____ Who, in the 1920s, struck out ten batters in a relief appearance?
   a. His brother pitched on the same team.
   b. They won 214 major league games between them.

27. _____ Walter Johnson pitched 21 years with one club. So did one other American League pitcher. Who was he?
   a. He never played in a World Series.
   b. Yet he won 260 career games.

28. _____ Who was traded after he player-managed his team to the world title?
   a. He won batting titles with two different teams.
   b. He was a second baseman.

29. _____ Who made the "$30,000 Muff?"
   a. He did it while playing with the 1912 Giants.

    b. Later in that inning, he made one of the greatest catches in series history.

30. _____ Who has been the only Tiger manager in 76 years to lead his team into the series in back-to-back years?

    a. He was a .320 lifetime hitter.

    b. He played in five series in seven years.

31. _____ Who was the Cardinal pitcher who lost a two-hitter?

    a. George McQuinn's two-run homer was the key hit.

    b. He bounced back to win Game Five, 2–0.

32. _____ Who has been the only Red manager to win back-to-back world titles?

    a. He played just one season in the majors.

    b. With the 1959 Phillies.

33. _____ Who was the youngest pitcher ever to hurl in the series?

    a. He was 19 at the time.

    b. He has a famous brother who is still playing.

34. _____ Who missed the opening assignment of a series because it fell on a Jewish religious holiday?

    a. He had a .655 lifetime winning percentage.

    b. He had an .097 lifetime batting average.

35. _____ Who hit for the highest series average (.391) in 20 or more games?

    a. He got a record-tying 13 hits in one series.

    b. He played on two world title teams in the 1960s.

36. _____ Who was the pitcher who hit important doubles in the opening games of the 1973 and 1974 series?

    a. He won four series games for Oakland.

    b. He once hit a series home run.

37. _____ Who got a record six consecutive hits in the 1924 World Series?

    a. He hit seven home runs in three series.

    b. He got the series-winning hit for the Tigers in 1935.

38. _____ Who got seven consecutive hits in back-to-back series?

    a. He was a catcher.

    b. He was a Rookie of the Year and an MVP.

39. _____ Who batted in six runs in one series as a pinch-hitter?

    a. He did it in the 1950s.

    b. He helped his team to a four-game sweep.

40. _____ Who was the National Leaguer who hit the most homers in series play?
   a. He hit 11.
   b. He twice hit four homers in a series.

41. _____ Who pitched a one-hitter for the Cubs in 1906?
   a. He won 181 games.
   b. He was called "Big Ed."

42. _____ Who was the American League player who hit safely in 15 of the 16 games in which he played?
   a. He hit better than .300 and drove home 100 or more runs in three consecutive years.
   b. He once hit .529 in a series.

43. _____ Who was the infielder in the 1920s who cost two different teams world titles because of errors in seventh games?
   a. He managed the Yankees before he cost them the 1921 title.
   b. He was the MVP in one of those years (1925).

44. _____ Who won three pennants and two world titles in his first three years of managing?
   a. He was a catcher who hit .272 lifetime.
   b. He moved into the front office after his three straight successes.

45. _____ Who has been the only pitcher, in addition to Don Drysdale, to both win and lose 1–0 decisions in series play?
   a. He beat Jim Konstanty.
   b. He lost to Preacher Roe.

46. _____ Who was the most recent pitcher to win the final game of back-to-back series?
   a. The years were 1952–53.
   b. He starred as a starter and as a reliever.

47. _____ Who was the Yankee pitcher who picked up saves in the final game of the back-to-back series?
   a. The years were 1951–52.
   b. They called him "Sarge."

48. _____ Who lost a record two 1–0 games?
   a. He did it in 1905 and 1914.
   b. He won over 300 career games.

49. _____ Who picked off two runners in the sixth inning of the seventh game in 1968?
   a. He picked off Lou Brock and Curt Flood.
   b. He won three games in that series.

50. _____ Who was the first pitcher to win the seventh game of one series and lose the seventh game of the following series?

  a. He won the seventh game in 1924.
  b. He was 1–2 the year that his team won and 2–1 the season that his club lost.

51. _____ Who was the first pitcher to win the final game of two consecutive series?

  a. He did it in 1921 and 1922.
  b. He split eight decisions in series play for the Giants.

52. _____ Who pitched a one-hitter for the Cubs in 1945?

  a. He won 162 games.
  b. Rudy York got the hit.

53. _____ Who was intentionally passed in his only series at-bat?

  a. He played for the 1962 Giants at the time.
  b. He came up with the 1951 Browns.

54. _____ Who was the player who, after getting 11 hits in the 1951 World Series, was pinch-hit for three times in the 1954 classic?

  a. He got four hits and stole home in Game One of 1951.
  b. Dusty Rhodes pinch-hit for him.

55. _____ Who was the catcher whose passed ball cost his team a big victory in 1941?

  a. The pitcher was Hugh Casey.
  b. He later jumped to the Mexican Leagues.

56. _____ Who tagged Don Newcombe for three homers and eight RBIs in the same series?

  a. He did it in 1956.
  b. Two of the shots were two-run blasts in the final game.

57. _____ Who won the last game of the 1927 series as a starter and the last game of the 1932 series as a reliever?

  a. He won 13 games in relief in 1927.
  b. He also saved 13 games that season.

58. _____ Who was the pitcher who threw a one-hitter for the Yankees in 1947?

  a. He lost.
  b. He never started another major league game.

59. _____ Who was the only pitcher, in addition to Carl Hubbell, to beat the Yankees in the 1930s?

  a. He did it for the Giants in 1936.
  b. He was called "Prince Hal."

60. _____ Who was the Yankee pitcher who struck out a record five times in one World Series game?

    a. In 1928 he had a league-high 24 wins.

    b. He later became an umpire.

61. _____ Who batted into five outs in two consecutive at-bats in a World Series game?

    a. He hit into a triple play the first time.

    b. He hit into a double play the second time.

62. _____ Who pitched a one-hitter for the Red Sox in 1967?

    a. Julian Javier got the hit.

    b. A skiing accident didn't help his future.

63. _____ Who was the catcher off whom Pepper Martin stole seven bases in two series?

    a. He played in five series with two teams.

    b. He player-managed a team to a world title.

64. _____ Who, in the 1920s, won the sixth and seventh games of a series?

    a. He did it for the 1925 Pirates.

    b. He twice won 20 games for the Pirates.

65. _____ Who was the .257 regular-season hitter in 1953 who batted .500 in the series and delivered a record 12 hits for a six-game clash?

    a. He batted .257 lifetime, too.

    b. In five series, however, he hit .333.

66. _____ Who got picked off second base for the final out of a series?

    a. The year was 1942.

    b. The catcher was Walker Cooper.

67. _____ Who set a record when he struck out the first five batters to face him in a starting assignment?

    a. He was the MVP in 1942.

    b. He won more than 20 games three years in a row.

68. _____ Who was the Oriole short-inning man who did not allow a run in three consecutive series?

    a. He won ten games in relief in 1970.

    b. Despite an 0.00 ERA, he lost his only decision in post-season play.

69. _____ Who was the first pitcher to hit a home run in series play?

    a. He did it for the 1920 Indians.

    b. He won 31 games that year.

70. _____ Who was the National League pitcher who allowed only one run in 25 ⅓ innings of pitching in series play?

a. He did it in the 1970s . . .

b. . . . for the Reds.

71. _____ Who was the Pirate star who was benched by manager Donie Bush in the 1927 series?

a. He hit .321 over 18 years.

b. He got the series-winning hit in 1925 for the Pirates.

72. _____ Who was the 40-year-old player who hit a game-winning home run in 1956?

a. He played on two world championship clubs in St. Louis.

b. He played on two world championship clubs in New York.

73. _____ Who hit the single that scored Enos Slaughter from first base for the winning run in the 1946 series?

a. He won a batting title.

b. His brother won one, too.

74. _____ Who became the first player to hit two home runs in two different games in the same series?

a. He hit .400 in the 1980 World Series.

b. He was named after Willie Mays.

75. _____ Who was the only National League pitcher to throw two complete-game wins in the 1970s?

a. He did it for the Pirates.

b. Mysteriously, his career came to an end because, a one-time location pitcher, he couldn't throw strikes anymore.

76. _____ Who pitched the opening game of back-to-back series for reverse teams?

a. He defeated the Yankees in 1976.

b. He lost to the Dodgers in 1977.

77. _____ Who, on his special night, got four hits, including a home run?

a. The year was 1973.

b. He ended up his career as a deluxe pinch-hitter.

78. _____ Who was the only pitcher to hit a grand slam in the series?

a. He won 20 or more games four years in a row.

b. He hit two home runs in World Series play.

79. _____ Who was the Yankee third baseman who repeatedly bailed out Ron Guidry in Game Three of the 1978 series with defensive gems?

a. He hit more home runs than any other third baseman in American League history.

b. They called him "Puff."

80. _____ Who was the Red Sox outfielder who dove into the right-field seats to rob Joe Morgan of a home run in 1975 and then doubled off Ken Griffey trying to return to first base after the catch?

   a. He has a strong throwing arm.
   b. He hits the long ball.

81. _____ Who, in Game Three of 1969, made two sensational catches—on balls hit by Elrod Hendricks and Paul Blair—that rank with the classic catches of series past?

   a. He also homered in that game.
   b. He came to the Mets from the White Sox.

82. _____ Who was the Tiger left fielder whose perfect throw cut down Lou Brock, trying to score, in the key play of Game Five in 1968?

   a. He played 18 years in the majors.
   b. He hit 325 career homers.

83. _____ Who was the third baseman whose diving backhand stab of Zoilo Versalles' smash down the third-base line, and subsequent tag of third for the inning-ending force, took Sandy Koufax out of his only jam in his 2–0 seventh-game victory over the Twins in 1965?

   a. He pushed Jackie Robinson out of his second-base job.
   b. He died while he was a coach with the Dodgers.

84. _____ Who was the outfielder whose outstanding running backhand stop of Willie Mays's double prevented Matty Alou from scoring and enabled the Yankees' Ralph Terry to preserve a 1–0 lead for the world title?

   a. He came up with Cleveland.
   b. He bowed out with St. Louis.

85. _____ Who was the infielder—noted for his good glove—whose three errors paved the way for the Pirates in 1979?

   a. He took Brooks Robinson's place at third.
   b. He moved on to the Angels.

86. _____ Who was the Yankee first baseman who lost a crucial throw from third baseman Clete Boyer because of the glare of the shirt-sleeves in the third-base boxes?

   a. He replaced Bill Skowron.
   b. The following year, he hit a grand slam home run against the Cardinals.

87. _____ Who was the Cardinal outfielder who, first, lost Jim Northrup's fly ball in the sun and, second,

slipped as the ball sailed by him for the game-winning triple in Game Seven of 1968?

    a. He was a great defensive outfielder.

    b. He tested baseball's reserve clause.

88. _____ Who stole six bases in a five-game series?

    a. He played with the 1907 Cubs.

    b. He was called "The Human Mosquito."

89. _____ Who was the player whose pinch-hit single in the 14th inning drove home the winning run in the classic's longest game?

    a. He did it for the Red Sox . . .

    b. . . . giving Babe Ruth the win.

90. _____ Who was the youngest pitcher to throw a complete-game win?

    a. He was 20 when he did it for the Athletics.

    b. His nickname was "Bullet Joe."

91. _____ Who pitched back-to-back complete games twice in the same series?

    a. He won three games and lost two.

    b. He pitched five complete games.

92. _____ Who was the three-game winner who allowed seven hits in one inning?

    a. He won 34 games that year.

    b. He was the roommate of Tris Speaker's during all of his 14 years in the majors.

93. _____ Who won five games and posted a .333 batting average in series play?

    a. He once won 31 games in a season.

    b. They called him "Colby Jack."

94. _____ Who was the first pitcher to lose three games in a series?

    a. He pitched for the 1919 White Sox.

    b. He was banned from baseball for allegedly conspiring to lose games.

95. _____ Who pinch-hit three times in a World Series and walked each time?

    a. He did it for the Senators . . .

    b. . . . in 1924.

96. _____ Who played on five losing teams in five tries?

    a. He caused a 1908 playoff in the National League.

    b. He has gone down in baseball's history as the sport's perennial "Sad Sack."

97. _____ Who was the player who hit two home runs in the 1924 series, despite the fact that he hit only 9 in 12 major league seasons?

   a. He was a young manager.

   b. He ended up an old manager.

98. _____ Who retired the first 22 batters in order?

   a. He was 5–0 in series play.

   b. He pitched in series 18 years apart.

99. _____ Who was the first player to hit a pinch-hit home run in series play?

   a. He hit a total of 12 homers in series play.

   b. He, like Frankie Frisch, hit ten doubles.

100. _____ Who was the Cardinal rookie who made four hits in one series game?

   a. He grew up with Yogi Berra.

   b. He later became a famous announcer.

The Shutout Series

If you don't believe that there was a dead ball era, you should glance at the statistics of the 1905–07 World Series, and then zero in on the records of the first of those classics.

In 16 games during the 1905–07 time span, there was not one home run hit in post-season play. To say that the pitchers dominated the hitters is to underscore the obvious.

Take the 1905 series, for example. The victorious Giants allowed the formidable Athletics just three runs in 45 innings of play. And none of the runs was earned. Christy Mathewson, the ace of John McGraw's staff, pitched a record three shutouts against Connie Mack's vaunted heroes. "Bix Six" was so completely in control that he allowed just 14 hits and a walk in 27 innings of pitching.

Joe McGinnity, also of the Giants, was almost as good as his celebrated teammate. He pitched a shutout, allowed only ten hits in 17 innings of pitching—a 22-game winner hurled one inning of relief in the "Iron Man's" first outing—and posted an 0.00 ERA. But his record was not perfect—he split his two decisions. In Game Two he was victimized by his defense, which allowed three unearned runs, and by his pitching opponent, who threw a four-hit shutout. (All five games ended in shutouts.)

Who was that Giant relief pitcher who later hurled a no-hitter for nine innings in the opening game of 1909—he lost the game in 13 innings, 3–0— and who was the Athletic shutout pitcher who went on to set a record by pitching nine consecutive complete games in World Series play?

(Answer appears on page 322.)

Chapter Seventeen

MAJOR LEAGUE CLUBS

CHICAGO CUBS

Infielders

True or False.

1. _____ Frank Chance, Charlie Grimm, and Phil Cavarretta ended their careers with lifetime batting averages in the .290s.

2. _____ Rogers Hornsby hit a club-high .380 in 1929.

3. _____ Ernie Banks played more games at shortstop than he did at first base.

4. _____ Heinie Zimmerman was the third baseman in the Tinker-to-Evers-to-Chance infield.

5. _____ Billy Herman compiled a lifetime average of .300 or better.

6. _____ Bill Madlock was the only Cub to win two batting titles.

Outfielders

Fill in the blanks.

7. _____ Who was the Bruin who won four home run crowns?

8. _____ Who is the present-day player who is nicknamed "Sarge"?

9. _____ Who won back-to-back home run titles in 1943–44?

10. _____ Who was the .320 lifetime hitter—he played two and one-half seasons with the Cubs—who ended his career with 300 home runs?

11. _____ Who was the Cub outfielder who played in 1,117 consecutive games to set a then-National League record?

12. _____ Who was the one-time Cub—he batted .285 lifetime with 213 career home runs—who played in World Series with the Cubs, Dodgers, and Braves?

Catchers

Matching.
13. _____ Johnny Kling   a. He managed the Cubs and the Tigers.
14. _____ Gabby Hartnett   b. He managed the Braves.
15. _____ Bob Scheffing   c. He player-managed the Cubs to a pennant.

Pitchers

Multiple Choice.
16. _____ Who was the pitcher against whom Babe Ruth "called his shot" in the 1932 World Series?
   a. Charlie Root b. Pat Malone c. Hippo Vaughn d. Guy Bush.
17. _____ Name the 176-game winner who was called the "Mississippi Mudcat."
   a. Bill Lee b. Guy Bush c. Hooks Wyse d. Lon Warneke
18. _____ Who was the losing pitcher—Fred Toney of the Reds was the winner—in the only nine-inning double no-hit game in major league history?
   a. Grover Alexander b. Hank Borowy c. Larry French d. Hippo Vaughn
19. _____ A winner of 162 major league games, he picked up a victory and a save in the 1945 World Series.
   a. Hank Borowy b. Lon Warneke c. Claude Passeau d. Charlie Root
20. _____ Who was the three-time 20-game winner who later became an umpire?
   a. Pat Malone b. Guy Bush c. Lon Warneke d. Bill Lee
21. _____ Who was the Cub pitcher who won 20 or more games in each of his first six full seasons in the majors?
   a. Ferguson Jenkins b. Ed Reulbach c. Mordecai Brown d. Johnny Schmitz
22. _____ Name the five-time 20-game winner who turned in the best single-season ERA (1.04) in National League history.

212

a. Ferguson Jenkins b. Grover Alexander c. Bob Rush
d. Mordecai Brown

23. _____ A 21-game winner for the Yankees and the Cubs in 1945, he split four World Series decisions that year.

a. Lon Warneke b. Claude Passeau c. Hank Borowy
d. Johnny Schmitz

24. _____ This 300-plus winner led the league in 1920, with the Cubs, in wins (27) and ERA (1.91).

a. Mordecai Brown b. Grover Alexander c. Guy Bush
d. Charlie Root

25. _____ The only National League pitcher to lead the loop in winning percentage for three consecutive seasons, he was the only pitcher to throw shutouts in both ends of a doubleheader.

a. Grover Alexander b. Ed Reulbach c. Pat Malone
d. Larry French

MONTREAL EXPOS

Infielders

Matching.

1. _____ Ron Fairly
2. _____ Dave Cash
3. _____ Ron Hunt
4. _____ Maury Wills
5. _____ Bob Bailey
6. _____ Larry Parrish

a. In 1971 he was hit by pitches a record 50 times.

b. A former Expo infielder, he's hit well over 200 career home runs.

c. He came up with the Pirates; he bowed out with the Red Sox. In between, he averaged 21 homers a year over a five-year span for the Expos.

d. In the three years before he joined the Expos, he led the league in at-bats with an average of 685 per season.

e. In his only season with the Expos, he led the team in stolen bases.

f. This veteran of 21 years—and four World Series—averaged 15 home runs a year in his five seasons with the Expos.

Outfielders

Multiple Choice.

7. _____ Who hit a single-season-high .334 for the Expos?
a. Ken Singleton b. Tim Raines c. Mack Jones d. Manny Mota

8. _____ Name the Expo who drove home 123 runs in one season.
a. Boots Day b. Tim Wallach c. Rusty Staub d. Larry Parrish

9. _____ Who was the outfielder with the strong arm who averaged 24 home runs a year from 1977–79?
a. Ellis Valentine b. Warren Cromartie c. Andre Dawson d. Rico Carty

214

10. _____ Who is the present-day outfielder who has played for eight teams and, from 1983–86, four clubs?

a. Dave Collins b. Mitch Webster c. George Wright d. Gary Ward

11. _____ Who was the Expo who set a record when he pinch-hit safely 25 times in 1977?

a. Jerry White b. Warren Cromartie c. Sam Mejias d. Jose Morales

12. _____ Who, in 1971, hit a then-club-high .311, drove home 97 runs, and moved to the Mets in 1972?

a. Manny Mota b. Rico Carty c. Rusty Staub d. Tommy Davis

Catchers

True or False.

13. _____ Barry Foote was the first-string catcher for the Expos before Gary Carter took over full-time in 1977.

14. _____ Tim McCarver played at least two full seasons with Montreal.

15. _____ Gary Carter tied a record with five home runs in two consecutive games.

Pitchers

Fill in the blanks.

16. _____ Who won the most games (20) in one season for Montreal?

17. _____ Who was the pitcher who struck out the most batters (251) in one season for the Expos?

18. _____ Name the starting pitcher whom the Expos traded to the Reds for Tony Perez.

19. _____ Who was the only relief pitcher, in addition to Goose Gossage, to register at least 20 saves a season from 1982–86?

20. _____ Who was the relief pitcher who led the loop in appearances for two consecutive years before he set records for games by a fireman with the Dodgers and the Twins?

21. _____ Who was the Rookie of the Year in 1979?

22. _____ Who pitched two no-hitters for the Expos?

23. _____ Who no-hit the Giants in 1981?
24. _____ Who was the 158-game winner who two times led the National League in losses?
25. _____ Who, along with Ken Singleton, was traded to the Orioles, where he won 20 games in his only year with Baltimore, for Dave McNally and Rich Coggins?

NEW YORK METS

Infielders

True or False.

1. _____ Gil Hodges ended his career with the Mets.
2. _____ Ron Hunt hit a key home run for the Mets in the final game of the 1969 World Series.
3. _____ Bud Harrelson hit .250 or over lifetime.
4. _____ Wayne Garrett came to the Mets in the deal for Nolan Ryan.
5. _____ Ed Kranepool was a lifetime Met.
6. _____ Donn Clendenon hit three home runs in the 1969 World Series.

Outfielders

Fill in the blanks.

7. _____ Who, in addition to Gary Carter, drove home a club-high 105 runs one year?
8. _____ Who stroked a club-high 39 homers in a season?
9. _____ Who hit a team-high .340 one year?
10. _____ Who was the former "Whiz Kid"— he hit .308 lifetime—who ended his career with the Mets?
11. _____ Who is the Met who averaged 27 home runs per year in his first four years in the majors?
12. _____ Who hit two home runs to defeat Steve Carlton in a game in which the Card lefty struck out a then-record 19 batters?

Catchers

Matching.
13. _____ Yogi Berra
14. _____ Jerry Grote
15. _____ John Stearns

a. He was born in St. Louis.
b. He was born in San Antonio.
c. He was born in San Francisco.

Multiple Choice.

16. _____ Who holds the club record for season wins (25) and strikeouts (289)?

    a. Jerry Koosman b. Nolan Ryan c. Tom Seaver d. Jon Matlack.

17. _____ Who was the pitcher who gave up Roberto Clemente's 3,000th—and final—hit?

    a. Jon Matlack b. Tug McGraw c. Danny Frisella d. Gary Gentry

18. _____ Who was the pitcher who coined the expression "You gotta believe"?

    a. Tom Seaver b. Bob Apodaca c. Tug McGraw d. Jerry Koosman

19. _____ Which one of the following pitchers won four of his 363 wins with the Mets?

    a. Mickey Lolich b. Warren Spahn c. Juan Marichal d. Early Wynn

20. _____ The pitcher who threw the historic 61st home run pitch to Roger Maris in 1961, he later lost 20 games for the 1964 Mets.

    a. Tracy Stallard b. Bill Monbouquette c. Dick Schwall d. Mike Fornieles

21. _____ Who became the first pitcher to go 3–0 in a championship series?

    a. Tug McGraw b. Jesse Orosco c. Nolan Ryan d. Dwight Gooden

22. _____ Who has posted the most wins (14) in one season out of the Met bull pen?

    a. Tug McGraw b. Jesse Orosco c. Roger McDowell d. Doug Sisk

23. _____ Twice a 20-game loser for the Mets, he split four World Series decisions with three different teams.

    a. Jack Fisher b. Roger Craig c. Al Jackson d. Pedro Ramos

24. _____ Which one of the following pitchers is 3–0 in World Series play?

    a. Jon Matlack b. Tom Seaver c. Gary Gentry d. Jerry Koosman

25. _____ Who became the first pitcher to fan 200 batters in his first three seasons in the majors?

    a. Dwight Gooden b. Nolan Ryan c. Tom Seaver d. Jerry Koosman

PHILADELPHIA PHILLIES

Infielders

True or False.

1. _____ Dolph Camilli won a home run title with the Phillies.

2. _____ Dave Cash registered more official at-bats (699) in one season than any other National League player.

3. _____ Larry Bowa hit .300 in a season.

4. _____ Mike Schmidt has led the National League in home runs a loop-high eight times.

5. _____ Emil Verban was the "Whiz Kid" second baseman in 1950.

6. _____ Willie Jones hit more home runs in a season than Dick Allen did.

Outfielders

Fill in the blanks.

7. _____ Who hit .400 three times with the Phillies?

8. _____ Who was the Phillie slugger who two times led the National League in home runs three years in a row?

9. _____ Who didn't win the RBI title despite the fact that he drove home 170 runs?

10. _____ Name the Phillie who hit a league-leading .398 one year?

11. _____ Whose tenth-inning home run on the last day of the 1950 season won the pennant for the Phillies?

12. _____ A .308 lifetime hitter, he won two batting titles with the Phillies in the 1950s.

Catchers

Matching.

13. _____ Curt Davis   a. He was Steve Carlton's favorite receiver.
14. _____ Andy Seminick
15. _____ Tim McCarver   b. He was the "Whiz Kids' " receiver?

c. He hit .333 career-wise for the Phillies, .308 overall.

Pitchers

Multiple Choice.

16. _____ Who was the pitcher who won a record 28 games in his rookie year?

a. Grover Alexander b. Harry Coveleski c. Eppa Rixey d. Bucky Walters

17. _____ Name the 500-plus home run hitter who ended his career with the Phillies as a pitcher.

a. Babe Ruth b. Ernie Banks c. Eddie Mathews d. Jimmie Foxx

18. _____ "The Giant Killer," he defeated New York five times in one week.

a. Cal McLish b. Chris Short c. Harry Coveleski d. Art Mahaffey

19. _____ Who was the first relief pitcher to win the MVP Award?

a. Mike Marshall b. Jim Konstanty c. Tug McGraw d. Joe Black

20. _____ Excluding Warren Spahn and Steve Carlton, he won more games than any other National League left-hander.

a. Eppa Rixey b. Curt Simmons c. Chris Short d. Jim Kaat

21. _____ Who was the Phillie pitcher who threw a career-record 502 home runs?

a. Steve Carlton b. Bucky Walters c. Jim Bunning d. Robin Roberts

22. _____ An American League transplant, he notched the 250th win of his 283-win career with the Phils.

a. Jim Bunning b. Mickey Lolich c. Jim Kaat d. Jim Lonborg

23. _____ Who was the pitcher who threw a perfect game for the Phils?

a. Jim Bunning b. Schoolboy Rowe c. Jim Lonborg d. Curt Simmons

220

24. _____ Who was the pitcher who led the league in wins (27) one year and losses (20) the following season?
   a. Grover Alexander b. Steve Carlton c. Jim Lonborg d. Curt Simmons

25. _____ Which one of the following pitchers was a Cy Young Award winner?
   a. Jim Lonborg b. Robin Roberts c. Jim Bunning d. Jim Kaat

PITTSBURGH PIRATES

Infielders

Fill in the blanks.

1. _____ Who was the first baseman who set a record when he drilled home runs in eight straight games?

2. _____ Who was the second baseman who hit two game-winning home runs in the 1960 World Series?

3. _____ Who was the Pirate shortstop who hit a club-high .385 in 1935?

4. _____ Who was the .320 lifetime hitter whom many experts consider to be the best all-round third baseman ever to play the game?

5. _____ A four-time home run champ in the American League, he finished his career in 1947 when he hit 25 home runs for the Pirates. Who was he?

6. _____ Name the infielder who won batting titles a National League-high eight times.

Outfielders

Matching.

7. _____ Tommy Leach
8. _____ Max Carey
9. _____ Paul Waner
10. _____ Jerry Lynch
11. _____ Roberto Clemente
12. _____ Lloyd Waner

a. He led the National League in stolen bases ten times.

b. A .317 lifetime hitter, he won four batting titles.

c. He set a then-record by hitting 18 pinch-hit career homers.

d. A .333 lifetime hitter, he won three batting crowns.

e. He collected over 200 hits in each of his first three years in the majors.

f. In 1902 he won the home run crown with six home runs, the lowest figure in history.

Catchers

Multiple Choice.
13. _____ He caught in the 1909 World Series.
  a. George Gibson b. Al Lopez c. Earl Smith d. Johnny Gooch
14. _____ He caught in the 1925 and the 1927 World Series.
  a. Al Lopez b. George Gibson c. Earl Smith d. Hal Smith
15. _____ He caught in the 1960 World Series.
  a. Manny Sanguillen b. Johnny Gooch c. Earl Smith d. Smoky Burgess

Pitchers

True or False.
16. _____ Rip Sewell (143–97) was known primarily for his knuckleball.
17. _____ Bob Friend had a winning major league record.
18. _____ Roy Face was the first reliever to pick up three saves in the same series.
19. _____ Vernon Law was the winning pitcher in the seventh game of the 1960 World Series.
20. _____ Murry Dickson led the National League in losses more times than any other Senior Circuit hurler.
21. _____ Steve Blass led his league in winning percentage one year.
22. _____ Deacon Phillippe had the most decisions in one World Series.
23. _____ Howie Camnitz registered more career wins than Sam Leever did.
24. _____ Wilbur Cooper recorded more lifetime victories than Babe Adams did.
25. _____ Larry French (197–171) never won 20 games in a season.

ST. LOUIS CARDINALS

Infielders

Multiple Choice.

1. _____ Which one of the following first basemen won one home run title, two RBI crowns, and hit over .300 in nine of his first ten years in the majors?
   a. Jim Bottomley b. Rip Collins c. Johnny Mize d. Stan Musial

2. _____ Which one of the following second basemen hit .400 three times?
   a. Frankie Frisch b. Red Schoendienst c. Emil Verban d. Rogers Hornsby

3. _____ Identify the shortstop whom they called "The Ground Hog."
   a. Specs Toporcer b. Marty Marion c. Leo Durocher d. Dick Groat

4. _____ Which one of the following players hit a grand slam home run in a World Series game?
   a. Pepper Martin b. Whitey Kurowski c. Ken Boyer d. Joe Torre

5. _____ Select the player from the following first basemen who performed for the 1934 "Gashouse Gang."
   a. Rip Collins b. Johnny Hopp c. Johnny Mize d. Stan Musial

6. _____ Who, among the following players, hit a home run that won an All-Star Game?
   a. Bill White b. Red Schoendienst c. Dick Groat d. Joe Torre

Outfielders

True or False.

7. _____ Stan Musial was the last National League player to win three consecutive batting titles.

8. _____ Joe Medwick won a Triple Crown.

9. _____ Enos Slaughter retired with a lifetime average that was under .300.

10. _____ Lou Brock broke Ty Cobb's stolen base record (96 thefts) when he stole 118 bases in 1974.

11. _____ Terry Moore played center field, between left fielder Stan Musial and right fielder Enos Slaughter, in the early 1940s.

12. _____ Chick Hafey, Joe Medwick, Harry Walker, and Curt Flood won batting titles.

Catchers

Fill in the blanks.

13. _____ Who was the catcher who threw out Babe Ruth, in an attempted steal, to end the 1926 World Series?

14. _____ Name the receiver who played in three consecutive World Series for the Cardinals.

15. _____ Who was the rookie receiver who stroked four hits in a game in the 1946 World Series?

Pitchers

Matching.

16. _____ Jesse Haines
17. _____ Grover Alexander
18. _____ Burleigh Grimes
19. _____ Dizzy Dean
20. _____ Mort Cooper
21. _____ Max Lanier
22. _____ Harry Brecheen
23. _____ Bob Gibson
24. _____ Steve Carlton
25. _____ Johnny Beazley

a. Nine times he struck out more than 200 batters in a season, and he pitched 13 shutouts in one year.

b. In five full seasons with the Cardinals, he averaged 24 victories a season.

c. He picked up three wins, one of them coming in relief, in a series.

d. With another team he won 30 or more games three straight years.

e. He, like Grover Alexander, won two games against the Yankees in 1926.

f. He missed the 1947–48 seasons because he was banned from baseball for "jumping" to the Mexican Leagues in 1946.

225

g. He won only 31 career contests, but he copped 21 of them, in addition to two series victories, in 1942.

h. In 1942 he led the league in ERA (1.78) and shut-outs (10).

i. At the age of 38, he won two World Series games for the Cardinals.

j. He struck out 19 batters in a 10-inning game, but lost.

ATLANTA BRAVES

Infielders

Multiple Choice.

1. _____ Whom did they call "The Baby Bull"?
   a. Felipe Alou b. Deron Johnson c. Tito Francona d. Orlando Cepeda

2. _____ Identify the player who hit more home runs (43) in one season than any other second baseman in the history of the game.
   a. Milt Bolling b. Felix Millan c. Bob Aspromonte d. Davy Johnson

3. _____ Who is the Brave infielder who with another team led the league in fielding at two different positions?
   a. Dennis Menke b. Ken Oberkfell c. Marty Perez d. Glenn Hubbard

4. _____ Which one of the following third basemen played in five World Series?
   a. Clete Boyer b. Eddie Mathews c. Darrell Evans d. Dennis Menke

5. _____ Who was the Brave who hit a season-high 47 homers and a season-high 135 RBIs?
   a. Orlando Cepeda b. Eddie Mathews c. Deron Johnson d. Willie Montanez

6. _____ Who is the first baseman who once hit 30 home runs in a season for the Phillies and, in a brief stint with the Braves, hit .321 in 1976 and 20 home runs in 1977?
   a. Darrell Evans b. Darrel Chaney c. Willie Montanez d. Jerry Royster

Outfielders

True or False.

7. _____ Mike Lum was the only batter ever to pinch-hit for Hank Aaron.

8. _____ Hank Aaron hit more home runs in Atlanta than he did in Milwaukee.

9. _____ Felipe Alou was called "The Road Runner."

10. _____ Dale Murphy has been the youngest back-to-back MVP winner in National League history.

11. _____ Rico Carty put big numbers on the board (.330 batting average and 22 home runs) as a rookie.

12. _____ Ken Griffey played on back-to-back World Series winners.

Catchers

Fill in the blanks.

13. _____ Name the catcher who hit .315 with 36 home runs and 101 RBIs in 1966.

14. _____ Who was the rookie catcher who hit 33 home runs in 1971?

15. _____ Who is the catcher who hit home runs in five consecutive games?

Pitchers

Matching.

16. _____ Tony Cloninger
17. _____ Phil Niekro
18. _____ Gene Garber
19. _____ Milt Pappas
20. _____ Hoyt Wilhelm
21. _____ Denny McLain
22. _____ Andy Messersmith
23. _____ Rick Mahler
24. _____ David Palmer
25. _____ Joe Niekro

a. He pitched a five-inning rain-abbreviated perfect game.

b. He drove home nine runs in one game.

c. He was the only 200-game winner who never won 20 games in a season.

d. He led the league in wins (21) and losses (20) in the same year.

e. He has more than 200 career saves.

f. His 7–0 start in 1985 was among the best in Braves' history.

g. He played out his option and signed with the Braves in an historic free agent deal.

h. The last 30-game winner in the majors, he ended up his career in Atlanta.

i. He won 20 games in back-to-back years for another club.

j. He played with nine major league teams.

CINCINNATI REDS

Infielders

Matching.

1. _____ Ted Kluszewski
2. _____ Joe Morgan
3. _____ Lonny Frey
4. _____ Pete Rose
5. _____ Frank McCormick
6. _____ Connie Ryan

a. He succeeded Eddie Stanky as manager of the Rangers.
b. He won the MVP Award in 1940.
c. He won back-to-back MVP titles.
d. He got five hits in a game a National League record-tying nine times.
e. He played second base for the pennant-winning clubs of 1939–40.
f. He averaged 43 home runs a year for a four-year span.

Outfielders

Multiple Choice.

7. _____ Who was the player who made a bigger name for himself in professional football than he did in professional baseball?

    a. Harry Craft b. Ival Goodman c. Greasy Neale d. Wally Berger

8. _____ Which one of the following players has led the National League in RBIs?

    a. Cesar Geronimo b. George Foster c. Vada Pinson d. Ken Griffey

9. _____ In one season he hit .377, the club high.

    a. Cy Seymour b. Frank Robinson c. Edd Roush d. Curt Walker

10. _____ An ineffective pitcher for the Athletics, he switched to the outfield with the Reds and posted a .301 lifetime batting average, which included a .351 mark over a three-year period (1924–26).

a. Rube Bressler b. Curt Walker c. Ival Goodman d. Harry Craft

11. _____ Name the .323 lifetime hitter who won two batting titles.

    a. Frank Robinson b. Vada Pinson c. Edd Roush d. Cy Seymour

12. _____ Who was the Red MVP winner who posted a .294 lifetime average and slugged 586 home runs?

    a. Edd Roush b. Wally Berger c. Vada Pinson d. Frank Robinson

Catchers

True or False.

13. _____ Johnny Bench has won more than one home run crown.

14. _____ Bubbles Hargrave was one of two catchers to win the batting title.

15. _____ Ernie Lombardi had a lifetime batting average of .300 or better.

Pitchers

Fill in the blanks.

16. _____ Who was the only pitcher to throw consecutive no-hitters?

17. _____ The youngest player ever to appear in a major league game, he led the National League in shutouts (5) in 1955.

18. _____ Who was the two-time 20-game winner who struck out more than 200 batters four years in a row?

19. _____ Name the 198-game winner who began his major league career as a third baseman.

20. _____ A one-time 27-game loser, he reeled off three straight 20-game winning seasons for the 1938–40 Reds.

21. _____ Called "The Whip," he led the league in wins (22), complete games (23), and strikeouts (193) in 1947.

22. _____ Who was the 1985 starter who became the first rookie 20-game winner in the majors since the Yankees' Bob Grim in 1954?

23. _____ In the 1972 World Series he, with relief aid from Clay Carroll in the ninth inning, pitched the Reds to their only 1–0 win in post-season play.

24. _____ Who was the first Little League product to pitch in the major leagues?

25. _____ Who is the Red relief specialist who notched 29 saves in 1986?

HOUSTON ASTROS

Infielders

Fill in the blanks.

1. _____ Who was the first baseman—the American League's RBI champ in 1976—who averaged 27 home runs per year during his three-year stay in Houston?

2. _____ Who was the .288 lifetime hitter who finished his career with the Astros after setting a record of appearing at the plate 600 or more times for 12 consecutive years in the American League?

3. _____ Who, going into the 1987 season, was the Astros' all-time leader with 70 pinch-hits?

4. _____ Who was the Astro third baseman who three times hit more than 20 home runs in a season?

5. _____ Who was the former first baseman with the Astros who wrote a confessional best seller, *Joe, You Coulda Made Us Proud*?

6. _____ Who was the Houston rookie second baseman (1965) who reached double figures in doubles (22), triples (12), and home runs (14)?

Outfielders

Matching.

7. _____ Cesar Cedeno
8. _____ Rusty Staub
9. _____ Jimmy Wynn
10. _____ Jose Cruz
11. _____ Terry Puhl
12. _____ Greg Gross

a. He was the .314 hitter who was named National League Rookie Player of the Year by *The Sporting News* in 1974.

b. He tied a record when he didn't make one error in a 157-game season.

c. He hit a homer in his first game with the Astros and has topped .300 six times with them.

d. He stole 61 bases, a club record, one year.

e. He hit .333, the club high, one season.

f. He clubbed 37 home runs, the team top, one year.

Catchers

Multiple Choice.

13. _____ This veteran of 16 campaigns played in two Word Series with both the Mets and the Dodgers, but he played his first two years in the majors with the Astros.

    a. Jerry Grote b. Ed Herrman c. John Bateman d. Johnny Edwards

14. _____ A long-ball hitter with defensive liabilities, he was traded to the Yankees during the 1977 season.

    a. Joe Ferguson b. Cliff Johnson c. Ed Herrman d. John Bateman

15. _____ Name the catcher who was traded for Larry Dierker.

    a. Cliff Johnson b. Jerry Grote c. Ed Herrman d. Joe Ferguson

234

True or False.

16. _____ Joe Niekro is the Astros' all-time single-season winner.

17. _____ Don Wilson pitched two no-hitters for the Astros.

18. _____ Mike Cuellar came up to the majors with Houston.

19. _____ Larry Dierker had a 20-win season with the Astros.

20. _____ Dave Smith established club save records for single season (33) and career (100) recently.

21. _____ Jim Bouton finished his career with the Astros.

22. _____ Nolan Ryan established a modern mark when he struck out the first eight batters in a game.

23. _____ Bob Knepper's 17 wins in 1986 is the all-time high for an Astro lefty.

24. _____ Bo Belinsky pitched a no-hitter for Houston.

25. _____ Mike Scott's 306 strikeouts in 1986 is the all-time high for the Astros.

LOS ANGELES DODGERS

Infielders

Matching.

1. _____ Steve Garvey
2. _____ Charlie Neal
3. _____ Maury Wills
4. _____ Ron Cey
5. _____ Gil Hodges
6. _____ Davey Lopes

a. He drove home 100 or more runs for seven consecutive years.
b. He stole 11 bases in the World Series.
c. He hit four home runs in a Championship Series.
d. He hit .370 in the 1959 World Series.
e. He's hit more than 300 home runs.
f. He won the stolen base title six consecutive years.

Outfielders

Multiple Choice.

7. _____ Who was called "The Reading Rifle"?
   a. Manny Mota b. Carl Furillo c. Dick Allen d. Rick Monday

8. _____ Who was the Dodger who hit two pinch-hit home runs in the 1959 World Series?
   a. Chuck Essegian b. Ron Fairly c. Jimmy Wynn d. Gino Cimoli

9. _____ Name the Dodger who hit 407 lifetime home runs.
   a. Duke Snider b. Wally Moon c. Frank Howard d. Tommy Davis

10. _____ Who's hit more than 30 home runs three times?
    a. Mike Marshall b. Dusty Baker c. Pedro Guerrero d. Ken Landreaux

11. _____ A seven-year member of the Dodgers, he hit better than 40 home runs three straight years for another club.
    a. Frank Howard b. Jimmy Wynn c. Tommy Davis d. Dick Allen

12. _____ Winner of back-to-back batting titles, he drove home a club-high 153 runs in one season.
   a. Tommy Davis b. Duke Snider c. Frank Howard d. Jimmy Wynn

Catchers

True or False.

13. _____ Johnny Roseboro spent his entire career with the Dodgers.

14. _____ Steve Yeager and John Ferguson both had lifetime batting averages that were above .250.

15. _____ Jeff Torborg hit higher than .250 in his career.

Pitchers

Fill in the blanks.

16. _____ From 1959–65 he struck out more than 200 batters six of seven times.

17. _____ Who tied Carl Hubbell's record in the All-Star Game when he struck out five consecutive American League batters?

18. _____ Who threw the 715th home run pitch to Hank Aaron?

19. _____ Who in a recent year chalked up an 11–0 record at Dodger Stadium?

20. _____ Who posted a record 21 consecutive seasons of more than 100 strikeouts?

21. _____ Who did the Dodgers get from the White Sox for Dick Allen?

22. _____ Name the 148-game winner who won his last four World Series decisions, including a seventh-game clincher.

23. _____ Who was the 16–3 relief pitcher who led the National League in winning percentage (.842) and games (69) in 1963 while he saved 21 contests?

24. _____ Who was the Dodger reliever who was nicknamed "The Vulture"?

25. _____ Who was the Dodger lefty, a two-time 20-game winner, who ended his career with 196 wins and 195 losses?

SAN DIEGO PADRES

Infielders

True or False.

1. _____ Nate Colbert hit more home runs in one season than any other Padre.

2. _____ Alan Wiggins stole a club-high 70 bases.

3. _____ Garry Templeton receives few bases on balls.

4. _____ Graig Nettles, in back-to-back seasons in which he played 150 or more games, failed to hit a triple.

5. _____ Steve Garvey has hit more than 300 career homers.

6. _____ Kevin Mitchell, who took Graig Nettles's position at third base, is the son of a former basketball teammate of Nettles's at San Diego State.

Outfielders

Fill in the blanks.

7. _____ Who led the league in hits in both 1984 and 1986?

8. _____ Who was selected by the Atlanta Hawks in the NBA draft, the Utah Stars in the ABA draft, and the Minnesota Vikings in the NFL draft?

9. _____ Nicknamed "Downtown," he twice hit 20 or more home runs in a season for the Padres. What's his real name?

10. _____ Who was the long-ball hitter who tied a record by playing on four different teams in the same year?

11. _____ Who is the current player who averaged 20 home runs per season in his first three years in the majors?

12. _____ Who was the 1975–76 outfielder who played for the Cardinals in the 1967–68 World Series and the Reds in the 1970 and 1972 fall classics?

Catchers

Matching.
13. _____ Gene Tenace
14. _____ Fred Kendall
15. _____ Terry Kennedy

a. He was part of a package deal for George Hendrick.
b. He is the son of a former major leaguer.
c. He averaged 17 home runs a year for the Padres in four seasons.

Pitchers

Multiple Choice.
16. _____ He won the Cy Young Award.
    a. Randy Jones b. Ed Whitson c. Rick Wise d. John Montefusco

17. _____ He won Cy Young awards in both leagues.
    a. Rollie Fingers b. LaMarr Hoyt c. Randy Jones d. Gaylord Perry

18. _____ Identify the Padre pitcher who struck out a club-record 231 batters in one season.
    a. Butch Metzger b. Johnny Podres c. Clay Kirby d. Steven Arlen

19. _____ Who was the winner over the Yankees in the 1976 World Series who was 13–30 in his short stay with the Padres?
    a. Butch Metzger b. Dave Roberts c. Fred Norman d. Clay Kirby

20. _____ Who was the pitcher whose 12 consecutive victories at the start of his career are a record?
    a. Bruce Metzger b. Pat Dobson c. Rich Folkers d. Johnny Podres

21. _____ Who is the pitcher who was suspended in 1986 for criticizing the owner's product?
    a. Ed Whitson b. Eric Show c. Goose Gossage d. Dave Dravecky

22. _____ Who was the winner of 148 career games and four World Series starts who finished his career by posting a 5–6 record with the Padres?
    a. Don Larsen b. Mudcat Grant c. Johnny Podres d. Jim Bouton

23. _____ Who was the Cy Young Award winner in the

American League who was released by the Padres before the 1987 season?

    a. Joe Niekro b. Goose Gossage c. LaMarr Hoyt d. Rollie Fingers

24. _____ Who led the league in saves in back-to-back years?

    a. Bob Shirley b. Tim Lollar c. Rollie Fingers d. Goose Gossage

25. _____ Who was the two-game winner for the Brewers in the 1982 World Series who pitched his first three years with the Padres?

    a. Rollie Fingers b. Tim Lollar c. Mike Caldwell d. Joe Niekro

SAN FRANCISCO GIANTS

Infielders

Multiple Choice.

1. _____ Who was the slugger who tied Ted Williams for tenth place on the all-time home run list?
   a. Orlando Cepeda b. Willie McCovey c. Willie Montanez d. Dave Kingman

2. _____ Which one of the following players hit a grand slam in World Series play?
   a. Chuck Hiller b. Don Blasingame c. Ron Hunt d. Hal Lanier

3. _____ Which one of the following players was the first San Francisco Giant shortstop?
   a. Chris Speier b. Tito Fuentes c. Jose Pagan d. Daryl Spencer

4. _____ Who tied a league record when he drove home six runs in one inning?
   a. Jim Davenport b. Bill Madlock c. Jim Ray Hart d. Darrell Evans

5. _____ Which one of the following hit .300 for three different teams?
   a. Willie McCovey b. Orlando Cepeda c. Darrell Evans d. Jose Pagan

6. _____ In three consecutive years he hit .300 in three different cities.
   a. Willie Montanez b. Jim Ray Hart c. Ron Hunt d. Tito Fuentes

Outfielders

True or False.

7. _____ Willie Kirkland hit the first home run at Candlestick Park.

8. _____ Dave Kingman struck out more times (189) in one season than any other player in the history of the game.

9. _____ Willie Mays hit more home runs in one season in New York than he did in San Francisco.

10. _____ Bobby Murcer was traded to the Giants in a deal for Bobby Bonds.

11. _____ Harvey Kuenn won a batting title with the Giants.
12. _____ All three Alou brothers—Matty, Felipe, and Jesus—once played in the same outfield at the same time.

Catchers

Fill in the blanks.
13. _____ Who was the Giant catcher who hit 27 home runs one year?
14. _____ Name the former Red backstop who hit 17 and 21 home runs in his two full seasons with the Giants?
15. _____ Who is the present-day catcher who topped National League receivers with a .995 fielding percentage in 1986?

Matching.

16. _____ John Montefusco
17. _____ Gaylord Perry
18. _____ Juan Marichal
19. _____ Stu Miller
20. _____ Jack Sanford
21. _____ Billy Loes
22. _____ Don Larsen
23. _____ Ruben Gomez
24. _____ Billy O'Dell
25. _____ Billy Pierce

a. A former Yankee, he beat the Bombers in the 1962 World Series.

b. He won a club-record 16 consecutive games in 1962.

c. He pitched the last Giant no-hitter.

d. Joe Adcock "ran him off" the mound one day.

e. He pitched two of his four 20-game-win seasons with the Giants.

f. He was a uniformed witness on the days Gil Hodges, Joe Adcock, Rocky Colavito, and Willie Mays hit four home runs in a game.

g. He won 20 or more games six times in a seven-year period of time.

h. In 1961 he led the league's relief pitchers in wins (14), winning percentage (.737), and saves (17).

i. A 19-game winner for the pennant-winning 1962 club, he led the league's relief pitchers in wins in both 1964 and 1965.

j. Two times a 20-game winner in the American League, he helped the Giants win the 1962 pennant by posting a 16–6 record.

BALTIMORE ORIOLES

Infielders

Fill in the blanks.

1. _____ From 1960–62 this slugging first base-man hit 100 home runs, including a career-high 46 in 1961.

2. _____ Name the second baseman who hit .280 or better for three consecutive pennant winners.

3. _____ Who was the infielder who set a club record when he stole 57 bases in 1964?

4. _____ In 1969 he hit .500 in the league Championship Series, and in 1970 he hit .583; in 1970 he hit .429 in the World Series, and in 1971 he hit .318.

5. _____ A consistent Gold Glove winner, he turned in an American League record lifetime fielding average of .977 at his position.

6. _____ Three times an RBI champ, this long-ball-hitting right-handed hitter (247 career homers) was the first starting third baseman with the Orioles.

Outfielders

Matching.

7. _____ Bob Nieman
8. _____ Dick Williams
9. _____ Paul Blair
10. _____ Frank Robinson
11. _____ Gene Woodling
12. _____ Ken Singleton

a. A .284 lifetime hitter, "Young Reliable" played on five world championship teams.

b. In 1958 he hit .325, which remained the Orioles' all-time batting high for one season until 1977.

c. He hit 49 home runs in one season, the club's all-time high.

d. A journeyman outfielder with a .260 lifetime average, he later managed three different teams to four pennants and two world titles.

e. He presently holds the club's all-time single-season (.328) batting high.

f. Considered the best defensive outfielder in the American League during his time, he turned slugger in the 1970 World Series, ripping the Red pitching staff for a .474 average.

Catchers

Multiple Choice.

13. _____ Which one of the following Oriole receivers had a couple of on-field run-ins with Billy Martin?
   a. Hal Smith b. Clint Courtney c. John Orsino d. Dick Brown

14. _____ A .255 lifetime hitter, he later emerged as one of the premiere batting instructors in the game.
   a. Charlie Lau b. Gus Triandos c. Hal Smith d. Dick Brown

15. _____ Who was the power-hitting backstop (167 home runs) whose career began to decline when Hoyt Wilhelm brought his knuckleball to Baltimore?

a. John Orsino b. Dick Brown c. Gus Triandos d. Hal Smith

Pitchers

True or False.

16. _____ Both Mike Cuellar and Dave McNally won 24 games, the club high, in one season.

17. _____ Jim Palmer holds the strikeout mark with 202 in a season.

18. _____ Wally Bunker was the youngest pitcher to hurl a shutout in World Series play.

19. _____ Chuck Estrada was traded to Cincinnati in the controversial deal for Frank Robinson.

20. _____ Stu Miller threw the pitch that Mickey Mantle hit for his 500th home run.

21. _____ Don Larsen won 21 games in his only season with the Orioles.

22. _____ Mike Flanagan won a Cy Young Award.

23. _____ Jim Palmer, Wally Bunker, and Dave McNally tossed shutouts against the Dodgers in the 1966 World Series.

24. _____ Hoyt Wilhelm, in a rare start, pitched a no-hitter against the Yankees in 1958.

25. _____ Robin Roberts had a losing record with the Orioles.

BOSTON RED SOX

Infielders

Matching.

1. _____ Billy Goodman
2. _____ Pete Runnels
3. _____ Vern Stephens
4. _____ Rico Petrocelli
5. _____ Jimmy Collins
6. _____ Pinky Higgins

a. He managed the Sox for eight seasons.
b. A .294 lifetime hitter, he managed Boston to its first pennant and series victory.
c. A batting champ, he ended his career with a *.300* lifetime average.
d. From 1969–71 he averaged almost 33 home runs per season.
e. He won batting titles two years apart.
f. A two-time RBI champ with Boston, he won another crown before coming to the Sox.

Outfielders

Multiple Choice.

7. _____ Though this .306 lifetime hitter played only seven years in the big time, he set a major league record when he rocked 67 doubles in one season.
   a. Duffy Lewis b. Ben Chapman c. Harry Hooper d. Earl Webb

8. _____ He was the only player ever to pinch-hit for Ted Williams.
   a. Gene Stephens b Carroll Hardy c. Sam Mele d. Al Zarilla

9. _____ He holds the club's stolen base record for one season.
   a. Dom DiMaggio b. Tris Speaker c. Tommy Harper d. Reggie Smith.

10. _____ In the same year that he led the league in stolen

bases (22), he rapped into 32 double plays, a major league record at that time.

a. Jackie Jensen b. Clyde Vollmer c. Fred Lynn d. Ken Harrelson

11. _____ Hollywood made a movie, *Fear Strikes Out*, about a segment of his life.

a. Jimmie Foxx b. Hoot Evers c. Ted Williams d. Jimmy Piersall

12. _____ He won three batting titles with a combined mark of .315 for those years.

a. Dale Alexander b. Carl Yastrzemski c. Elmer Flick d. Ted Williams

Catchers

True or False.

13. _____ Bill Carrigan, who hit .257 during a ten-year career with the Red Sox, later managed Boston to back-to-back world titles.

14. _____ Rick Ferrell handled the pitching serves of his brother, Wes, with the Red Sox.

15. _____ Birdie Tebbetts was the starting catcher on the great Red Sox teams of the late 1940s.

Pitchers

Fill in the blanks.

16. _____ Which Red Sox pitcher threw the first perfect game of the modern era?

17. _____ Who won two games, including a one-hitter, in the 1967 World Series?

18. _____ Son of a Hall of Famer, he pitched for Boston from 1956–59. Who was he?

19. _____ Name the relief pitcher who led the American League bull pen specialists in wins in each of his first three years in the majors (1962–64) and who struck out more batters than he pitched innings in each of those seasons.

20. _____ Who was the pitcher who lost the playoff game, between the Indians and the Red Sox, that decided the 1948 pennant?

21. _____ Who set the league record for shut-outs by southpaws (9) in one season?

22. _____ Name the pitcher who won his 300th—and final—game with the Red Sox.

23. _____ A two-time 20-game loser with the Red Sox, he went on to win seven World Series games with another American League team. Who was he?

24. _____ Who was the pitcher who, including the regular season and series, won 37 games and lost six in 1912?

25. _____ Who was the pitcher who came on in relief, with a runner who had walked on first base with no one out in the first inning, and proceeded to pitch a perfect game?

CLEVELAND INDIANS

Infielders

Fill in the blanks.

1. _____ Who was the first baseman who drove home 162 runs, a club record, in one season?

2. _____ Who was the second baseman who made an unassisted triple play in the 1920 World Series?

3. _____ When Lou Boudreau was traded to the Red Sox, who took his place at shortstop?

4. _____ Name the third baseman who made two great defensive plays against Joe DiMaggio on the night "The Yankee Clipper's" 56-game batting streak was broken.

5. _____ Can you name the last Indian who won a batting title?

6. _____ Who was the batter who hit the ball that Willie Mays ran down in the 1954 World Series?

Outfielders

Matching.

7. _____ Elmer Flick
8. _____ Joe Jackson
9. _____ Tris Speaker
10. _____ Earl Averill
11. _____ Jeff Heath
12. _____ Larry Doby

a. He was the first black player to compete in the American League.

b. He won a batting title with a .306 average.

c. He never won a batting title, even though he hit .408 in one season and .356 lifetime.

d. He hit at least one home run in every major league park that was in use during his career.

e. He stopped Ty Cobb's string of nine consecutive batting titles when he led the league with a .386 average in 1916.

f. He had a son who played in the big leagues.

Catchers

Multiple Choice.

13. _____ Who caught Bob Feller when "Rapid Robert" no-hit the Yankees, 1–0, in 1946, and provided the only run in the game with a home run?
   a. Buddy Rosar b. Frank Hayes c. Rollie Hemsley d. Jim Hegan

14. _____ Name the catcher who handled six different 20-game winners during his career with the Tribe.
   a. Steve O'Neill b. Luke Sewell c. Jim Hegan d. Johnny Romano

15. _____ Which one of the following catchers had the highest lifetime average?
   a. Buddy Rosar b. Luke Sewell c. Jim Hegan d. Russ Nixon

Pitchers

True or False.

16. _____ Jim Bagby won more games in one season than any other Indian pitcher.

17. _____ Herb Score never won 20 games in a season.

18. _____ Johnny Allen won 15 of 16 decisions in 1937 to set an American League mark (.938) for winning percentage in one season.

19. _____ The two pitchers who joined forces to halt Joe DiMaggio's 56-game hitting streak were Jim Bagby and Al Smith.

20. _____ Bob Feller, Bob Lemon, Early Wynn, and Mike Garcia all won 20 or more games in the same season.

21. _____ Gene Bearden, who pitched Cleveland to a pennant and a World Series crown in 1948 when he posted a record of 20–7, never before or after registered a winning record.

22. _____ Bob Feller pitched more no-hitters than any other right-handed pitcher.

23. _____ Both Jim and Gaylord Perry turned in 20-win seasons with the Tribe.

24. _____ Wes Ferrell had more consecutive 20-win seasons than did Bob Feller, Bob Lemon, or Early Wynn.

25. _____ Early Wynn finished his career with the Indians.

DETROIT TIGERS

Infielders

Multiple Choice.

1. _____ One year he drove home 183 runs, the club high; the following season, he clubbed 58 home runs, the team high.
   a. Norm Cash b. Hank Greenberg c. Walt Dropo d. George Burns

2. _____ He was the last Tiger to win a batting title.
   a. George Kell b. Harvey Kuenn c. Al Kaline d. Norm Cash

3. _____ Which one of the following players has been one of only two players who competed in every game of a 154-game schedule without hitting into a double play?
   a. Dick McAuliffe b. Lu Blue c. Tom Tresh d. George Kell

4. _____ Who was the only third baseman, in addition to George Brett and Carney Lansford, to win a batting title?
   a. Marv Owen b. Ray Boone c. Eddie Yost d. George Kell

5. _____ Name the league's batting titlist (1959) who was traded after the season for the league's home run hitter.
   a. Charlie Gehringer b. Harvey Kuenn c. Al Kaline d. Norm Cash

6. _____ The Tigers won 18 of their 23 batting titles before one of their infielders won the coveted award. Who was that 1937 standout?
   a. Harvey Kuenn b. George Kell c. Charlie Gehringer d. Hank Greenberg

Outfielders

True or False.

7. _____ Sam Crawford was the only modern-day player to lead the National League and the American League in both triples and home runs.

8. _____ Ty Cobb and Harry Heilmann have been the only teammates to hit .400.

9. _____ Al Kaline compiled a .300 lifetime average.

10. _____ In the seventh inning of the seventh game of the 1968 World Series, Rocky Colavito got the key triple that broke up a pitching duel between Mickey Lolich and Bob Gibson and paced the Bengals to a 4–1 victory.

11. _____ Hoot Evers, Johnny Groth, and Vic Wertz, outfielders for the Tigers, all hit .300 or better in the same season.

12. _____ Ty Cobb was the youngest player to win a major league batting title.

Catchers

Fill in the blanks.

13. _____ Who set a record when he hit 18 home runs in one month?

14. _____ Who was the playing manager who compiled a lifetime batting average of .320?

15. _____ Who was the starting receiver for the Tigers' 1968 world champions?

Matching.

16. _____ Mark Fidrych
17. _____ Denny McLain
18. _____ Mickey Lolich
19. _____ Jim Bunning
20. _____ Frank Lary
21. _____ Bob Cain
22. _____ Virgil Trucks
23. _____ Hal Newhouser
24. _____ Schoolboy Rowe
25. _____ George Mullin

a. He was the pitcher who tried to keep the ball low to Bill Veeck's midget, Eddie Gaedel.

b. He tied an American League record by winning 16 consecutive decisions.

c. He was the only modern-day pitcher to lose 20 games with a pennant winner.

d. He was the only Tiger pitcher to win the Rookie of the Year Award.

e. He was known as "The Yankee Killer."

f. He won Cy Young awards in back-to-back seasons.

g. He was the only Tiger pitcher to strike out 300 or more batters in a season.

h. Two of the five games he won in one season were no-hitters.

i. He won more than 100 games in each league, and he struck out more than 1,000 batters in each loop.

j. He led the league in wins three straight years.

MILWAUKEE BREWERS

Infielders

True or False.

1. _____ George Scott led the American League in home runs one year.

2. _____ Jim Gantner has more than 1,000 career hits.

3. _____ Robin Yount has more than 2,000 hits.

4. _____ Paul Molitor holds the team record for most steals (45) in a season.

5. _____ Cecil Cooper is the team leader in season batting average and RBIs.

6. _____ Don Money never hit more than 20 home runs in a season for the Brewers.

Outfielders

Fill in the blanks.

7. _____ Who was the Hall of Famer who played the last two years of his 23-year record-studded career with the Brewers?

8. _____ Who is the player who hit 33 home runs in his rookie season?

9. _____ Who hit a season-high 45 homers in 1979?

10. _____ Who was the infielder-outfielder, known more for his base-stealing exploits than his power, who blasted 31 home runs in 1970, the first year of the franchise?

11. _____ Who tied Reggie Jackson for the home run lead in 1980?

12. _____ Who tied Reggie Jackson for the home run lead in 1982?

Catchers

Matching.

13. _____ Darrell Porter
14. _____ Ellie Rodriguez
15. _____ Charlie Moore

a. His best batting average with Milwaukee was .285.
b. His best mark with the Brewers was .254.
c. His best season with Milwaukee was .301.

Pitchers

Multiple Choice.

16. _____ Who won a club-high 22 games in 1978?
   a. Jim Slaton b. Ken Sanders c. Mike Caldwell d. Jim Lonborg

17. _____ Who leads the Brewer moundsmen with 207 strikeouts in a season?
   a. Ken Brett b. Billy Champion c. Bill Travers d. Ted Higuera

18. _____ Who was the former bonus baby who lost 18 games in 1970?
   a. Lew Krausse b. Gene Brabender c. Skip Lockwood d. John O'Donoghue

19. _____ Who was the Milwaukee pitcher who was killed in an Arizona dune buggy crash on January 1, 1976?
   a. Danny Frisella b. Milt Tracy c. Dan Story d. Jim Clancy

20. _____ Name the former Cy Young Award winner who was 14–12 in his only season with the Brewers?
   a. Chris Short b. Jim Lonborg c. Bill Parsons d. Al Downing

21. _____ Who won 20 games in his rookie season?
   a. Ted Higuera b. Mike Caldwell c. Moose Haas d. Jim Slaton

22. _____ Who won the MVP Award?
   a. Mike Caldwell b. Rollie Fingers c. Pete Vuckovich d. Pete Ladd

23. _____ Who won the Cy Young Award?
   a. Don Sutton b. Mike Caldwell c. Pete Vuckovich d. Moose Haas

24. _____ Who is the present-day 300-game winner who once pitched for the Brewers?

a. Phil Niekro b. Tom Seaver c. Steve Carlton d. Don Sutton

25. _____ Who was the former All-Star Game pitcher who chalked up a career-high 16 saves in 1986?

a. Mark Clear b. Juan Nieves c. Dan Plesac d. Bill Wegman

NEW YORK YANKEES

Infielders

Fill in the blanks.

1. _____ Who was the first baseman who re-placed Lou Gehrig in the lineup after "The Iron Horse" ended his string of 2,130 consecutive games?

2. _____ Who was the second baseman whose twelfth hit of the 1953 World Series scored Hank Bauer with the winning run in the ninth inning of the sixth and decisive game?

3. _____ Name the shortstop who was given his release on Old Timers' Day in 1956.

4. _____ Who was the Yankee third baseman who won four home run titles with another team?

5. _____ Who was the infielder whose only two hits in a World Series were home runs?

6. _____ Who was the first baseman who hit .293 and banged eight home runs in eight series?

Outfielders

Matching.

7. _____ Joe DiMaggio
8. _____ Hank Bauer
9. _____ Roger Maris
10. _____ Elston Howard
11. _____ Tommy Henrich
12. _____ Babe Ruth

a. He came to the Yankees in a trade with Kansas City.

b. Primarily a catcher, he also played the outfield and first base in the series.

c. He won two home run titles.

d. He was called "Old Reliable."

e. He got a second chance, after a quick pitch, and hit a home run.

f. He drove home all four of his team's runs in a series win.

Catchers

Multiple Choice.
13. _____ One year he hit .362, the all-time high for catchers.
   a. Bill Dickey b. Yogi Berra c. Thurman Munson d. Elston Howard
14. _____ He hit two two-run home runs in the seventh game of a World Series win.
   a. Wally Schang b. Bill Dickey c. Yogi Berra d. Aaron Robinson
15. _____ He hit .373, the third all-time best, in series play.
   a. Ralph Houk b. Yogi Berra c. Bill Dickey d. Thurman Munson

Pitchers

True or False.
16. _____ Bill Bevens, after he lost both a no-hitter and the game on the last pitch of a 1947 series game, never again won an outing in the major leagues.
17. _____ Don Larsen struck out Duke Snider for the last out of his perfect game in the 1956 World Series.
18. _____ Johnny Sain saved the last game in both the 1951 and the 1952 World Series.
19. _____ Whitey Ford both won and lost more games than any other pitcher in series competition.
20. _____ Red Ruffing hit more home runs than any other major league pitcher.
21. _____ Herb Pennock and Lefty Gomez won a combined total of 11 games without dropping a decision in series play.
22. _____ Allie Reynolds pitched more no-hitters than any other Yankee hurler.
23. _____ Before 1977, Jim Bouton was the last Yankee pitcher to win a World Series game.
24. _____ Joe Page, Johnny Murphy, Luis Arroyo, and Lindy McDaniel were relief pitchers, in the presented order, for the Yankees.
25. _____ Spud Chandler and Sparky Lyle both won MVP awards.

TORONTO BLUE JAYS

Infielders

Matching.

1. _____ Tony Fernandez
2. _____ Willie Upshaw
3. _____ Damaso Garcia
4. _____ Alfredo Griffin
5. _____ John Mayberry
6. _____ Danny Ainge

a. A Brigham Young graduate, he's played major league baseball and NBA basketball.

b. In his four years in Toronto, he averaged over 22 home runs a season.

c. He was the first player in Blue Jay history to surpass 200 hits (213) in a season.

d. He hit 27 home runs and drove home 104 runs in 1983.

e. He was the co-winner of the Rookie of the Year Award in 1979.

f. He stole a club-high 54 bases in 1982.

Outfielders

Multiple Choice.

7. _____ Who hit a then club-high .315 in 1983?
   a. Jesse Barfield b. George Bell c. Lloyd Moseby d. Dave Collins

8. _____ Who hit a club-high 47 home runs in one year?
   a. John Mayberry b. Ron Fairly c. Rico Carty d. George Bell

9. _____ Who drove home a club-record 134 runs one year?
   a. Rico Carty b. George Bell c. Jesse Barfield d. John Mayberry

10. _____ Who was the one-time Blue Jay who struck out three out of three times for the Yankees in a World Series?
   a. Bob Bailor b. Otto Velez c. Barry Bonnell d. Al Woods

11. _____ Who in one of his two seasons with Toronto hit .308 and hit a league-high 15 triples?
   a. Dave Collins b. Al Woods c. Barry Bonnell d. Tommy Hutton

12. _____ Who at age 39—in his only season with Toronto—batted .279, hit 19 home runs, and drove home 64 runs?
   a. Rico Carty b. Tommy Hutton c. Ron Fairly d. Bob Bailor

Catchers

True or False.

13. _____ Alan Ashby was the first full-time catcher of the Blue Jays.

14. _____ Rick Cerone, among others, was traded by the Blue Jays to the Yankees for Chris Chambliss, among others, who never played a game for Toronto.

15. _____ Ernie Whitt has hit 20 home runs in a season.

Pitchers

Fill in the blanks.

16. _____ Who was the former Blue Jay who won a club-high 17 games twice?

17. _____ Who is the pitcher who struck out a club-high 198 batters in one season?

18. _____ Who became the first starting left-handed pitcher to win for the Blue Jays since Paul Mirabella in 1980?

19. _____ Who, with a glittering 1.72 ERA, fell five innings short of qualifying for the American League title one year?

20. _____ Who led Toronto in saves in his first three seasons with the club?

21. _____ Who became the first Toronto pitcher to go over 100 career wins?

22. _____ Who was the 1982 Cy Young Award winner who was 7–7 in his only season with the Blue Jays?

23. _____ Who was the Blue Jay reliever who, with a National League team, won a league-high 15 games out of the bull pen one year and then turned around and lost a league-high nine games the following season?

24. _____ Who was the one-time no-hit pitcher

with the Dodgers who finished up with the Blue Jays in 1977, their maiden season?

25. _____ Who was the Blue Jays' "big" winner in their initial season?

CALIFORNIA ANGELS

Infielders

Multiple Choice.

1. _____ Which one of the following first basemen did not perform for the Angels?

    a. Steve Bilko b. Ted Kluszewski c. Vic Power d. Dick Stuart

2. _____ Which one of the following second basemen did not perform for the Angels?

    a. Rocky Bridges b. Jerry Adair c. Bobby Knoop d. Sandy Alomar

3. _____ Which one of the following shortstops did not compete for the Angels?

    a. Freddie Patek b. Jim Fregosi c. Joe Koppe d. Leo Cardenas

4. _____ Which one of the following third basemen did not suit up for the Angels?

    a. Joe Foy b. Eddie Yost c. Aurelio Rodriguez d. Ken McMullen

5. _____ Which one of the following infielders did not appear on the roster of the Angels?

    a. Lee Thomas b. Joe Adcock c. Bob Oliver d. Pete Runnels

6. _____ Which one of the following infielders did not take the field for the Angels?

    a. Norm Siebern b. Jerry Remy c. Dick Green d. Rick Burleson

Outfielders

True or False.

7. _____ Leon Wagner hit more home runs (37) in one season than any other Angel.

8. _____ Bobby Bonds stole more bases in one season than any other Angel.

9. _____ Alex Johnson hit for the highest Angel average in one season.

10. _____ Joe Rudi, Don Baylor, and Bobby Bonds were all free agents when the Angels signed them.

11. _____ Frank Robinson hit 30 home runs in one season for the Angels.

12. _____ Brian Downing holds the American League record for most consecutive errorless (244) games.

Catchers

Fill in the blanks.

13. _____ Name the Angel catcher who is the son of a former big leaguer.

14. _____ Name the Angel receiver who was California's starting catcher for the most seasons.

15. _____ Name the Angel backstop who later managed Cleveland to three sixth-place finishes.

Pitchers

Matching.

16. _____ Dean Chance
17. _____ Bo Belinski
18. _____ Don Sutton
19. _____ Andy Messersmith
20. _____ Clyde Wright
21. _____ Nolan Ryan
22. _____ Frank Tanana
23. _____ Bill Singer
24. _____ Rudy May
25. _____ George Brunet

a. He won 22 in 1970 for the Angels; he lost 20 in 1974 for the Twins.

b. He pitched four no-hitters for the Angels.

c. He was the first Angel pitcher to win 20 games in a season.

d. He was the first Angel pitcher to throw a no-hitter.

e. After spending the majority of his first 11 years with the Angels, he started for the Yankees in the historic opening of the new stadium in 1976.

f. Before excelling for the Dodgers, he spent four years with the Angels, winning 20 games in 1971.

g. He won 20 games for the Dodgers in 1969 before he equaled that total for the Angels in 1973.

h. He started his 700th game, the second all-time high, for the Angels in 1986.

i. Twice this lefty flame-thrower has struck out more than 250 batters in a season.

j. Twice he led the American League in losses.

CHICAGO WHITE SOX

Infielders

Matching.
1. _____ Dick Allen
2. _____ Eddie Collins
3. _____ Luke Appling
4. _____ Bill Melton
5. _____ Nelson Fox
6. _____ Buck Weaver

a. He played the most consecutive major league games (98) without striking out.
b. He played on four world championship teams.
c. He batted .333 in his last big-league season.
d. He had a career slugging average of .534.
e. He was the first Pale Hose player to win a home run title.
f. One year he hit only six home runs but drove home 128 runs.

Outfielders

Multiple Choice.
7. _____ He never hit less than .300 in his entire career.
   a. Rip Radcliff b. Wally Moses c. Bibbs Fall d. Joe Jackson

8. _____ He set the then-American League record for strikeouts (175) in one season.
   a. Gus Zernial b. Smead Jolley c. Dave Nicholson d. Larry Doby

9. _____Once part of a famous outfield, he finished his career with the White Sox, batting .302 over his last five seasons.
   a. Happy Felsch b. Harry Hooper c. Mule Haas d. Minnie Minoso

10. _____ Which one of the following outfield trios had ballhawks who each hit .300 or better in the same season?
    a. Dixie Walker, Mike Kreevich, and Rip Radcliff b. Mule Haas, Al Simmons, and Rip Radcliff c. Smead

Jolley, Red Barnes, and Carl Reynolds d. Nemo Leibold, Happy Felsch, and Joe Jackson

11. _____ Which one of the following White Sox outfielders copped the batting crown with another team?

a. Bob Fothergill b. Taft Wright c. Wally Moses d. Ralph Garr

12. _____ Which one of the following players was hit by more pitches than any other American League player before Don Baylor?

a. Al Simmons b. Minnie Minoso c. Johnny Mostil d. Jim Landis

Catchers

True or False.

13. _____ Ray Schalk
14. _____ Moe Berg
15. _____ Mike Tresh

a. He became a double agent after his baseball career.
b. He called the signals for four pitchers who won 20 or more games in the same season.
c. He was the father of a son who hit four World Series home runs.

Pitchers

Fill in the blanks.

16. _____ Who was the White Sox pitcher who threw a perfect game?

17. _____ Who holds the club record for wins (40) and strikeouts (269)?

18. _____ Name the pitcher who won 260 games in 21 years, all with the White Sox.

19. _____ Can you recall the promising young hurler who lost a leg in a 1938 hunting accident?

20. _____ A 21-game winner for the 1920 White Sox, he was a holdout for the entire 1922 season and a suspended player for the following three years. Who was he?

21. _____ Who was the Black Sox pitcher who lost all three of his decisions in the tainted 1919 World Series?

22. _____ Who is the recent-day pitcher who both won and lost 20 games in the same season?

23. _____ Who was the 200-game winner who used to hook up with Whitey Ford in some classic pitching duels in the 1950s?

24. _____ Who won three games in a World Series?

25. _____ Who was the "steady" White Sox pitcher who later played on five consecutive world championship teams with the Yankees?

KANSAS CITY ROYALS

Infielders

Multiple Choice.

1. _____ Name the first baseman who holds the season club high in home runs.
   a. Bob Oliver b. John Mayberry c. Steve Balboni d. Tommy Davis

2. _____ Who has been the only second baseman in American League history to win seven Gold Gloves?
   a. Frank White b. Cookie Rojas c. Jackie Hernandez d. Jerry Adair

3. _____ In nine seasons at shortstop for the Royals, he averaged 37 steals.
   a. Jackie Hernandez b. Freddie Patek c. Bobby Knoop d. U. L. Washington

4. _____ Who became the sixth player to collect 20 or more doubles, triples, and home runs in the same season?
   a. Frank White b. John Mayberry c. Willie Aikens d. George Brett

5. _____ Who set the record for at least one strikeout in 13 consecutive games?
   a. John Mayberry b. Frank White c. Cookie Rojas d. Steve Balboni

6. _____ Who hit a record two home runs in each of two World Series games in 1980?
   a. Willie Aikens b. John Mayberry c. George Brett d. Frank White

Outfielders

True or False.

7. _____ Lou Piniella won the Rookie of the Year Award.

8. _____ Amos Otis drove home more runs (133) in one season than any other Royal player.

9. _____ Willie Wilson hits a high percentage of inside-the-park home runs.

10. _____ Hal McRae won a batting title.

11. _____ Amos Otis hit three home runs in a World Series.

269

12. _____ None of the present-day Royal outfielders' fathers played in the major leagues.

Catchers

Fill in the blanks.
13. _____ Who was the recent-day catcher who led the American League with a .995 fielding percentage?
14. _____ Who had a career-high .291 batting average, 20 home runs, and 112 RBIs in 1979?
15. _____ Who stole a record 36 bases for catchers in 1982?

Matching.

16. _____ Steve Busby
17. _____ Mark Littell
18. _____ Larry Gura
19. _____ Dennis Leonard
20. _____ Paul Splittorff
21. _____ Bret Saberhagen
22. _____ Mark Gubicza
23. _____ Dan Quisenberry
24. _____ Jim Colborn
25. _____ Dick Drago

a. He averaged five wins a year during the early years of the franchise.

b. He pitched two no-hitters.

c. He struck out a club-high 244 batters in one year.

d. He was the youngest recipient of the World Series MVP Award.

e. The Yankees traded him for Fran Healy.

f. He threw the pitch that Chris Chambliss hit for the playoff-deciding homerun in 1976.

g. He won two games and lost none in the three Championship Series from 1976–78.

h. He logged the highest number of saves (212) from 1980 through 1985.

i. A 20-game winner with the Brewers, he pitched a no-hitter in his only full season with the Royals.

j. In 1986 this double-figure winner in his first three major league seasons won nine of his last ten, including his last five.

MINNESOTA TWINS

Infielders

Matching.

1. _____ Rod Carew
2. _____ Gary Gaetti
3. _____ Zoilo Versalles
4. _____ Harmon Killebrew
5. _____ Bob Allison
6. _____ Billy Martin

a. He won six home run titles.

b. He hit two home runs on the opening day of the season.

c. Four times he got 200 hits, including a career-high 239 in 1977.

d. From 1963–65 he led the league in triples.

e. A veteran of four world championship teams, he finished his career with the Twins, a team he later managed to a division title.

f. He was the only American League player to win the Rookie of the Year Award and the three-base crown in the same year.

Outfielders

Multiple Choice.

7. _____ From 1956–58 he led the league in strikeouts.

   a. Jimmy Hall b. Don Mincher c. Bob Allison d. Jim Lemon

8. _____ Who is the recent-day Twin who collected 223 hits in a season?

   a. Kirby Puckett b. Tom Brunansky c. Mickey Hatcher d. Gary Ward

9. _____ He hit 20 home runs in 1976, including an historic one at Yankee Stadium.

   a. Steve Braun b. Lyman Bostock c. Larry Hisle d. Dan Ford

272

10. _____ He made a great sliding catch against the Dodgers in the 1965 World Series.
a. Sandy Valdespino b. Ted Uhlaender c. Bob Allison d. Bill Tuttle

11. _____ Who was the player who hit 33 circuit clouts in 1963, the all-time high for a Twin lefty before Ken Hrbek?
a. Jimmy Hall b. Lenny Green c. Ted Uhlaender d. Tony Oliva

12. _____ From 1959–64 he averaged 119 RBIs per year.
a. Tony Oliva b. Harmon Killebrew c. Bob Allison d. Cesar Tovar

Catchers

True or False.

13. _____ Butch Wynegar made the All-Star team in his rookie year.

14. _____ Johnny Roseboro had a higher lifetime batting average than Earl Battey did.

15. _____ In their most productive long-ball seasons, Roseboro hit more home runs than Battey did.

Pitchers

Fill in the blanks.

16. _____ Who was the Twin pitcher who won more games in one season than any other Minnesota hurler?

17. _____ Name the pitcher who struck out 258 batters, the club high, in one season.

18. _____ Can you recall the pitcher whom Billy Martin "punched out" in 1969?

19. _____ Which of the Perry brothers enjoyed 20-win seasons in 1969–70 for the Twins?

20. _____ Who was the first Minnesota pitcher to register back-to-back 20-win seasons?

21. _____ Who was the pitcher who won two games in the 1965 World Series?

22. _____ Name the pitcher who was a 20-game winner with the Angels before he was a 20-game winner with the Twins.

23. _____ Who was the Twin relief pitcher who starred with the Dodgers before he led the American League in saves in 1969 (31) and 1970 (34)?

24. _____ Who was the relief pitcher who bounced from club to club before he averaged 18 saves a year for the 1965–68 Twins?

25. _____ Who was the only Twin pitcher to lose 20 games in a season?

OAKLAND A'S

Infielders

Fill in the blanks.

1. _____ Who played in four World Series, on four championship teams, with two different teams?

2. _____ Who hit two home runs in his first major league game?

3. _____ Who, in 1986, played in 162 games for the second straight year, batted .285, and stole 33 bases?

4. _____ Who was the Oakland infielder of the 1970s who ended his career with 242 home runs?

5. _____ Who was traded to the A's when the Red Sox had to make room for the emerging Wade Boggs?

6. _____ Who was one of the two major leaguers who has played all nine positions in a game?

Outfielders

Matching.

7. _____ Tony Armas
8. _____ Rick Monday
9. _____ Dave Kingman
10. _____ Bill North
11. _____ Gonzalo Marquez
12. _____ Herb Washington

a. He was the A's designated runner in the 1974 World Series.

b. He tied for a home run title.

c. Three times he pinch-hit singles in the 1972 World Series.

d. The 1976 stolen base champ, he averaged 53 thefts per season in his first four years in the majors.

e. In 1986 he hit over 30 home runs for the third straight year; the following year, he was out of baseball.

f. He was the first player to be selected in the free agent draft.

Catchers

Multiple Choice.

13. _____ Who was the only player to be traded for a manager?
   a. Dave Duncan b. Gene Tenace c. Ray Fosse d. Manny Sanguillen

14. _____ Which one of the following catchers compiled the highest single-season average with the A's?
   a. Dave Duncan b. Ray Fosse c. Phil Roof d. Frank Fernandez

15. _____ Which one of the following catchers hit the most home runs in one season?
   a. Dave Duncan b. Ray Fosse c. Phil Roof d. Frank Fernandez

Pitchers

True or False.

16. _____ Catfish Hunter was the last pitcher to throw a perfect game.

17. _____ Vida Blue was the youngest player to win the MVP Award.

18. _____ Catfish Hunter won all of his four World Series decisions with the A's.

19. _____ Jay Howell has recorded 29 saves in a season.

20. _____ Ken Holtzman never won 20 games for the A's.

21. _____ Holtzman matched Hunter's total of four World Series wins with Oakland.

22. _____ Vida Blue has won the most games in one season for the A's.

23. _____ Blue never won a World Series game.

24. _____ Rollie Fingers has been the only pitcher to hurl in all seven games of a World Series.

25. _____ Fingers has recorded the most saves by any pitcher in series history.

SEATTLE MARINERS

Infielders

True or False.

1. _____ Ken Phelps was the Mariners' starting first baseman until he broke a bone in his hand.

2. _____ If a player is batting very low, an announcer may say he's under the (Mario) "Mendoza Line."

3. _____ Rey Quinones went to the Mariners in a deal for Jerry Remy.

4. _____ Julio Cruz tied an American League record for most consecutive stolen bases (32) without being caught stealing.

5. _____ Al Davis's 116 RBIs in 1984 were the most ever by a rookie.

6. _____ Jim Presley is a good contact hitter.

Outfielders

Fill in the blanks.

7. _____ Who is the present-day player who went his first 398 major league at-bats without hitting a home run?

8. _____ Who hit a club-high 32 home runs in 1985?

9. _____ Who hit a club-high .326 in 1981?

10. _____ Who was the rookie with 25 home runs whom the Mariners traded after the 1986 season?

11. _____ Who was the slugger with 325 career home runs who hit 29 circuit clouts for the Mariners in 1979?

12. _____ Who is the former Mariner who shined in post-season play for the 1986 Red Sox?

Catchers

Matching.

13. _____ Jerry Narron
14. _____ Jim Essian
15. _____ Bob Kearney

a. He led American League catchers in total chances (897) in 1984.

b. He became the Yankees' catcher after Thurman Munson's tragic death.

c. A veteran of six major league clubs, he batted .275 in his only year in Seattle.

Pitchers

Multiple Choice.

16. _____ Who struck out a club-high 262 batters in one season?
   a. Mark Langston b. Mike Moore c. Pete Ladd d. Mike Morgan

17. _____ Who won a club-record 19 games in one season?
   a. Mike Morgan b. Bill Swift c. Mark Langston d. Mike Moore

18. _____ Who struck out a record 20 Mariner batters in 1986?
   a. Bert Blyleven b. Bret Saberhagen c. Ron Guidry d. Roger Clemens

19. _____ Who was the former Mariner pitcher who was once suspended for "doctoring" a baseball?
   a. Rick Honeycutt b. Jim Colborn c. Gaylord Perry d. Bill Caudill

20. _____ Who was the Mariner pitcher who led the league in strikeouts (209) in 1982?
   a. Gaylord Perry b. Floyd Bannister c. Dick Drago d. Jim Colborn

21. _____ Who was the former Mariner moundsman who won a Championship Series game and a World Series game with another club?
   a. Jim Beattie b. Ken Clay c. Shane Rawley d. Jim Colborn

22. _____ Who won his 300th game with the Mariners?
   a. Don Sutton b. Tom Seaver c. Phil Niekro d. Gaylord Perry

23. _____ Who established a major league record for most games (78) by a pitcher in his rookie season?
   a. Matt Young b. Bill Caudill c. Ed Vande Berg d. Dick Drago

24. _____ Who racked up 102 saves from 1982–85?
   a. Matt Young b. Bill Caudill c. Ed Vande Berg d. Dick Drago

25. _____ Who was traded to the Yankees for Gene Nelson, Bill Caudill, and a player to be named later?
   a. Jim Beattie b. Mike Kekich c. Shane Rawley d. Bill Caudill

TEXAS RANGERS

Infielders

Matching.

1. _____ Pete O'Brien
2. _____ Lenny Randle
3. _____ Buddy Bell
4. _____ Bump Wills
5. _____ Scott Fletcher
6. _____ Toby Harrah

a. He stole a club-record 52 bases in one season.
b. He hit a club-high 23 home runs by a left-handed hitter.
c. After failing to hit over .256 in five seasons with the White Sox, he moved to Texas in 1986 and led the Rangers with a .300 average.
d. He was traded after a one-sided fight with former manager Frank Lucchesi.
e. A shortstop, he hit 27 home runs one year.
f. This third baseman averaged .302 for the six full seasons he played in Texas.

Outfielders

Multiple Choice.

7. _____ Name the player who set the club record for home runs in one season.
   a. Rico Carty b. Larry Parrish c. Gary Ward d. Frank Howard.

8. _____ Name the rookie who hit 30 home runs in 1986.
   a. Pete Incaviglia b. Al Oliver c. Frank Howard d. Rico Carty

9. _____ Who was the outfielder who, after playing in three consecutive World Series, became expendable and was traded to Texas?
   a. Rico Carty b. Tom Grieve c. Mickey Rivers d. Willie Horton

10. _____ Which one of the following Texas players hit .300 lifetime?

    a. Al Oliver b. Elliot Maddox c. Ken Henderson d. Larry Bittner

11. _____ Who is the present-day player who, going into the 1987 season, had three times hit more than 20 home runs in a season for the Rangers?

    a. Oddibee McDowell b. Pete Incaviglia c. Toby Harrah d. Larry Parrish

12. _____ Name the player who hit 262 home runs before he joined the Rangers as a designated hitter.

    a. Al Oliver b. Frank Howard c. Ken Henderson d. Willie Horton

Catchers

True or False.

13. _____ Dick Billings was the Rangers' initial catcher in their franchise history.

14. _____ John Ellis hit 20 or more home runs in a season for Texas.

15. _____ Darrell Porter played on pennant-winning teams on two clubs outside of Texas.

Pitchers

Fill in the blanks.

16. _____ Who won 25 games, the club's all-time high, in one season?

17. _____ Who struck out 233 batters, the team's all-time high, in one year?

18. _____ Who was the former Texas mounds-man who started the first game of the 1976 World Series?

19. _____ Who is the former Texas hurler who was just 23–23 with the Rangers despite the fact that he has won well over 200 games?

20. _____ Name the one-time 19-game winner who was traded to Cleveland in the Gaylord Perry deal.

21. _____ Who is the 39-year-old pitcher who won a career-high 18 games in 1987?

22. _____ Who was the former Ranger pitcher who started World Series games for the Pirates and the Yankees?

23. _____ Who in 1985 led all American League relievers with 111 strikeouts?

24. _____ Who is the relief pitcher who set a record for rookies when he appeared in 80 games?

25. _____ Bert Blyleven pitched a no-hitter for the Rangers in 1977. Who pitched the first—and only other—no-hitter for Texas?

A Man for All Seasons

A baseball executive who never played in the major leagues had the Midas touch when it came to getting the most out of ballplayers; undoubtedly he "touched," either directly or indirectly, every era that we've covered in this book.

In the late 1890s he discovered Honus Wagner, who later won eight batting championships for the Pirates. In 1903 and 1904 he managed the Tigers to second-division finishes. But he put together the machinery that later (1907–09) produced three straight pennants. In 1918 he took over the managerial duties of the Red Sox, and he led them to a pennant and world title. But more important, in the same year he switched Babe Ruth from a regular-turn pitcher to an everyday first baseman–outfielder.

This baseball administrator managed the Red Sox through 1920. In the interim between 1918 and 1920, he had seen a pattern beginning to take shape. Red Sox owner Harry Frazee, who was in financial trouble, was unloading pennant-winning ballplayers to the Yankees. So when Yankee owner Jake Ruppert offered him the general manager's job in New York, he moved to the Bronx.

In 1921, his first year in New York, the Yankees won their first pennant. In his additional 24 years in the Yankee G.M. job, the Bronx Bombers won 13 pennants and 10 world championships. The pride that he helped to build in the pinstripe uniform has carried over to the present time; the Yankees have gone on to win 19 additional pennants and 12 world titles.

If you can name this "man for all seasons," you most probably have "touched" all of the bases in this book. Who was he?

(Answer appears on page 322.)

Chapter Eighteen

THE RECORD BOOK

This chapter is divided into three parts. The first section deals only with American League records. The second section deals only with National League marks. (In some cases, where players from both leagues share a major league record, statements about each player may appear under their respective league.) The third section deals only with major league marks. Let's see how many of the record-holders you can call to mind.

100. AMERICAN LEAGUE RECORDS

1. _____ Who compiled the highest average (.422) in one season?
   a. George Sisler b. Napoleon Lajoie c. Harry Heilmann d. Ty Cobb
2. _____ Who collected 107 pinch-hits in his career?
   a. Dave Philley b. Johnny Mize c. Gates Brown d. Bobby Brown
3. _____ Who had one or more hits in 135 games one year?
   a. Johnny Pesky b. George Brett c. Rod Carew d. Wade Boggs
4. _____ Who was the right-handed batter who had 200 or more hits in five consecutive years?
   a. Joe DiMaggio b. Jimmie Foxx c. Al Simmons d. Hank Greenberg
5. _____ Who was the left-handed batter who had 200 or more hits in five consecutive seasons?

a. Charlie Gehringer b. George Sisler c. Joe Jackson
d. Lou Gehrig

6. _____ Who hit for the cycle three times?
a. Bob Meusel b. Nellie Fox c. Larry Doby d. Harvey
Kuenn

7. _____ Who got seven consecutive pinch-hits?
a. Dave Philley b. Merv Rettenmund c. Sam Leslie d. Bill
Stein

8. _____ Who collected 187 singles in one season?
a. Willie Wilson b. Ty Cobb c. Wade Boggs d. George
Sisler

9. _____ Who was the right-handed batter who hit 64
doubles in one season?
a. Hank Greenberg b. Luke Appling c. George Burns
d. Vern Stephens

10. _____ Who was the right-handed batter who hit 573
career home runs?
a. Frank Robinson b. Harmon Killebrew c. Hank Greenberg d. Jimmie Foxx

11. _____ Who hit 16 career pinch-hit home runs?
a. Cliff Johnson b. Gates Brown c. Johnny Mize d. Merv
Rettenmund

12. _____ Who was the rookie who hit 49 home runs?
a. Mark McGwire b. Joe DiMaggio c. Ted Williams d. Roy
Sievers

13. _____ Who was the left-handed batter who hit four
consecutive home runs in a nine-inning game?
a. Jim Gentile b. Norm Cash c. Luke Easter d. Lou
Gehrig

14. _____ Who was the right-handed batter who hit four
consecutive home runs in a nine-inning game?
a. Hank Greenberg b. Pat Seerey c. Clyde Vollmer
d. Rocky Colavito

15. _____ Who, in addition to Bob Nieman, hit two home
runs in his first major league game?
a. Cesar Tovar b. Bert Campaneris c. Hal McRae d. Gorman
Thomas

16. _____ Who hit five home runs, out of five hits, in five
games?
a. Bob Meusel b. Ken Williams c. Gus Zernial d. Dick
Wakefield

17. _____ Who was the Twin who three times hit pinch-hit
grand slams in his career?
a. Rich Reese b. Jimmy Hall c. Bob Allison d. Jim
Lemon

18. _____ Who totaled 400 bases five times in his career?
a. Jimmie Foxx b. Babe Ruth c. Lou Gehrig d. Joe DiMaggio

19. _____ Who had five long hits in one game?
a. Ted Williams b. Jim Rice c. Lou Boudreau d. Fred Lynn

20. _____ Who was the right-handed batter who drove home 183 runs in one season?
a. Hank Greenberg b. Al Simmons c. Joe DiMaggio d. Frank Howard

21. _____ Who was the catcher who drove home 133 runs one year?
a. Yogi Berra b. Gus Triandos c. Carlton Fisk d. Bill Dickey

22. _____ Who drove home at least one run in 13 consecutive games?
a. Cass Michaels b. George Kell c. Dale Mitchell d. Taft Wright

23. _____ Who drove home 11 runs in one game?
a. Earl Averill b. Hal Trosky c. Tony Lazzeri d. Ben Chapman

24. _____ Who walked seven consecutive times?
a. Eddie Yost b. Billy Rogell c. Jimmy Dykes d. Lou Gehrig

25. _____ Who drew 33 intentional walks one year?
a. Jimmie Foxx b. Ted Williams c. Harmon Killebrew d. Roger Maris

26. _____ Who hit 17 sacrifice flies in 1971?
a. Roy White b. Frank Robinson c. Reggie Jackson d. Brooks Robinson

27. _____ Who is the pitcher who started 33 games one year but didn't finish one of them?
a. Frank Tanana b. Wilbur Wood c. Milt Wilcox d. Ed Whitson

28. _____ Who was the pitcher who finished up a game with 17 innings of relief?
a. Schoolboy Rowe b. Ed Rommel c. Ed Walsh d. George Pipgras

29. _____ Who won 24 games in his rookie season?
a. Bob Grim b. Edgar Summers c. Carl Mays d. Urban Shocker

30. _____ Who was the Indian pitcher who won 17 consecutive games?
a. Bob Feller b. Early Wynn c. Bob Lemon d. Johnny Allen

31. _____ Who was the Oriole pitcher who won 17 consecutive games?

a. Mike Cuellar b. Mike Flanagan c. Jim Palmer d. Dave McNally

32. _____ Who was the starting pitcher who won nine consecutive games at the start of his career?

a. Whitey Ford b. Ned Garver c. Ellis Kinder d. Hal Newhouser

33. _____ Who was the Yankee pitcher who won 23 consecutive games from the Athletics?

a. Bob Shawkey b. Joe Bush c. Waite Hoyt d. Carl Mays

34. _____ Who was the Yankee relief pitcher who won 12 consecutive games one season?

a. Joe Page b. Bob Grim c. Luis Arroyo d. Ron Davis

35. _____ Who was the Yankee who won 12 consecutive games in his rookie season?

a. Atley Donald b. Spud Chandler c. Bump Hadley d. Monte Pearson

36. _____ Who won 15 consecutive games at the end of the season?

a. Schoolboy Rowe b. Ted Lyons c. Alvin Crowder d. Tommy Bridges

37. _____ Who was the Senator pitcher who lost 19 consecutive games?

a. Bob Groom b. Bob Porterfield c. Sid Hudson d. Walt Masterson

38. _____ Who was the Athletic pitcher who lost 19 consecutive games?

a. Carl Scheib b. Lou Brissie c. John Nabors d. Alex Kellner

39. _____ Who was the two-time batting champ who, as a pitcher, allowed 13 runs in one inning?

a. Lefty O'Doul b. Jimmie Foxx c. Pete Runnels d. Luke Appling

40. _____ Who led the league in lowest ERA four consecutive years?

a. Whitey Ford b. Lefty Grove c. Hal Newhouser d. Bob Feller

41. _____ Who pitched five consecutive shutouts?

a. Jack Chesbro b. Ed Walsh c. Cy Young d. Doc White

42. _____ Who pitched an 18-inning 1–0 shutout?

a. George Earnshaw b. Walter Johnson c. Lefty Grove d. Stan Coveleski

43. _____ Who retired 33 consecutive batters one year?

a. Mike Caldwell b. Larry Gura c. Steve Busby d. Mike Boddicker

44. _____ Who allowed 374 career home runs?

a. Mike Torrez b. Bert Blyleven c. Jim Hunter d. Dizzy Trout

45. _____ Who was the left-handed pitcher who struck out 2,679 batters?

a. Mickey Lolich b. Hal Newhouser c. Whitey Ford d. Lefty Grove

46. _____ Who was the rookie left-hander who struck out 245 batters in a season?

a. Mel Parnel b. Herb Score c. Billy Pierce d. Ron Guidry

47. _____ Who is the present-day left-hander who struck out 18 batters in a game?

a. Frank Tanana b. Ted Higuera c. Bruce Hurst d. Ron Guidry

48. _____ Who struck out 18 batters in one game but lost?

a. Nolan Ryan b. Bob Feller c. Bob Turley d. Luis Tiant

49. _____ Who, in a rare relief assignment, struck out 14 batters in one game?

a. Denny McLain b. Sam McDowell c. Luis Tiant d. Mel Stottlemyre

50. _____ Who was the left-handed pitcher who threw 45 consecutive scoreless innings?

a. Doc White b. Walter Johnson c. Lefty Gomez d. Lefty Grove

101. NATIONAL LEAGUE RECORDS

1. _____ Who had a slugging average of .756 one year?
   a. Chuck Klein b. Hack Wilson c. Rogers Hornsby d. Joe Medwick

2. _____ Who had one or more hits in 135 games one year?
   a. Paul Waner b. Pete Rose c. Chuck Klein d. Honus Wagner

3. _____ Who had 200 or more hits for five consecutive years?
   a. Pete Rose b. Chuck Klein c. Paul Waner d. Lloyd Waner

4. _____ Who twice had six hits in six at-bats?
   a. Stan Musial b. Jim Bottomley c. Bill Terry d. Lefty O'Doul

5. _____ Who had 14 hits in two consecutive double-headers?
   a. Bill White b. Enos Slaughter c. Terry Moore d. Marty Marion

6. _____ Who hit for the cycle three times?
   a. Stan Musial b. Pete Reiser c. Roberto Clemente d. Babe Herman

7. _____ Who led the league in doubles eight times?
   a. Honus Wagner b. Pete Rose c. Stan Musial d. Paul Waner

8. _____ Who was the left-handed batter who hit 521 career homers?
   a. Duke Snider b. Willie McCovey c. Mel Ott d. Willie Stargell

9. _____ Who hit 18 career pinch-hit homers?
   a. Gus Bell b. Red Schoendienst c. Jerry Lynch d. Rusty Staub

10. _____ Who was the switch-hitter who banged 36 home runs in one season?
    a. Ted Simmons b. Howard Johnson c. Reggie Smith d. Pete Rose

11. _____ Who was the pitcher who twice hit seven home runs in a season?
    a. Don Newcombe b. Warren Spahn c. Don Drysdale d. Ken Brett

12. _____ Who hit 34 home runs at his home grounds one year?

a. Ted Kluszewski b. Mel Ott c. Eddie Mathews d. Ralph Kiner

13. _____ Who hit 30 or more home runs for nine consecutive years?
a. Hank Aaron b. Eddie Mathews c. Willie McCovey d. Willie Mays

14. _____ Who hit 101 home runs in back-to-back seasons?
a. Johnny Mize b. Willie Mays c. Hack Wilson d. Ralph Kiner

15. _____ Who was the left-handed batter who hit 96 home runs in back-to-back seasons?
a. Mel Ott b. Willie McCovey c. Ted Kluszewski d. Eddie Mathews

16. _____ Who hit 17 home runs in one month?
a. Willie McCovey b. Ernie Banks c. Willie Mays d. Johnny Mize

17. _____ Who was the one-time Cardinal who hit five home runs in a doubleheader?
a. Johnny Mize b. Rogers Hornsby c. Stan Musial d. Joe Cunningham

18. _____ Who was the Padre who hit five home runs in a doubleheader?
a. Nate Colbert b. Willie McCovey c. Graig Nettles d. Steve Garvey

19. _____ Who was the Expo who hit pinch-hit homers in both ends of a doubleheader?
a. Harold Breeden b. Andre Dawson c. Ellis Valentine d. Larry Parrish

20. _____ Who five times hit three home runs in a Senior Circuit game?
a. Joe Morgan b. Ernie Banks c. Johnny Mize d. Bill Nicholson

21. _____ Who was the pitcher who three times hit two home runs in a game?
a. Steve Carlton b. Don Newcombe c. Rick Wise d. Tony Cloninger

22. _____ Who hit for 450 total bases in one season?
a. Hack Wilson b. Mel Ott c. Hank Aaron d. Rogers Hornsby

23. _____ Who three times had more than 400 total bases in a season?
a. Stan Musial b. Hank Aaron c. Chuck Klein d. Bill Terry

24. _____ Who had 25 total bases in two consecutive games?

a. George Foster b. Dave Kingman c. Joe Adcock d. Tony Perez

25. _____ Who was the Pirate who hit four or more long hits in a game four times?
    a. Willie Stargell b. Ralph Kiner c. Roberto Clemente d. Bob Robertson

26. _____ Who walked 1,799 times?
    a. Jimmy Wynn b. Eddie Stanky c. Joe Morgan d. Richie Ashburn

27. _____ Who walked 100 times in his rookie year?
    a. Maury Wills b. Jim Gilliam c. Richie Ashburn d. Willie McCovey

28. _____ Who was walked seven consecutive times?
    a. Ralph Kiner b. Willie Mays c. Johnny Mize d. Mel Ott

29. _____ Who was the right-handed all-fields hitter who walked seven consecutive times?
    a. Eddie Stanky b. Al Dark c. Harvey Kuenn d. Dick Groat

30. _____ Who was the Brave who walked at least once in 15 consecutive games?
    a. Joe Adcock b. Darrell Evans c. Hank Aaron d. Billy Bruton

31. _____ Who struck out 1,936 times during his career?
    a. Bobby Bonds b. Dave Kingman c. Willie Stargell d. Vince DiMaggio

32. _____ Who struck out only 173 times in 18 years?
    a. Tommy Holmes b. Paul Waner c. Pete Reiser d. Lloyd Waner

33. _____ Who was the pitcher who struck out 62 times in a season?
    a. Jerry Koosman b. Bob Buhl c. Sandy Koufax d. Russ Meyer

34. _____ Who grounded into 30 double plays in one year?
    a. Joe Medwick b. Ernie Lombardi c. Roy Campanella d. Walker Cooper

35. _____ Who stole home 33 times during his career?
    a. Pete Reiser b. Jackie Robinson c. Max Carey d. Pee Wee Reese

36. _____ Who got caught stealing 36 times in one year?
    a. Maury Wills b. Ron LeFlore c. Miller Huggins d. Tim Raines

37. _____ Who pitched 434 innings one year?
    a. Christy Mathewson b. Grover Alexander c. Joe McGinnity d. Dazzy Vance

38. _____ Who was the 22-game winner for the Dodgers who had an .880 winning percentage one year?

    a. Whit Wyatt b. Carl Erskine c. Preacher Roe d. Don Newcombe

39. _____ Who was the Giant pitcher who won six opening-day games?

    a. Juan Marichal b. Carl Hubbell c. Sal Maglie d. Christy Mathewson

40. _____ Who pitched 90 career shutouts?

    a. Warren Spahn b. Grover Alexander c. Christy Mathewson d. Bob Gibson

41. _____ Who was the pitcher who lost 13 1–0 games?

    a. Burleigh Grimes b. Lee Meadows c. Bill Hallahan d. Bill Lee

42. _____ Who pitched 21 consecutive hitless innings one year?

    a. Don Drysdale b. Sal Maglie c. Johnny Vander Meer d. Ewell Blackwell

43. _____ Who allowed nine career grand slams?

    a. Jerry Reuss b. Don Sutton c. Robin Roberts d. Steve Carlton

44. _____ Who was the Cardinal pitcher who allowed nine walks in a shutout game?

    a. Wilmer Mizell b. Dizzy Dean c. Howie Pollet d. Harry Brecheen

45. _____ Who was the right-hander who struck out 313 batters in one season?

    a. Tom Seaver b. J. R. Richard c. Dizzy Dean d. Don Drysdale

46. _____ Who is the present-day pitcher, in addition to Nolan Ryan, who struck out 18 batters in one game?

    a. Bill Gullickson b. Fernando Valenzuela c. Dwight Gooden d. Mike Scott

47. _____ Who was the left-handed pitcher who struck out 15 batters in his first game?

    a. Steve Carlton b. Fernando Valenzuela c. Karl Spooner d. Tommy John

48. _____ Who was the right-handed pitcher who struck out 15 batters in his first major-league game?

    a. Dizzy Dean b. Tom Seaver c. Bob Gibson d. J. R. Richard

49. _____ Who hit 154 batters during his career?

    a. Bobo Newsom b. Steve Carlton c. Don Drysdale d. Sam Jones

50. _____ Who was the catcher who fielded .992 over a 14-year career?
   a. Johnny Edwards b. Roy Campanella c. Johnny Bench
   d. Gabby Hartnett

102. MAJOR LEAGUE RECORDS

1. _____ Who played the most games in one season?
   a. Pete Rose b. Maury Wills c. Bobby Richardson d. Rickey Henderson

2. _____ Who was the left-handed batter who hit for the highest single-season batting average?
   a. Bill Terry b. Ted Williams c. George Sisler d. Joe Jackson

3. _____ Who hit for the highest single-season average as a switch-hitter?
   a. Jimmy Collins b. Eddie Murray c. Pete Rose d. Mickey Mantle

4. _____ Who scored one or more runs in 18 consecutive games?
   a. Red Rolfe b. Nellie Fox c. Bobby Richardson d. Red Schoendienst

5. _____ Who was the right-handed batter who got 253 hits in one season?
   a. Rogers Hornsby b. Jimmie Foxx c. Heinie Manush d. Al Simmons

6. _____ Who had seven hits in a nine-inning game?
   a. Bill Mazeroski b. Johnny Ray c. Willie Randolph d. Rennie Stennett

7. _____ Who had five hits in his first major-league game?
   a. Cecil Travis b. Joe Cronin c. Casey Stengel d. Bob Nieman

8. _____ Who hit for the cycle in both leagues?
   a. Frank Robinson b. Bob Watson c. Nellie Fox d. Davey Lopes

9. _____ Who got three hits in one inning?
   a. Sammy White b. Gene Stephens c. Pee Wee Reese d. Stan Musial

10. _____ Who got two hits in one inning in his first major-league game?
    a. Bob Nieman b. Bert Campaneris c. Billy Martin d. Junior Gilliam

11. _____ Who reached base 16 consecutive times?
    a. George Brett b. Ted Williams c. Eddie Yost d. Garry Templeton

12. _____ Who got nine consecutive pinch-hits?

a. Dave Philley b. Rusty Staub c. Del Unser d. Davy Johnson

13. _____ Who was the pitcher who had eight hits in two consecutive games?
a. George Earnshaw b. Wes Ferrell c. Red Ruffing d. Don Newcombe

14. _____ Who sprayed 198 singles in one season?
a. Willie Wilson b. Wade Boggs c. Lloyd Waner d. Nelson Fox

15. _____ Who hit six doubles in a doubleheader?
a. Pete Rose b. Stan Musial c. Tris Speaker d. Hank Majeski

16. _____ Who hit 36 triples in one season?
a. Sam Crawford b. J. Owen Wilson c. Joe Jackson d. Earle Combs

17. _____ Who two times hit three triples in one game in one season?
a. Kiki Cuyler b. George Stirnweiss c. Dave Brain d. Ty Cobb

18. _____ Who hit 20 pinch-hit home runs?
a. Johnny Mize b. Rusty Staub c. Bob Cerv d. Cliff Johnson

19. _____ Who hit 30 or more home runs for 12 consecutive years?
a. Hank Aaron b. Harmon Killebrew c. Babe Ruth d. Jimmie Foxx

20. _____ Who hit 20 or more home runs for 20 consecutive years?
a. Frank Robinson b. Hank Aaron c. Ted Williams d. Jimmie Foxx

21. _____ Who hit 114 home runs in back-to-back years?
a. Babe Ruth b. Hank Aaron c. Willie Mays d. Ralph Kiner

22. _____ Who was the pitcher who hit three home runs in a game?
a. Tony Cloninger b. Rick Wise c. Red Ruffing d. Jim Tobin

23. _____ Who was the pitcher who five times hit two home runs in a game?
a. Bob Lemon b. Wes Ferrell c. Don Newcombe d. Don Drysdale

24. _____ Who was the part-time player who hit four consecutive home runs in three consecutive games?
a. George Shuba b. Gino Cimoli c. John Blanchard d. Chuck Essegian

25. _____ Who was the pitcher who hit home runs in four consecutive games?

   a. Warren Spahn b. Red Lucas c. Walter Johnson d. Ken Brett

26. _____ Who got six home runs, out of six hits, in six consecutive games?

   a. Mike Schmidt b. Del Ennis c. Frank Hurst d. Willie Jones

27. _____ Who hit three home runs in his first two major league games?

   a. Buddy Hassett b. Dolph Camilli c. Joe Cunningham d. Jim Tobin

28. _____ Who hit a grand slam in his first major league game?

   a. Bobby Bonds b. Bobby Murcer c. Dwayne Murphy d. Tony Armas

29. _____ Who had 17 total bases in an extra-inning game?

   a. Willie Mays b. Rudy York c. Mike Schmidt d. Rocky Colavito

30. _____ Who was the Indian who had seven consecutive long hits?

   a. Elmer Smith b. Larry Doby c. Al Rosen d. Andre Thornton

31. _____ Who was the White Sox who had seven consecutive long hits?

   a. Richie Allen b. Earl Sheely c. Bill Melton d. Sherman Lollar

32. _____ Who had one or more long hits in 14 consecutive games?

   a. Walker Cooper b. Johnny Mize c. Sid Gordon d. Paul Waner

33. _____ Who drove home at least one run in 17 consecutive games?

   a. Ray Grimes b. George Stirnweiss c. Taft Wright d. Elmer Valo

34. _____ Who was the right-handed hitter who walked 151 times in a season?

   a. Jimmy Wynn b. Eddie Stanky c. Eddie Yost d. Jimmie Foxx

35. _____ Who was the Tiger who walked at least once in 18 consecutive games?

   a. Roy Cullenbine b. Harvey Kuenn c. Charlie Gehringer d. Jake Woods

36. _____ Who struck out only 113 times in a 14-year career?

a. Luke Appling b. Richie Ashburn c. Earle Combs
d. Joe Sewell

37. _____ Who had 67 sacrifices in one season?
a. Ray Chapman b. Phil Rizzuto c. Nellie Fox d. Eddie
Yost

38. _____ Who hit 114 sacrifice flies in his career?
a. Gil Hodges b. Brooks Robinson c. Frank Robinson
d. Willie McCovey

39. _____ Who hit 19 sacrifice flies in 1954?
a. Joe Adcock b. Gil Hodges c. Andy Pafko d. Eddie
Mathews

40. _____ Who pitched for 25 years?
a. Gaylord Perry b. Phil Niekro c. Grover Alexander
d. Jim Kaat

41. _____ Who started 37 games in a season but didn't
complete one of them?
a. Steve Bedrosian b. Bob Buhl c. Vern Bickford d. Joe
Cowley

42. _____ Who pitched in 13 consecutive games?
a. Mike Marshall b. Rollie Fingers c. Bruce Sutter
d. Goose Gossage

43. _____ Who pitched 39 consecutive complete games in
one year?
a. Ed Walsh b. Jack Chesbro c. Joe McGinnity d. Jack
Taylor

44. _____ Who pitched 464 innings in one season?
a. Vic Willis b. Ed Walsh c. Joe McGinnity d. Jack
Chesbro

45. _____ Who registered 341 career saves?
a. Sparky Lyle b. Elroy Face c. Bruce Sutter d. Rollie
Fingers

46. _____ Who, at the start of his career, pitched 22 consecutive scoreless innings?
a. Hank Borowy b. Dave Ferris c. Tex Hughson d. Howie
Pollett

47. _____ Who allowed 11 walks in a shutout win?
a. Wilmer Mizell b. Lefty Gomez c. Spud Chandler
d. Mario Russo

48. _____ Who pitched 21 consecutive scoreless innings in
one game?
a. Leon Cadore b. Carl Hubbell c. Walter Johnson d. Joe
Oeschger

49. _____ Who pitched a 21-inning game without allowing
a walk?

a. Stan Coveleski b. Babe Adams c. Carl Mays d. Jim Hunter

50. _____ Who struck out seven consecutive batters in his first major league game?

a. Mort Cooper b. Ron Davis c. Sammy Stewart d. Nolan Ryan

Three Men on Third

Babe Herman looked like a knightly champion when he stepped into the batter's box—he hit .393 in 1930 and he batted .324 lifetime—but when he played the outfield or ran the bases, he seemed to develop some chinks in his armor.

Fly balls, the stories go, used to either bounce off his head or carom off his shoulders with great regularity. Some baseball observers have said that his glove was a mere ornament on his hand.

His base running didn't help the Brooklyn franchise lose its nickname of "Bums," either. Take the case of the day in 1926, for example, when the Dodgers hosted the Braves. The bases were full of Dodgers when Herman, a rookie at the time, advanced mightily to the plate. Hank DeBerry led off third, Dazzy Vance danced off second, and Chick Fewster leaned off first.

Herman did not disappoint them. He rocketed a ball high off the right-field wall. DeBerry scored easily. Vance could have, too, but he changed his mind after taking a wide turn around third. He retreated to third base where he met Fewster sliding into the "hot corner." In the meantime, Herman got a good start out of the box. He put his head down and raced around the bases with reckless abandon. Sliding into third, with what he thought was a sure triple, he was perplexed to bump into his two teammates. You might call the Dodgers' base running, in that instance, a "comedy of errors," or you might label Herman's aggressive dash an example of a "rookie's mistake."

But the third baseman was confused, too. He knew that two of the runners didn't belong there, but he didn't know which two runners were trespassing. So he did the obvious: he tagged all three of the runners. And the umpire called two of them out. But which two? Who, do you think, had the right to be there?

(Answer appears on page 322.)

Chapter Nineteen

THE HALL OF FAME

103. CLUES TO COOPERSTOWN

From Barrow to Youngs

Match the following 50 Hall of Famers with the descriptions that follow.

Jackie Robinson	Josh Gibson
Zack Wheat	Ed Barrow
Herb Pennock	Eppa Rixey
Carl Hubbell	Fred Clarke
John McGraw	Jesse Haines
Bob Lemon	Babe Ruth
Bill Dickey	Ross Youngs
Hank Greenberg	Johnny Evers
Dazzy Vance	Satchel Paige
Al Simmons	Chick Hafey
Bill Terry	Edd Roush
Mel Ott	Goose Goslin
Branch Rickey	Max Carey
Heinie Manush	Frankie Frisch
Frank Baker	Lefty Gomez
Jimmy Collins	Sam Rice
Dave Bancroft	George Sisler
Red Faber	Monte Irvin
Bob Feller	Pie Traynor
Harry Hooper	Ray Schalk
Cool Papa Bell	Lou Boudreau
Nap Lajoie	Rabbit Maranville
Joe Cronin	Charlie Gehringer
Lou Gehrig	George Kelly
Ted Lyons	Robin Roberts

1. _____ This celebrated National League screwball artist won 253 major league games (24 in succession), pitched a 1–0 18-inning win against the Cardinals in 1933 (it wrapped up the pennant), and gained baseball immortality in the 1934 All-Star Game when he struck out Babe Ruth, Lou Gehrig, Jimmie Foxx, Al Simmons, and Joe Cronin in succession.

2. _____ This slugging American League first baseman scored more than 100 runs in 13 consecutive seasons, batted in more than 100 runs in 13 consecutive seasons, and played in every one of his team's games for 13 consecutive seasons while, at one time or another, leading the league in almost every conceivable batting title.

3. _____ The third best winning percentage (.671) pitcher of all time, he also won 12 league home run titles.

4. _____ Part of a double-play trio immortalized in a famous poem, he had the good judgment to retrieve Al Bridwell's apparent hit and touch second base to force Fred Merkle on a play that pushed the Giants into a one-game playoff that they lost to the Cubs in 1908.

5. _____ A six-time home run champion, he hit more National League round-trippers with one team than any other left-handed batter.

6. _____ This American League outfielder, who won two batting titles (1930–31) and hit .334 lifetime, batted better than .380 four times, and hit better than .300 for four American League teams.

7. _____ Though he never played in a World Series, he twice hit over .400, sported a .340 lifetime average, hit safely a record 257 times in one season, earned the reputation of being the best defensive first baseman of his time, and produced two sons who played in the majors.

8. _____ The last National Leaguer to hit over .400, he has been the Giants' most successful manager since John McGraw: he led New York to three pennants and one world title.

9. _____ A four-time home run champion who lost four peak years to the military service, he was discharged in mid-season of 1945, just in time to lead his team to pennant and World Series victories.

10. _____ Winner of 286 major league games, he claims that his most satisfying victory was his pennant-clinching decision against the Dodgers in 1950.

11. _____ One of the most exciting base runners of all time, he led the Dodgers to six pennants and one

World Series victory between 1947–56; however, his greatest contribution came in 1949 when he was named the MVP for leading the league in batting (.342) and stolen bases (37). In that same year he drove home 124 runs and he scored 122 runs.

12. _____ Though he never won a World Series game, he did win 266 lifetime contests, hurled three no-hitters, and pitched 12 one-hitters in his 18-year major league career.

13. _____ In a 22-year career divided between the Phillies and the Reds, he won 266 games, the most victories by a National League southpaw until Warren Spahn recorded 363 triumphs.

14. _____ A pennant-winning manager in his first year, he was sold two years later, by Clark Griffith (his father-in-law), to the Red Sox for $250,000.

15. _____ Untainted catcher for the infamous Black Sox of 1919, he led American League receivers in putouts for nine years; fielding, eight years; and he caught over 100 games a season for 11 consecutive years.

16. _____ One of the four men who have won four consecutive home run titles, he starred in the infield for the Athletics (1908–14) and the Yankees (1916–22).

17. _____ One of the best defensive catchers who ever played the game, one of the best average-hitting catchers who ever played the game (.313), one of the best home run-hitting catchers who ever played the game (202), he played on eight world championship clubs.

18. _____ Shortstop for the "Miracle Braves," he played with five National League teams over a 23-year span, during which time he established the major league shortstop record for putouts (5,139), and placed second in assists (7,354) and total chances (13,124).

19. _____ A three-time 20-game winner, he set a National League record when he led the loop in strikeouts for seven consecutive years.

20. _____ In 21 years of pitching in the American League, his team finished in the first division only five times (its highest finish was third); however this durable right hander won 260 games, a club record.

21. _____ Possessor of a 29-game batting streak, he played 18 years in the Dodgers' outfield while posting a .317 career batting mark and winning the 1918 batting championship with a .335 batting average.

22. _____ This Pirate outfielder, who stole 738

lifetime bases, led the National League in thefts for ten years. In 1922 he stole successfully 51 out of 53 times.

23. _____ A great defensive outfielder with the Reds and Giants (1916–31), he was also an accomplished batter, hitting .323 lifetime and winning batting championships in 1917 and 1919.

24. _____ He played in more games, registered more at-bats, scored more runs, collected more hits, slashed more doubles, slammed more triples, ran more total bases, and batted in more runs than any other Senator player.

25. _____ Second on the Tigers to Ty Cobb in games played, at-bats, runs, hits, doubles, and total bases, he starred in the 1934–35 World Series and won the batting championship in 1937.

26. _____ Though he led the league in only one offensive department (triples, 19, in 1923), he batted .320 lifetime and gained baseball's admiration as the greatest defensive third baseman in National League history.

27. _____ A 240-game winner for the Athletics, Red Sox, and Yankees, he excelled in World Series play with a spotless 5–0 record. He also saved three games in series competition.

28. _____ A .316 lifetime hitter, and manager of "The Gashouse Gang" that won the pennant and series in 1934, he was traded to the Cardinals for Rogers Hornsby.

29. _____ Considered by many to be the greatest third baseman ever to play the game, he revolutionized the style of third base play while compiling a .294 lifetime average and managing the Red Sox to back-to-back pennants in 1903–04.

30. _____ The first successful "boy manager"— he won consecutive pennants from 1901–3 and in 1909—he played 15 years in the Pirates' outfield while recording a .312 lifetime average.

31. _____ A .334-hitting third baseman, he gained greater fame when he led his charges to ten pennants and three World Series victories.

32. _____ Winner of batting championships in 1901, 1903, and 1904, he once hit .422 for the Athletics, the highest single-season batting average in American League history.

33. _____ This .322 lifetime hitter for the Giants batted .300 in nine of his ten years in the majors while leading New York to five pennants and two world titles. At the age of 30, he died of a kidney ailment.

34. _____ Winner of 254 games, he was one of

the four White Sox pitchers who won 20 games in 1920. During 15 of his 20 seasons in the majors, his team finished in the second division. He was also the last of the legal spitball pitchers in the American League.

35. _____ He played on five pennant winners with the Senators and the Tigers while compiling a .316 lifetime average. In 1928 he won the batting title with a .379 mark. Eleven times he drove home 100 runs.

36. _____ Though he did not get to the majors until he was 30, this outfielder for the Giants won an RBI title and finished his career with a .293 mark. In the 1951 series he batted .458 and stole home once.

37. _____ First baseman for the Giants, Reds, and Dodgers (1915–32), he batted .297. He once hit three home runs in three consecutive innings. At another time he banged seven home runs in six games.

38. _____ The oldest rookie in the history of the game (42), he posted a 6–1 record in 1948 to help the Indians win the pennant. At the age of 59, he pitched his last game for the Athletics. Dizzy Dean called him the greatest pitcher he had ever seen.

39. _____ This American League left-hander was 6–0 in World Series play and 3–1 in all-star action. He was also a four-time 20-game winner with an overall record of 189–102.

40. _____ The last player-manager who led his team to a pennant and World Series victory, he owns a .295 lifetime average. He had his greatest year in 1948 when he hit .355, got four hits in the playoff game, and won the Most Valuable Player award.

41. _____ He recorded a .317 lifetime average despite poor eyesight. For six consecutive years he batted better than .329. In 1929 the flyhawk, who played with both the Cardinals and the Reds, hit safely ten consecutive times to tie a league record.

42. _____ They called him "Beauty," because in his time he was considered a shortstop without peer. In 1922 he set a record when he handled 984 chances at short-stop for the Giants. He averaged 5.97 chances a game during his major league career.

43. _____ Considered the best defensive out-fielder, next to Tris Speaker, during his time, he was re-sponsible for talking Ed Barrow into converting Babe Ruth into an outfielder. Along with Speaker and Duffy Lewis, he played in one of the most famous outfields of all time. A

great World Series performer, he turned in his best season's batting marks in 1921 and 1924 with the White Sox.

44. _____ He didn't come up to the majors until he was 27, but he won 210 games before he pitched his last major league ball at the age of 44. In the 1926 World Series he beat the Yankees twice.

45. _____ He was likened to Willie Keeler with the bat, Tris Speaker in the field, and Ty Cobb on the bases. Yet this all-round performer never got a chance to show his skills in the majors. He was limited to 29 summers of Negro ball and 21 winters of off-season play.

46. _____ He won four batting titles and hit almost 800 home runs in the Negro leagues. Twice he hit more than 70 home runs in a season. He died at the age of 35, the year Jackie Robinson was admitted to the major leagues.

47. _____ A player, manager, and general manager, "The Mahatma" reached greatness in the game as an innovative administrator. He established the first farm system with the Cardinals, broke the color line when he signed Jackie Robinson, and created dynasties in St. Louis and Brooklyn.

48. _____ The manager of the 1918 Red Sox world championship team, he is more singularly remembered for having discovered Honus Wagner, converting Babe Ruth into an outfielder, and establishing a dynasty as general manager of the Yankees.

49. _____ Winner of two games in the 1948 World Series and loser of two games in the 1954 World Series, he started out as a third baseman and ended up winning 207 major league games.

50. _____ A .330 lifetime hitter, he won one batting title (Tigers), collected 200 hits four times, and batted .300 for four major league clubs.

From Aaron to Kell

Match the following 47 Hall of Famers with the descriptions that follow.

Hank Aaron   Ed Delahanty
Grover Alexander Joe DiMaggio
Luis Aparicio   Don Drysdale
Luke Appling   Rick Ferrell
Earl Averill   Elmer Flick
Ernie Banks   Chief Bender

Yogi Berra	Whitey Ford
Jim Bottomly	Jimmie Foxx
Mordecai Brown	Willie McCovey
Jesse Burkett	Burleigh Grimes
Roy Campanella	Lefty Grove
Frank Chance	Gabby Hartnett
Jack Chesbro	Harry Heilmann
Roberto Clemente	Billy Herman
Ty Cobb	Rogers Hornsby
Mickey Cochrane	Waite Hoyt
Eddie Collins	Jim Hunter
Earle Combs	Travis Jackson
Stan Coveleski	Hugh Jennings
Sam Crawford	Walter Johnson
Kiki Cuyler	Addie Joss
Ray Dandridge	Al Kaline
Dizzy Dean	Willie Keeler
	George Kell

1. _____ A winner of 239 games during the regular season and five games in World Series play, he won 20 or more games six consecutive years (1906–11), posted an ERA of 1.04 in 1906—the lowest mark for any pitcher with more than 250 innings of pitching—and he didn't allow an earned run in the 1907–08 series.

2. _____ In 1941 he won his 300th—and last—game with the Boston Red Sox.

3. _____ A multi-time batting champ, he once batted .360 over an eight-year span (1920–27) without winning a crown.

4. _____ A four-time batting champ, he hit safely in 14 consecutive World Series games, and he finished his career with *3,000* hits.

5. _____ He once hit 50 home runs in a season, but he didn't win the home run crown; he finished his regular-season career with a .609 slugging average, and he finished his World Series career with a .609 slugging average.

6. _____ A lifetime .321 hitter, he played in three World Series with the Pirates and the Cubs, and in his best overall year (1925), he batted .357, hit a league-leading 26 triples, scored a league-leading 144 runs, and stole 41 bases.

7. _____ A .281 lifetime hitter, he caught 1,805 games over an 18-year career with three American League teams, some of which were spent handling the pitches of a brother who six times won 20 games.

8. _____ The Cubs have not won a World Series since this .297 career hitter led them to back-to-back crowns (1907–08) as their player-manager.

9. _____ Third on the all-time hit list (3,771), he also won four home run crowns, three of the times with the number of four-base blows he hit corresponding to the number (44) he wore on his back.

10. _____ A three-time winner of the home run crown, he hit more home runs than any other left-handed batter in National League history.

11. _____ He ranks first in World Series games, at-bats, hits, and doubles; second in runs and runs batted in; and third in home runs and walks.

12. _____ A .304 lifetime hitter, he got a career-high 227 hits in 1935, and played in four World Series with the Cubs and Dogers at three-year intervals (1932–35–38–41).

13. _____ A 300-game winner, he posted ERAs below 2.00 for six consecutive years (1915–20).

14. _____ His lifetime ERA was 1.88, the second all-time low, but unfortunately he died young, at the age of 31.

15. _____ In the 1921 World Series he didn't allow an earned run in 27 innings of pitching, but he won only two of three decisions, losing the final game, 1-0, on an error by Roger Peckinpaugh.

16. _____ A 236-game lifetime winner, he posted the best all-time winning percentage (.690) in modern-day ball.

17. _____ A 210-game lifetime winner, he failed to complete a game in World Series play only one out of ten times, the last time, after completing a record nine games in a row.

18. _____ In 1904 this old Highlander started 51 games, finished 48 contests, and won 41 games, all-time bests.

19. _____ A five-time 20-game winner, he won three games for the Indians in the 1920 World Series, and lost two games for the Senators in the 1925 post-season classic.

20. _____ The second all-time winner with 416 victories, he won the last game of the 1924 World Series, and lost the curtain-caller the following year.

21. _____ He didn't pitch his first full season in the National League until he was 30 years old, yet he went on to win 270 major league games.

22. _____ He was the last National League pitcher (1934) to win 30 games in a season.

23. _____ From 1962–65 he had 40 or more starts every year, and he pitched over 300 innings in each of those seasons.

24. _____ A .341 lifetime hitter, he three times batted .400 in the 1890s before leading the league with a .382 mark for the 1901 Cards.

25. _____ A catcher in the National League for 20 years, he hit 236 career homers, high at his position until Roy Campanella ended up with 242.

26. _____ He was the only player to win batting titles in both leagues, hitting .408 for the 1899 Phillies and .376 for the 1902 Senators.

27. _____ This catcher four times hit more than 30 home runs in a season, and in 1953 he drove home a league-leading 142 RBIs.

28. _____ He led the American League in stolen bases his first nine years (1956–64) in the circuit.

29. _____ He won batting titles in 1936 and 1943, the only ones that a player on his team has won.

30. _____ He hit .333 lifetime but never won a batting crown.

31. _____ Four times he hit more than 20 triples in a season, and twice—once in each league—he won the home run crown.

32. _____ In the 11 full seasons that this .318 career hitter played in the majors, he averaged 104 RBIs a year.

33. _____ A .320 lifetime hitter, he played in five World Series, four of them in the 1930s, and player-managed a team to back-to-back penants.

34. _____ From 1924 to 1929 this .310 lifetime hitter—who had seasons of most hits, doubles, triples, home runs, and RBIs—averaged 126 runs batted in a year.

35. _____ A middle infielder, he averaged 44 home runs a year from 1957–60.

36. _____ Until Don Mattingly eclipsed it, he held the Yankee team record of 231 hits in a season.

37. _____ Eight years in a row this .345 lifetime hitter collected more than 200 hits.

38. _____ He finished his career one home run shy of 400.

39. _____ This .315 lifetime hitter once (1905) won a batting title with a mark of .306.

40. _____ A second baseman, he hit 301 career homers.

41. _____ This .325 lifetime hitter, in his first

five years in the majors, averaged better than one RBI for every game he played.

42. _____ This .312 lifetime hitter became the first manager to lead his team to three consecutive penants (1907–09); he was also the first of only two skippers to lead his club to three consecutive World Series defeats.

43. _____ A .306 lifetime batter, this infielder hit better than .300 eight straight years and won the batting title in 1949.

44. _____ A defensive standout, this middle infielder played his entire career with one club and posted a .291 lifetime average.

45. _____ In 1921 he won the batting title, outhitting his manager by five points.

46. _____ People who saw him play say that Brooks Robinson couldn't match his defensive skills at third base, but unfortunately he didn't get the opportunity to showcase them in the big leagues.

47. _____ In World Series play he won four-of-four decisions for a West Coast team and one-of-three for an East Coast club.

From Killebrew to Wynn

Match the following 46 Hall of Famers with the descriptions that follow.

Harmon Killebrew	Tris Speaker
Ralph Kiner	Joe Tinker
Chuck Klein	Rube Waddell
Sandy Koufax	Honus Wagner
Fred Lindstrom	Bobby Wallace
Mickey Mantle	Ed Walsh
Juan Marichal	Lloyd Waner
Rube Marquard	Paul Waner
Eddie Mathews	Ted Williams
Christy Mathewson	Hack Wilson
Willie Mays	Billy Williams
Joe McGinnity	Early Wynn
Joe Medwick	Walter Alston
Johnny Mize	Charles Comiskey
Stan Musial	Clark Griffith
Eddie Plank	Bucky Harris
Pee Wee Reese	Miller Huggins

Brooks Robinson   Al Lopez
Frank Robinson   Connie Mack
Red Ruffing   Joe McCarthy
Joe Sewell   Bill McKechnie
Duke Snider   Wilbert Robinson
Warren Spahn   Casey Stengel

1. _____ In back-to-back years (1903–04) he pitched more than 400 innings in each season.

2. _____ In his last five years (1962–66) he posted ERAs under 2.00.

3. _____ He finished his career with *300* victories.

4. _____ This 201-game winner pitched in five World Series with the Giants and Dodgers, winning two games and losing five.

5. _____ Six times he won more than 20 games in a season for the Giants.

6. _____ He held the American League strike-out record for one season (349) until Nolan Ryan broke it.

7. _____ Four times—three times in a row—he won 30 or more games in a season.

8. _____ Eight times he won 20 or more games for Connie Mack.

9. _____ The most games he won in a season was 23, but he won 20 or more games in a year a record 13 times.

10. _____ He won six consecutive games in World Series play.

11. _____ He hit more than 500 career homers, including 40 or more in his second, third, and fourth years in the majors.

12. _____ In his first five full seasons in the majors (1929–33) he won four home run crowns.

13. _____ He led the National League in home runs in back-to-back years with two clubs.

14. _____ He played on five consecutive World Series losers before he played on a winning team.

15. _____ A .324 lifetime batter, he led the National League in doubles and RBIs from 1936–38.

16. _____ He hit .365 one year (1957) but finished second to Ted Williams in the batting race.

17. _____ He hit more right-handed home runs (586) than any other player except Willie Mays and Hank Aaron.

18. _____ He averaged 37 home runs a season in his ten-year career.

19. _____ A .333 lifetime hitter, he won batting crowns in 1927, 1934, and 1936.

20. _____ At age 18 he got four hits in a World Series game against Walter Johnson.

21. _____ After the Giants traded him to the Cubs, he promptly proved that his former team had made a mistake by winning three home run titles in his first three years in the Windy City.

22. _____ In the four years that he won home run crowns he averaged 50 circuit clouts a season.

23. _____ From 1953–57 he hit 40 or more home runs in each season.

24. _____ Eight times he hit more than 40 home runs in a season but never hit 50.

25. _____ He broke into Cleveland's lineup after Ray Chapman was killed by a Carl Mays pitch.

26. _____ At the age of 37 this .344 lifetime hitter batted .389.

27. _____ A .329 lifetime batter, he had a career average that was higher than any other player at his position.

28. _____ This .331 lifetime hitter player in four World Series (1942–46) in a five-year period of time.

29. _____ This .316 lifetime batter collected more than 200 hits in four of his first five years in the majors.

30. _____ In his first two league Championship Series (1969–70), this .267 lifetime batter hit .500 and .583.

31. _____ A .344 lifetime hitter, he won a batting title at the age of 40.

32. _____ A .263 lifetime hitter, he played in consecutive World Series from 1906–08.

33. _____ A one-time 40-game winner, he posted the lowest career ERA (1.82) of all time.

34. _____ This super defensive shortstop played 25 years, most of them with the Browns; he was called "Rhody."

35. _____ He won back-to-back pennants with Cincinnati.

36. _____ He won two pennants and finished a runner-up ten times.

37. _____ He won World Series on both coasts, one in the East and three in the West.

38. _____ He won World Series 23 years apart.

39. _____ In 24 years of managing he won nine pennants—one in the National League and eight in the

American League—and never finished lower than fourth in the standings.

40. _____ Called "The Tall Tactician," he finished first nine times, but ended up last 17 times.

41. _____ A one-time coach for John McGraw, with whom he played with the Orioles, he later managed Brooklyn to two pennants.

42. _____ Called "The Old Roman," he once managed St. Louis to four straight pennants; he was later the owner of the White Sox during the Black Sox scandal.

43. _____ No stranger to highs and lows, he won ten pennants but finished up his managerial career with four consecutive tenth-place finishers.

44. _____ Called "The Old Fox," he managed just one winner in 20 years, but he also became an owner who presided over three pennant winners and one World Series champ.

45. _____ Called "The Mighty Mite," he twice led one team to three consecutive pennants.

46. _____ Thirteen years in a row he hit 20 or more round-trippers—he slugged 426 lifetime—but he never won a home run crown.

What Have you Done Lately?

Career-wise, Dusty Rhodes was a less-than-mediocre pinch-hitter, but for one season, 1954, he was probably the best clutch-hitting pinch-hitter in baseball history.

In 1954, the year the Giants won the pennant and swept the Indians in the World Series, Rhodes seemed to come through almost every time he stepped to the plate with men on base in a clutch situation. Actually, he made 15 hits in 45 at bats, in pinch-hitting situations, for a .333 average. Overall, he batted .341 and he belted 15 home runs.

In the World Series that year, he made four hits in six plate appearances. Pinch-hitting, he batted safely all three times he stepped to the plate. All three pinch-hits were timely. In Game One he hit a three-run homer in the bottom of the tenth to provide the winning margin in a 5–2 contest. In Game Two his pinch-hit single tied the score at 1–1. Inserted in left field, he proceeded to hit a long home run en route to a Giant 3–1 win. In Game Three he delivered a pinch-hit single with the bases loaded to score the runs that turned out to be the tying and winning counters.

But after that season his star faded. Four years later, he was out of the big leagues. His seven-year pinch-hitting average was an anemic .212.

Another irony of Rhodes's 1954 performance was that in each one of his pinch-hitting appearances he batted for a Giant star—now a Hall of Famer—who in the 1951 World Series clubbed the ball for a .458 mark and stole home in the opening game.

Who was that Giant superstar of 1951—he got seven hits in the first two games—who bowed in favor of the Giant superstar of 1954?

(Answer appears on page 322.)

Chapter Twenty

RETIRED UNIFORM NUMBERS

NATIONAL LEAGUE

We'll give you the teams, the number of "numbers" they've retired, and the players' uniform numbers. You identify the players.

Atlanta (4)

1. _____ (21)
2. _____ (35)
3. _____ (41)
4. _____ (44)

Chicago (2)

1. _____ (14)
2. _____ (26)

Cincinnati (2)

1. _____ (1)
2. _____ (5)

Houston (2)

1. _____ (22)
2. _____ (40)

Los Angeles (8)

1. _____ (1)
2. _____ (4)
3. _____ (19)
4. _____ (24)
5. _____ (32)
6. _____ (39)
7. _____ (42)
8. _____ (56)

New York (2)

1. _____ (14)
2. _____ (37)

Philadelphia (2)

1. _____ (1)
2. _____ (36)

Pittsburgh (8)

1. _____ (1)
2. _____ (4)
3. _____ (8)
4. _____ (9)
5. _____ (20)
6. _____ (21)
7. _____ (33)
8. _____ (40)

St. Louis (5)

1. _____ (6)
2. _____ (14)
3. _____ (17)
4. _____ (20)
5. _____ (45)

San Francisco (5)

1. _____ (4)
2. _____ (11)
3. _____ (24)
4. _____ (27)
5. _____ (44)

AMERICAN LEAGUE

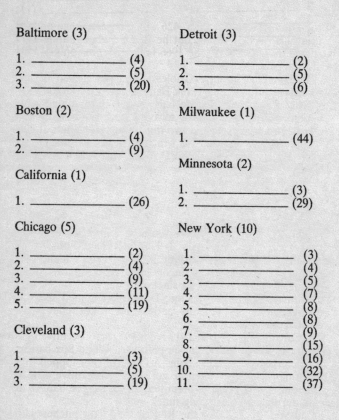

Baltimore (3)

1. ————————— (4)
2. ————————— (5)
3. ————————— (20)

Boston (2)

1. ————————— (4)
2. ————————— (9)

California (1)

1. ————————— (26)

Chicago (5)

1. ————————— (2)
2. ————————— (4)
3. ————————— (9)
4. ————————— (11)
5. ————————— (19)

Cleveland (3)

1. ————————— (3)
2. ————————— (5)
3. ————————— (19)

Detroit (3)

1. ————————— (2)
2. ————————— (5)
3. ————————— (6)

Milwaukee (1)

1. ————————— (44)

Minnesota (2)

1. ————————— (3)
2. ————————— (29)

New York (10)

1. ————————— (3)
2. ————————— (4)
3. ————————— (5)
4. ————————— (7)
5. ————————— (8)
6. ————————— (8)
7. ————————— (9)
8. ————————— (15)
9. ————————— (16)
10. ————————— (32)
11. ————————— (37)

Moe the Pro

Moe Drabowsky was just a .426 winning percentage pitcher during his 17-year career but he was a 1.000 winning percentage moundsman in the 1966 fall classic, his only World Series appearance.

In Game One of the Orioles' four-game sweep of the Dodgers, Bird manager Hank Bauer summoned Drabowsky to relieve starter Dave McNally in the third inning with Baltimore clinging tenuously to a 4–2 lead. Drabowsky was superb. He pitched six and two thirds innings of shutout ball en route to the Orioles' 5–2 win. But it was the manner in which Drabowsky stifled the Dodgers that raised the eyebrows of veteran World Series observers. He allowed just one hit, issued two free passes, and struck out *11* batters, a fall classic record for pitchers in relief.

Drabowsky's pitching performance turned out to be the catalyst that the Birds' staff needed. In Game Two, Jim Palmer blanked Los Angeles, 9–0; in Game Three, Wally Bunker zipped the Dodgers, 1–0; and in Game Four, Dave McNally whitewashed manager Walter Alston's men, 1–0. In the last 33⅔ innings of the 1966 Series, Baltimore's staff did not allow the Dodgers a single run.

At one point in Game One, Drabowsky fanned six consecutive Los Angeles batters, another record for relief pitchers in World Series play.

A Cincinnati pitcher of 1919 recorded six consecutive outs via the strikeout route, but he permitted White Sox batters to reach base during the skein. A Giant pitcher topped that performance in 1921 when he got seven consecutive outs in strikeout fashion, but he permitted three Yankee batters to walk during the intervening time.

Can you name either the Red or the Giant pitcher who recorded a World Series first? If you can name both of them you will be a 1.000 winning percentage pitcher—just like Moe Drabowsky!

(Answer appears on page 322.)

ANSWERS SECTION

Inner-Chapter Answers

Introduction: Warren Sandell, who according to *The New York Times* "had a propensity to throw home-run pitches," never made it to the major leagues.

Ruth's Shadow: Lou Gehrig

The Shot Heard 'Round the World: Larry Jansen

The Asterisk Pitcher: Hank Aaron, the runner on first base, thought that Joe Adcock's game-winning hit had remained in play; so, when he saw Felix Mantilla racing toward home, he assumed that the one run would automatically bring the game to an end. Consequently, shortly after rounding second base, he stopped and headed for the dugout. Adcock, who had not noticed Aaron's error in judgment, naturally passed his teammate. Since the hitter had illegally passed the base runner, he was ruled out by the umpire. Aaron, on the other hand, could have been called out for illegally running the base paths. If both runners had been called out before Mantilla crossed home plate, no run would count because the third out would have been recorded before the winning run scored. But Mantilla did score and the Braves did win.

And Harvey Haddix has become an asterisk!

Exceptions to the Rule: Bob Cain, pitcher; Bob Swift, catcher; and Bill Stewart, umpire

The Mystery Death: Willard Hershberger

A Checkered Career: Hank Gowdy

Classic Comebacks: Gaylord Perry (Giants) and Ray Washburn (Cardinals); Jim Maloney (Reds) and Don Wilson (Astros)

Baseball's Number Game: Lou Brock (.293) and Carl Yastrzemski (.285)

The Fateful Farewell: Al Gionfriddo was Furillo's pinch-runner, Eddie Miksis was Reiser's, and Eddie Miksis was the fielder.

The Iron Horse: Wally Pipp

To Catch a Thief: Bob O'Farrell

Two Strikes Against Him: Joe Sewell

Where Are the Iron Men: The pitchers are Steve Blass and Nelson Briles of the 1971 Pirates and Burt Hooton and Don Sutton of the 1977 Dodgers. Blass recorded the two complete games.

The Trivia Tandem: Larry McWilliams (starter) and Gene Garber (reliever)

The Black Sox: Ray Schalk, catcher; Eddie Collins, second baseman; and Red Faber, pitcher

The Shoe Polish Plays: Nippy Jones and Cleon Jones

The Shutout Series: Red Ames (Giants) and Chief Bender (Athletics)

A Man for All Seasons: Ed Barrow

Three Men on Third: Dazzy Vance, since there was no force, had rightful possession of the bag. Chick Fewster and Babe Herman, who were the trespassers, were declared out. Since that day, whenever someone says, "The Dodgers have three men on base," a listener with a keen sense of wit will invariably say, "Which one?"

What Have You Done Lately: Monte Irvin

Moe the Pro: Hod Eller (Reds) and Jesse Barnes (Giants)

1. From Anderson to Yount

1. Roger Clemens (1986)
2. Garry Templeton (1977–79 Cards)
3. Greg Minton (1978–82 Giants)
4. Buddy Bell (.299 for the 1979 Rangers)
5. Ron Guidry (Yankees)
6. Steve Carlton (1972 Phillies)
7. Robin Yount (Brewers)
8. Willie Wilson (Royals)
9. Pete Rose
10. Bill Gullickson (1982 Expos)
11. Davey Lopes (1975 Dodgers)
12. Willie Wilson
13. Don Baylor (1974 Orioles)
14. Bob Stanley (1982 Red Sox)
15. Fernando Valenzuela (1981 Dodgers)
16. Juan Samuel (1984 Phillies)
17. Phil Niekro (1977–80 Braves)
18. Gene Garber (1979 Braves)
19. Ted Simmons (180 at the beginning of 1988)
20. Terry Kennedy (Padres)
21. Mike Easler
22. Bruce Sutter (1977 Cubs)
23. Don Baylor
24. Frank Tanana (1978 Angels)
25. Rickey Henderson (1982 A's)
26. Dale Murphy (Braves)
27. Cal Ripken, Sr.
28. Rick Sutcliffe
29. Steve Sax
30. Juan Samuel (1983 Phillies)
31. Bill Campbell (1976 Twins)
32. Tim Wallach (1982 Expos)
33. Mookie Wilson (Jackson, Miss., in 1978)
34. Tom Seaver (1985)
35. Mike Schmidt
36. Jason Thompson
37. Wade Boggs (1982 Red Sox)
38. Dennis Eckersley (1981 Red Sox)
39. Mike Hargrove
40. Andre Thornton (1978 Indians)
41. Carlton Fisk (1985 White Sox)
42. Don Sutton
43. Darrell Evans (1973 Braves)
44. Jack Morris (20 and 232)
45. Dave Winfield (37)
46. Graig Nettles
47. Roy Smalley (1982)
48. Butch Wynegar (1976 Twins)

49. Dave Stieb (1983 Blue Jays)
50. Fred Lynn (1983)
51. Richard Dotson (He was 24 when he won 22 in 1983)
52. George Brett (1983 Royals)
53. Dave Righetti (1986 Yankees)
54. Hal McRae (1982 Royals)
55. Gary Gaetti (1981)
56. Ron Davis (1981 Yankees)
57. Carney Lansford (Red Sox)
58. Don Mattingly (1984)
59. Charlie Hough (Rangers)
60. Leon Durham (1982)
61. Charlie Lea
62. Keith Hernandez
63. Walt Terrell (1983 Mets)
64. John Denny (1983 Phillies)
65. Bill Madlock
66. Glenn Hubbard
67. Dave Parker (Pirates)
68. Mario Soto
69. Ray Knight
70. Steve Balboni
71. Nolan Ryan
72. Ken Landreaux
73. David Palmer (Expos)
74. Steve Garvey (1977 Dodgers)
75. Goose Gossage (1977 Pirates)
76. Bob and Ken Forsch
77. Gary Carter (1978 Expos)
78. Manny Trillo (Phillies)
79. Cecil Cooper
80. Sparky Anderson
81. Aurelio Lopez
82. Paul Molitor (Brewers)
83. Terry Puhl (1979)
84. John Tudor (1982–83)
85. John Candelaria
86. George Frazier (1981 Yankees)
87. Willie McGee (1982 Cards)
88. Claudell Washington (1979 White Sox, 1980 Mets)
89. Len Barker (1981)
90. Steve Bedrosian (1987 Phillies)
91. Pedro Guerrero (1981–82)
92. LaMarr Hoyt (1981–82)
93. Frank White
94. Rickey Henderson (A's)
95. Larry Parrish
96. Gary Ward (1983)
97. Bill Buckner (1980)
98. Willie Upshaw (104 in 1983)
99. Don Mattingly
100. Jesse Barfield

2. From Aikens to Yount

1. Jim Clancy
2. Doug DeCinces (1982)
3. Dick Schofield, Jr.
4. Harold Baines (He was 23 in 1982.)
5. Floyd Bannister (1982 Mariners)

6. Pat Corrales (Phillies–Indians)
7. John McNamara (Padres, A's, Reds, Angels, and Red Sox)
8. Davy Johnson (1973 Braves)
9. Chuck Tanner (1955 Braves)
10. Bob Knepper
11. Dwight Gooden (Mets)
12. Rick Manning (1977 Indians)
13. Rich Dauer (1978 Orioles)
14. Chet Lemon (1977)
15. Dwayne Murphy (1980 A's)
16. Jim Sundberg (1979 Rangers)
17. Rickey Henderson
18. Tim Raines
19. Eddie Murray (Orioles)
20. Dwight Evans (1981 Red Sox)
21. Willie Upshaw (Gene and Marvin Upshaw)
22. Ernie Whitt (Blue Jays)
23. Fred Lynn (1975 Red Sox)
24. Bob Boone (Angels)
25. Reggie Jackson (1973 A's, 1977 Yankees)
26. Carlton Fisk (White Sox)
27. Ron Kittle (1983)
28. John McNamara (Reds)
29. Dick Howser (1980 Yankees)
30. Davy Johnson
31. Chuck Tanner (for Manny Sanguillen)
32. Dick Williams (1967 Red Sox, 1972–73 A's, 1984 Padres)

33. Bert Blyleven (1977)
34. Ray Knight
35. Don Sutton
36. Tony LaRussa
37. Tom Seaver (1971)
38. Mike Schmidt
39. Steve Carlton (1972)
40. Kent Tekulve (1978–79)
41. Bruce Sutter
42. Dan Quisenberry (1983)
43. John Montefusco
44. John McNamara
45. Don Sutton
46. Darrell Evans (1976 Braves)
47. Pete Rose (1978 Reds)
48. Willie Wilson (1979 Royals)
49. Steve Garvey
50. Garry Templeton (1979 Cards)
51. Graig Nettles (1971 Indians)
52. Reggie Jackson
53. Graig Nettles (Padres)
54. Whitey Herzog
55. Garry Templeton (1979 Cards)
56. Willie Wilson (1980 Royals)
57. Jack Clark
58. Jim Rice (46 home runs, 213 hits in 1978)
59. George Brett (1979 Royals)
60. George Brett (1978)
61. Tom Seaver (1973 Mets)
62. Ron Guidry (1978 Yankees)
63. Steve Carlton (1972 Phillies)
64. Reggie Jackson

65. Pete Rose (1975 Reds)
66. Ron Guidry (.893 for the 1978 Yankees)
67. Goose Gossage (1975 White Sox, 1978 Yankees)
68. Jack Clark (1978)
69. Willie Randolph
70. Rudy Law (77 in 1983)
71. Ron Guidry (1.74 for the 1978 Yankees)
72. Pete Rose (1963 Reds)
73. Steve Carlton (1979 Phillies)
74. Willie Aikens (Royals)
75. George Brett
76. Reggie Jackson (1973, 1975 A's; 1980 Yankees; and 1982 Angels)
77. Lee Mazzilli
78. Rick Cerone
79. Dave Righetti
80. Carlton Fisk
81. Tom Seaver (1981 Reds)
82. Darryl Strawberry (1983)

83. Larry Herndon
84. Robin Yount (1982 Brewers)
85. Dave Righetti
86. Phil Niekro (At the start of the 1987 season, he was 48.)
87. Carlton Fisk (Red Sox and White Sox)
88. Ron Kittle (1983)
89. George Brett
90. Steve Balboni
91. Ron Davis (Yankees)
92. Charlie Hough
93. Andre Dawson (against the 1978 Braves)
94. Tim Wallach (1980)
95. Mike Schmidt
96. Bill Madlock (Cubs and Pirates)
97. Claudell Washington
98. Dave Concepcion
99. Lou Whitaker
100. Fred Lynn (1975 Red Sox)

3. From Aase to Youmans

1. Ryne Sandberg
2. Gary Matthews
3. Jody Davis (1983)
4. Shawon Dunston
5. Rick Sutcliffe
6. Lee Smith
7. Dennis Eckersley
8. Mike Fitzgerald
9. Andres Galarraga
10. Floyd Youmans
11. Tim Burke (1985)
12. Jeff Reardon
13. Tim Raines (1981)
14. Gary Carter

15. Darryl Strawberry
16. Kirk Gibson
17. Keith Hernandez (1986)
18. Dwight Gooden (1984–86)
19. Roger McDowell (1986)
20. Bob Ojeda (1986)
21. Jesse Orosco
22. Mike Schmidt
23. Juan Samuel (1984–86)
24. Steve Bedrosian (40 in 1987)
25. Tony Peña
26. Mike Diaz

27. Barry Bonds
28. Tommy Herr
29. Willie McGee (.353 for 1985 Cards)
30. Ozzie Smith
31. Vince Coleman (1985)
32. Jack Clark
33. John Tudor
34. Danny Cox (1985 Cards)
35. Bob Forsch
36. Todd Worrell (Cards)
37. Dale Murphy
38. Glen Hubbard (1978)
39. Ozzie Virgil (27)
40. Ken Griffey
41. Gene Garber
42. Rick Mahler
43. Dave Parker
44. Eric Davis
45. Ron Oester
46. Buddy Bell (194)
47. Bo Diaz
48. John Franco
49. Bill Doran (1986)
50. Mike Scott (1986)
51. Bob Knepper
52. Jim Deshaies (12 in 1986)
53. Dave Smith
54. Nolan Ryan
55. Steve Sax
56. Mike Marshall
57. Bill Madlock
58. Pedro Guerrero
59. Fernando Valenzuela
60. Bob Welch
61. Steve Garvey
62. Kevin Mitchell
63. Goose Gossage
64. Andy Hawkins
65. Will Clark (1986)
66. Jeff Leonard
67. Candy Maldonado
68. Mike Krukow
69. Mark Davis
70. Eddie Murray
71. Cal Ripken
72. Fred Lynn (1979 Red Sox)
73. Lee Lacy
74. Mike Boddicker (1984)
75. Don Aase (1986)
76. Mike Flanagan
77. Wade Boggs
78. Jim Rice
79. Marty Barrett (1986)
80. Don Baylor (Orioles, Angels, Yankees, and Red Sox)
81. Dwight Evans
82. Roger Clemens
83. Bruce Hurst
84. Joe Carter (1986)
85. Julio Franco
86. Tony Bernazard
87. Brett Butler
88. Brook Jacoby
89. Pat Tabler
90. Phil Niekro
91. Ernie Camacho
92. Tom Candiotti
93. Darrell Evans (1985)
94. Alan Trammell
95. Lou Whitaker
96. Jack Morris
97. Willie Hernandez (1984)
98. Robin Yount
99. Rob Deer
100. Paul Molitor

4. From Balboni to Witt

1. Ted Higuera
2. Mark Clear
3. Don Mattingly
4. Rickey Henderson
5. Willie Randolph
6. Dave Winfield
7. Dave Righetti
8. Jesse Barfield
9. Lloyd Moseby
10. George Bell
11. Dave Stieb
12. Wally Joyner (1986)
13. Doug DeCinces
14. Brian Downing
15. Gary Pettis (1984–86)
16. Mike Witt
17. Don Sutton
18. Harold Baines (1982–87)
19. Ossie Guillen
20. Carlton Fisk
21. Joe Cowley (1986)
22. Bob James
23. George Brett
24. Steve Balboni
25. Willie Wilson (1982)
26. Frank White
27. Kirby Puckett
28. Kent Hrbek
29. Gary Gaetti
30. Bert Blyleven
31. Jose Canseco
32. Pete Incaviglia
33. Larry Parrish
34. Mitch Williams
35. Bobby Witt

Chapter Two Answers

5. How Good Is .300?

Batting Champs

1. Mickey Mantle (.298)
2. Tommy Davis (.294)
3. Norm Cash (.271)
4. Hal Chase (.291)
5. George Stirnweiss (.268)
6. Carl Yastrzemski (.285)
7. Pete Runnels (.291)
8. Bobby Avila (.281)
9. Harry Walker (.296)
10. Dick Groat (.286)
11. Lou Boudreau (.295)
12. Mickey Vernon (.286)
13. Debs Garms (.293)
14. Heinie Zimmerman (.295)
15. Pete Reiser (.295)
16. Larry Doyle (.290)
17. Ferris Fain (.290)
18. Alex Johnson (.288)
19. Phil Cavarretta (.293)
20. Carl Furillo (.299)

.300 Hitters

1. Johnny Pesky (.307)
2. Enos Slaughter (.300)
3. Joe Cronin (.302)
4. Mel Ott (.304)
5. Bill Dickey (.313)
6. Lloyd Waner (.316)
7. Bob Meusel (.309)
8. Joe Jackson (.356)
9. Hack Wilson (.307)
10. Earl Averill (.318)
11. Sam Rice (.322)
12. Dale Mitchell (.312)
13. Hank Greenberg (.313)
14. Eddie Collins (.333)
15. Earle Combs (.325)
16. Babe Herman (.324)
17. Kiki Cuyler (.321)
18. Frankie Frisch (.316)
19. Pie Traynor (.320)
20. Mickey Cochrane (.320)

6. Who Did It Twice?

National League

1. Willie Mays
2. Harry Walker
3. Dixie Walker
4. Carl Furillo
5. Jackie Robinson

1. Lefty O'Doul
2. Tommy Davis
3. Henry Aaron
4. Ernie Lombardi
5. Richie Ashburn

American League

1. George Kell
2. Al Kaline
3. Norm Cash
4. Mickey Mantle
5. Harvey Kuenn

1. Jimmie Foxx
2. Luke Appling
3. Mickey Vernon
4. Pete Runnels
5. Ferris Fain

7. The Fabulous Fifties

1. Roger Maris
2. Babe Ruth
3. Babe Ruth
4. Jimmie Foxx
5. Hank Greenberg
6. Hack Wilson
7. Babe Ruth
8. Babe Ruth
9. Ralph Kiner
10. Mickey Mantle
11. Mickey Mantle
12. Willie Mays
13. George Foster
14. Both answers can be
15. Johnny Mize or Ralph Kiner
16. Willie Mays
17. Jimmie Foxx

8. The (500) Home Run Club

1. Hank Aaron
2. Babe Ruth
3. Willie Mays
4. Frank Robinson
5. Harmon Killebrew
6. Reggie Jackson
7. Mickey Mantle
8. Jimmie Foxx
9. Mike Schmidt
10. Both 10–11 can be Ted
11. Williams or Willie McCovey
12. Both 12–13 can be
13. Eddie Mathews or Ernie Banks
14. Mel Ott

9. They Hit for Power and Average

National League

1. Heinie Zimmerman
2. Rogers Hornsby
3. Rogers Hornsby
4. Chuck Klein
5. Joe Medwick
6. Johnny Mize

American League

1. Nap Lajoie
2. Ty Cobb
3. Babe Ruth
4. Jimmie Foxx
5. Lou Gehrig
6. Ted Williams
7. Ted Williams

8. Ted Williams
9. Mickey Mantle
10. Frank Robinson
11. Carl Yastrzemski

10. The 3000-Hit Club

1. Pete Rose
2. Ty Cobb
3. Hank Aaron
4. Stan Musial
5. Tris Speaker
6. Honus Wagner
7. Carl Yastrzemski
8. Eddie Collins
9. Willie Mays
10. Nap Lajoie
11. Paul Waner
12. Cap Anson
13. Lou Brock
14. Al Kaline
15. Roberto Clemente

11. Triple Crown Winners

1. Nap Lajoie
2. Ty Cobb
3. Rogers Hornsby
4. Rogers Hornsby
5. Chuck Klein or Jimmie Foxx
6. Chuck Klein or Jimmie Foxx
7. Lou Gehrig
8. Joe Medwick
9. Ted Williams
10. Ted Williams
11. Mickey Mantle
12. Frank Robinson
13. Carl Yastrzemski

12. Highest Lifetime Average for Position

National League

1. Bill Terry
2. Rogers Hornsby
3. Honus Wagner
4. Pie Traynor
5. Riggs Stephenson
6. Paul Waner
7. Lefty O'Doul
8. Eugene Hargrave

American League

1. Lou Gehrig and George Sisler
2. Nap Lajoie
3. Cecil Travis
4. Frank Baker
5. Ty Cobb
6. Joe Jackson
7. Ted Williams
8. Mickey Cochrane

13. Highest Single Season Average for Position

National League

1. Bill Terry
2. Rogers Hornsby
3. Arky Vaughan
4. Heinie Zimmerman
5. Lefty O'Doul
6. Babe Herman
7. Chuck Klein
8. Chief Meyers

American League

1. George Sisler
2. Nap Lajoie
3. Luke Appling
4. George Brett
5. Ty Cobb
6. Joe Jackson
7. Ted Williams
8. Bill Dickey

14. The Year They Hit the Heights

1. Rogers Hornsby
2. Ty Cobb
3. Ted Williams
4. Babe Ruth
5. Joe DiMaggio
6. Stan Musial
7. Mickey Mantle
8. Roberto Clemente
9. Jackie Robinson
10. Charlie Keller

15. Matching Averages

1. Ty Cobb
2. Rogers Hornsby
3. Tris Speaker
4. Babe Ruth
5. Bill Terry
6. Stan Musial
7. Honus Wagner
8. Jimmie Foxx
9. Mickey Cochrane
10. Mel Ott

16. Once Is Not Enough

1. Lou Gehrig
2. Rocky Colavito
3. Gil Hodges
4. Pat Seerey
5. Joe Adcock
6. Mike Schmidt
7. Willie Mays
8. Bob Horner

17. National League Home Run Kings

1. Mike Schmidt
2. Ralph Kiner
3. Mel Ott
4. Johnny Mize
5. Eddie Mathews or Johnny Bench

6. Eddie Mathews or
   Johnny Bench
7. Ted Kluszewski or
   Duke Snider

8. Ted Kluszewski or
   Duke Snider

18. American League Home Run Kings

1. Babe Ruth
2. Harmon Killebrew
3–8. Any combination of
   Jimmie Foxx, Frank
   Baker, Hank Green-
   berg, Reggie Jack-
   son, Ted Williams
   and Mickey Mantle
9–10. Either Lou Gehrig
   or Jim Rice

11–16. Any combination
   of Frank Howard,
   Tony Armas, Joe
   DiMaggio, Gorman
   Thomas, Larry
   Doby, and Dick
   Allen
17–20. Any combination of
   Roger Maris, George
   Scott, Graig Nettles,
   and Carl Yastrzemski

19. Would You Pinch-Hit?

1. No (.294)
2. No (.283)
3. No (.290)
4. No (.289)
5. Yes (.326)
6. No (.270)
7. Yes (.304)
8. No (.272)
9. Yes (.312)
10. Yes (.296)

11. Yes (.286)
12. Yes (.284)
13. No (.269)
14. No (.261)
15. Yes (.287)
16. Same (.276)
17. Yes (.304)
18. No (.264)
19. Yes (.293)
20. Yes (.273)

20. Decades of Batting Champs

National League

1. Pirates
2. Reds
3. Phillies
4. Reds

5. Cubs
6. Dodgers
7. Reds
8. Braves
9. Expos

1. Senators	6. Athletics
2. Indians	7. Red Sox
3. Tigers	8. Angels
4. White Sox	9. Red Sox
5. Yankees	

21. Sub-.320 Batting Leaders

1. Rod Carew	4. Elmer Flick
2. Frank Robinson	5. Carl Yastrzemski
3. George Stirnweiss	

22. .390-Plus Runners-up

1. Joe Jackson	4. Babe Herman
2. Ty Cobb	5. Al Simmons
3. Babe Ruth	

23. Stepping into the Box

1. L	16. L
2. R	17. R
3. S	18. R
4. R	19. S
5. S	20. S
6. L	21. L
7. S	22. R
8. R	23. S
9. L	24. L
10. S	25. R
11. R	26. S
12. L	27. R
13. L	28. L
14. R	29. S
15. L	30. S

24. Famous Home Run Pitches

1. Ralph Terry
2. Robin Roberts
3. Ralph Branca
4. Don Newcombe
5. Jack Billingham
6. Al Downing
7. Howie Pollet
8. Barney Schultz
9. Bob Lemon
10. Bob Purkey

25. The Pitching Masters

1. Cy Young
2. Walter Johnson
3. Christy Mathewson or Grover Alexander
4. Grover Alexander or Christy Mathewson
5. Warren Spahn
6. Eddie Plank
7. Gaylord Perry
8. Tom Seaver
9. Lefty Grove or Early Wynn
10. Lefty Grove or Early Wynn
11–13. Any combination of Steve Carlton, Phil Niekro, or Don Sutton

26. The Perfect Game

1. Ernie Shore
2. Jim Hunter
3. Jim Bunning
4. Cy Young
5. Addie Joss
6. Sandy Koufax
7. Don Larsen
8. Charlie Robertson
9. Mike Witt
10. Len Barker

27. Multiple No-Hitters

1. Nolan Ryan
2. Sandy Koufax
3. Bob Feller or Jim Maloney
4. Bob Feller or Jim Maloney
5–15. Any combination of the following: Johnny Vander Meer, Steve Busby, Ken Holtzman, Don Wilson, Dean Chance, Jim Bunning, Warren Spahn, Sam Jones, Carl Erskine, Allie Reynolds, Virgil Trucks

335

28. Back-to-Back 20-Game Winners

1. h
2. s
3. p
4. n
5. w
6. d
7. v
8. t
9. k
10. m
11. f
12. q
13. o
14. e
15. x
16. j
17. a
18. i
19. c
20. u
21. g
22. r
23. b
24. l
25. y
26. z

29. The Flamethrowers

1. Nolan Ryan
2. Sandy Koufax
3. Mickey Lolich
4. Sam McDowell
5. Bob Feller
6. Steve Carlton
7. Walter Johnson
8. Rube Waddell
9. Vida Blue
10. J. R. Richard
11. Mike Scott

30. Blue-Chip Pitchers

1. Whitey Ford (.690)
2. Allie Reynolds (.630)
3. Jim Palmer (.638)
4. Mort Cooper (.631)
5. Tom Seaver (.603)
6. Vic Raschi (.667)
7. Sal Maglie (.657)
8. Dizzy Dean (.644)
9. Sandy Koufax (.655)
10. Lefty Gomez (.649)

31. 200 Times a Loser

1. Cy Young
2. Bobo Newsom
3. Walter Johnson
4. Warren Spahn
5. Grover Alexander
6. Red Ruffing
7. Paul Derringer
8. Robin Roberts
9. Bob Friend
10. Early Wynn

32. Winding Up

1. L	16. R
2. L	17. L
3. R	18. L
4. L	19. R
5. R	20. L
6. R	21. L
7. L	22. L
8. L	23. R
9. R	24. R
10. R	25. R
11. R	26. R
12. R	27. L
13. L	28. R
14. L	29. L
15. R	30. L

Chapter Four Answers

33. Four Bases to Score

1. d
2. c
3. b
4. b
5. a
6. a
7. d
8. b
9. d (1910, 1913, and 1917)
10. a (1939–40)
11. c
12. d
13. b (117)
14. c
15. a
16. a
17. b (1901, Reds; 1908 and 1914, Tigers)
18. d (.410 with 1899 Phillies and .376 with 1902 Senators)
19. c (52 in 1977)
20. d
21. d
22. d (170–161)
23. a
24. c (for the 1948 Indians)
25. d
26. c
27. c (1951–52)
28. c (1962–63)
29. d
30. d
31. b
32. b

33. c
34. a
35. b
36. c (.401 in 1930)
37. d
38. a
39. d
40. b (1983)
41. c (.407 in 1920 and .420 in 1922)
42. b (30–7 in 1934)
43. a (.349)
44. d
45. a (41)
46. a (33–25 in 1925)
47. d (1947) He was two outs short of duplicating the feat.
48. d
49. a
50. d
51. b (51 in 1947)
52. a (9)
53. c (36)
54. b
55. a
56. c
57. b
58. b (1973)
59. b
60. c
61. b
62. d
63. d
64. d
65. a (1923)
66. a (1976)

67. c (1946–52)
68. c
69. d ((1968)
70. a
71. b (.422 in 1901)
72. a
73. c (1922)
74. b
75. d
76. b
77. d (1947)
78. d (1964)
79. d
80. a
81. b
82. d
83. b (Indians)

84. c
85. a
86. d
87. b
88. d
89. c (1226)
90. c
91. c (1964)
92. d
93. d (Hunter was 5–3 in series play.)
94. a (1915)
95. c
96. c (1952)
97. d (1959, with the White Sox)
98. d
99. d
100. c (1961)

34. From Ruth to Reggie

1. Hank Greenberg
2. Johnny Allen (1937)
3. Earl Averill
4. Monty Stratton (1938)
5. Ossie Vitt
6. Bob Feller
7. Frank Robinson
8. Hank Greenberg
9. Chris Chambliss
10. Hank Borowy
11. Phil Masi
12. Joe McCarthy
13. Don Kessinger (1979 White Sox)
14. Lou Boudreau (Cleveland, 1948)
15. Joe Gordon
16. Rocky Colavito
17. Stu Miller
18. Lou Boudreau
19. Ted Williams
20. Cal Abrams
21. Bobo Holloman (Browns, 1953)
22. Chuck Stobbs
23. Chuck Dressen
24. Johnny Antonelli
25. Willie Mays
26. Hank Aaron
27. Vic Wertz
28. Ruben Gomez
29. Pat Dobson
30. Tommy Byrne
31. Gil McDougald
32. Sal Maglie
33. Yogi Berra
34. Tony Kubek
35. Pirates (1925)

36. Royals (1985)
37. Harry Heilmann (.403 in 1923)
38. Johnny Roseboro
39. Casey Stengel
40. Tom Zachary
41. Tracy Stallard
42. Luis Arroyo
43. Johnny Blanchard
44. Frank Lary
45. Casey Stengel
46. Phil Linz
47. Juan Marichal
48. Don Drysdale
49. Willie Davis
50. Milt Pappas
51. Bob Turley
52. First Base
53. Happy Chandler
54. Frank Robinson
55. Norm Siebern
56. Al Rosen
57. Don Demeter
58. Bill McKechnie
59. Ken Harrelson
60. Denny McLain (31–6 in 1968)
61. Nippy Jones
62. Cleon Jones
63. Curt Flood
64. Rod Carew (1972)
65. Gene Tenace (1972)
66. Dick Williams
67. Yankees
68. Howard Ehmke
69. Phillies (1930)
70. Allie Reynolds
71. Babe Ruth

72. Philadelphia (Jimmie Foxx, A's; Chuck Klein, Phillies)
73. Bill Terry
74. Jerome and Paul Dean
75. Joe Medwick
76. Bobby Brown (1947, 1949–51)
77. Lefty O'Doul (254, 1929) and Bill Terry (254, 1930)
78. Rickey Henderson (130 in 1982)
79. Spud Chandler (.717)
80. Whitey Ford (8)
81. Bobby Richardson (209, 1962)
82. Duke Snider (1956)
83. Reggie Jackson (1980 Yankees)
84. David Dale Alexander (1932, Tigers and Red Sox)
85. Harry Walker (1947, Cardinals and Phillies)
86. Johnny Burnett (1932 Indians)
87. Bump Hadley (1937)
88. Leo Durocher (1941)
89. Jeff Heath
90. Maury Wills
91. Sandy Koufax (1966)
92. Bill Eckert
93. Charlie Grimm
94. Yogi Berra
95. Johnny Edwards
96. Rogers Hornsby
97. Lou Gehrig (1931)
98. Eddie Stanky (1945) and Jimmy Wynn (1969)
99. Jack Coombs (13, 1910 Athletics)
100. Joe Morgan

35. Baseball's Who's Who

1. Walter Johnson
2. Rogers Hornsby (1921–25)
3. Bill McKechnie (Pirates, 1925; Cardinals, 1928; and Reds, 1939–40)
4. Al Kaline of the Tigers, who was 20 in 1955
5. Ted Williams of the Red Sox, who was 40 in 1958
6. Mike Higgins of the 1938 Red Sox
7. Walt Dropo of the 1952 Tigers
8. Joe Jackson (1920)
9. Ty Cobb, whose .401 for the Tigers in 1922 finished second to George Sisler's .420
10. Tom Zachary of the 1929 Yankees
11. "Iron Man" Joe McGinnity of the 1903 Giants
12. Casey Stengel
13. Jimmie Foxx (A's, 1932–33; and Red Sox, 1938)
14. George "Specs" Toporcer of the 1921 Cardinals
15. Clint Courtney of the 1951 Yankees
16. Dizzy Dean
17. Harry Brecheen (0.83) of the Cardinals
18. Harry Heilmann of the 1921, 1923, 1925, and 1927 Tigers
19. Ted Williams of the 1941–42, 1947–48, and 1957–58 Red Sox
20. Eddie Robinson (1948)
21. Ralph Houk
22. Joe McCarthy
23. Casey Stengel
24. Johnny Frederick of the 1932 Dodgers
25. Joe Cronin of the 1943 Red Sox
26. Ed Reulbach of the 1906–08 Cubs
27. Lefty Grove of the 1929–31 Athletics
28. Grover Alexander
29. Mel Ott of the 1932, 1934, and 1937 Giants
30. Ralph Kiner of the 1947–48, and 1952 Pirates
31. Wes Ferrell
32. Walter Johnson
33. Luke Appling (1936 and 1943)
34. Mark Littell
35. Hal Newhouser (1944–45)
36. Rube Bressler
37. Harmon Killebrew
38. Hank Aaron
39. Norm Cash
40. Ernie Banks
41. Red Ruffing
42. Red Lucas

43. Lefty Grove
44. Jimmie Foxx: batting, 1933 (Athletics) and 1938 (Red Sox); home runs, 1932–33, 1935 (Athletics) and 1939 (Red Sox).
45. Mickey Mantle (1956)
46. Roy Face
47. Ted Williams (1941–42 and 1947)
48. Cy Young
49. Jim Bottomley
50. Roger Cramer
51. Jim Palmer of the 1973, 1975–76 Orioles
52. Tom Seaver of the 1969, 1973, 1975 Mets
53. Mike Marshall of the 1974 Dodgers
54. Steve Carlton of the 1972, 1977, 1980, and 1982 Phillies
55. Gaylord Perry (Indians, 1972; Padres, 1978)
56. Mark Fidrych of the 1976 Tigers
57. Bob Horner of the 1978 Braves
58. Wade Boggs of the 1985–87 Red Sox
59. Fred Lynn of the 1975 Red Sox
60. Stan Musial of the 1950–52 Cardinals
61. Wade Boggs
62. Bruce Sutter (1979)
63. Mike Schmidt of the 1974–76 Phillies
64. Roger Maris of the 1960–61 Yankees
65. Dale Murphy of the 1982–83 Braves
66. Mike Schmidt
67. Tony Gwynn, who hit .370 for the Padres in 1987
68. Pete Rose
69. Ferguson Jenkins (1967–72)
70. Gaylord Perry of the Giants, Indians, and Padres
71. Jim Palmer of the Orioles
72. Steve Carlton (310) of the 1972 Phillies
73. Sparky Lyle
74. Phil Niekro (21–20) of the 1979 Braves
75. Rod Carew (.388 with the Twins and .339 with the Angels)
76. Tom Seaver of the 1968–76 Mets

36. Matching Names

1. Bobby Thomson
2. Allie Reynolds
3. Ted Williams
4. Johnny Mize
5. Dom DiMaggio
6. Casey Stengel
7. Tommy Henrich
8. Vernon Law
9. Joe DiMaggio
10. Ty Cobb
11. Honus Wagner
12. Tris Speaker
13. Babe Ruth
14. Walter Johnson
15. Lou Gehrig
16. Carl Hubbell
17. Mickey Mantle
18. Luke Appling
19. Paul Waner
20. Frankie Frisch

37. First Names

1. Bill
2. Paul
3. Jerome
4. Larry
5. Elwin
6. George
7. Joe
8. Johnny
9. Lynwood
10. Edwin
11. Charles Dillon
12. Fred
13. Harry
14. Leroy
15. Enos
16. Charles
17. Edward
18. Leon
19. Robert
20. James

38. Middle Names

1. "The Hat"
2. "The Man"
3. "The Cat"
4. "The Dutch Master"
5. "The Barber"
6. "Louisiana Lightning"
7. "The Lip"
8. "The Whip"
9. "King Kong"
10. "Puddin' Head"
11. "The Crow"
12. "Home Run"
13. "Poosh 'Em Up"
14. "The Kid"
15. "Pie"
16. "Bobo"
17. "Birdie"
18. "Twinkletoes"
19. "Three Finger"
20. "Pee Wee"

39. Last Names

1. Medwick
2. Crawford
3. Jackson
4. Wood
5. Dugan
6. Piniella
7. Greenberg
8. Cochrane
9. Feller
10. Grimm
11. Reiser
12. Bottomley
13. Doby
14. Newhouser
15. Houk
16. Keeler
17. Murphy
18. Turner
19. Jones
20. Hubbell

40. Multiple Names

1. Dick Stuart
2. Leon Wagner
3. Willie Mays
4. Pete Rose
5. Brooks Robinson

1. "No-Neck"
2. "Catfish"
3. "Boog"
4. "Blue Moon"
5. "Mudcat"

1. Frank
2. Willie
3. Frank
4. Harmon
5. Ken

1. McDowell
2. Plank
3. McBride
4. Jackson
5. Mizell

41. Did They or Didn't They?

1. False (Don Drysdale hit seven twice.)
2. False (Johnny Bench)
3. True (1955)
4. False (Don Newcombe, 1956)
5. True (Ferguson Jenkins, Cubs, and Vida Blue, A's, in 1971)
6. True
7. True (51 in 1955 and 52 in 1965)
8. True
9. False (Don Mattingly, 1985)
10. True
11. True (1951, 1953, and 1955)
12. False (Hank Aaron)
13. True
14. True (1966)
15. False (Dan Bankhead did, too.)
16. True (1969, 1973, 1977–78)
17. True (.300 for 1980 Yankees)
18. False (Joe Black, 1952)
19. False (Elston Howard, 1963)
20. True (1949)
21. False (Lou Brock did not.)
22. True (Burt Hooton, Elias Sosa, and Charlie Hough)
23. True

24. False (Frank Robinson, 1966)
25. True
26. False (Larry Doby, 1948)
27. False (Jim Gilliam, 1953)
28. True (1957)
29. False (Jimmie Foxx, 50 in 1938)
30. False (Marshall Bridges, 1962)
31. True
32. False (Vida Blue, 301 in 1971)
33. True (7)
34. False (Mudcat Grant, 1965)
35. True (Maury Wills, Jim Gilliam, John Roseboro, Tommy Davis, Willie Davis, and Lou Johnson)
36. False (Mickey Lolich, 1968)
37. False (Willie Wilson, 705 in 1980)
38. True (284)
39. True (the 1950s, 1960s, 1970s, and 1980s)
40. False (Rod Carew, .328)
41. True (1965–67)
42. False (Max Carey had 738; Wills, 586.)
43. True
44. True
45. True (.302–.298)
46. False (Roberto Clemente, 1964–65)
47. True (1955)
48. False (He won two AL titles, 1972 and 1974.)

42. The Trailblazers

1. Thompson–Brown
2. Roberts
3. Thomas
4. Howard
5. Trice
6. Doby
7. Banks–Baker
8. Black
9. Green
10. Paula
11. Robinson
12. Jethroe
13. Alston–Lawrence
14. Thompson–Irvin
15. Virgil
16. Hairston

43. Black Clouters

1–3. Willie Mays, Hank Aaron, or Reggie Jackson
4. Willie McCovey or Jim Rice
5. Jim Rice or Willie McCovey
6–10. Any combination of Larry Doby, Dick Allen, Willie Stargell, Ernie Banks, or George Foster
11–15. Any combination of Frank Robinson, George Scott, Ben Oglivie, Jesse Barfield, or Andre Dawson

44. Single-Season Sluggers

1. Willie Mays
2. George Foster
3. Willie Mays
4. Frank Robinson
5. Hank Aaron
6. George Bell
7. Reggie Jackson
8. Nate Colbert
9. Dick Allen
10. Jimmy Wynn
11. Andre Dawson

45. National League Batting Champs

1. Robinson
2. Mays
3. Aaron
4. Aaron
5. Clemente
6. Davis
7. Davis
8. Clemente
9. Clemente
10. Alou
11. Clemente
12. Carty
13. Williams
14. Garr
15. Madlock
16. Madlock

17. Parker	21. Madlock
18. Parker	22. Gwynn
19. Madlock	23. McGee
20. Oliver	24. Raines
	25. Gwynn

46. American League Batting Champs

1. Avila	8. Carew
2. Oliva	9. Carew
3. Oliva	10. Carew
4. Robinson	11. Carew
5. Carew	12. Carew
6. Johnson	13. Carew
7. Oliva	14. Wilson

47. Rookies of the Year

1. Robinson	4. Mays
2. Newcombe	5. Black
3. Jethroe	6. Gilliam

48. The Hall of Fame

1–22. Any combination of the following players:

Jackie Robinson	John "Pop" Lloyd
Roy Campanella	Martin Dihigo
Satchel Paige	Willie Mays
Buck Leonard	Oscar Charleston
Josh Gibson	Hank Aaron
Cool Papa Bell	Lou Brock
Roberto Clemente	Bob Gibson
Monte Irvin	Juan Marichal
Judy Johnson	Frank Robinson
Ernie Banks	Willie McCovey
	Ray Dandridge
	Billy Williams

49. What's the Retirement Age?

1. 1950	9. 1963
2. 1971	10. 1947
3. 1957	11. 1958
4. 1956	12. 1955
5. 1965	13. 1960
6. 1956	14. 1960
7. 1961	15. 1962
8. 1955	

50. One-Town Men

1. Luke Appling	6. Mel Ott
2. Brooks Robinson	7. Al Kaline
3. Bill Terry	8. Ernie Banks
4. Stan Hack	9. Cecil Travis
5. Walter Johnson	10. Pee Wee Reese

51. The First Inning

1. Charlie Grimm	11. Bobby Bragan
2. Jimmy Dykes	12. Bob Kennedy
3. Lou Boudreau	13. Joe Gordon
4. Bill Rigney	14. Joe Schultz
5. Walter Alston	15. Gene Mauch
6. Harry Lavagetto	16. Preston Gomez
7. Mickey Vernon	17. Dave Bristol
8. Bill Rigney	18. Ted Williams
9. Harry Craft	19. Darrell Johnson
10. Casey Stengel	20. Roy Hartsfield

52. The Last Inning

1. Charlie Grimm
2. Marty Marion
3. Eddie Joost
4. Bill Rigney
5. Walter Alston
6. Harry Lavagetto
7. Bobby Bragan
8. Luke Appling
9. Joe Schultz
10. Ted Williams

53. Secondary Pursuits

1. c
2. g
3. e
4. j
5. o
6. a
7. k
8. b
9. m
10. n
11. h
12. d
13. i
14. f
15. l

54. Major League Owners

1. e
2. h
3. j
4. c
5. p
6. o
7. t
8. k
9. n
10. b
11. f
12. s
13. m
14. a
15. q
16. g
17. l
18. i
19. d
20. r

55. The Missing Link

1. Yogi Berra
2. Charlie Keller
3. Terry Moore
4. Duffy Lewis
5. Earle Combs
6. Carl Furillo
7. Ted Williams
8. Lou Piniella
9. Don Mueller
10. Matty Alou
11. Dick Sisler
12. Roger Maris
13. Jackie Jensen
14. Vic Wertz
15. Sid Gordon
16. Pete Reiser

17. Al Simmons
18. Harry Heilmann
19. Casey Stengel
20. Frank Robinson
21. Reggie Smith

22. Al Kaline
23. Joe Rudi
24. Cesar Cedeno
25. Jimmy Wynn

56. Who Played Third?

1. Brooks Robinson
2. Sal Bando
3. Mike Schmidt
4. Ron Cey
5. Red Rolfe
6. Jim Tabor
7. Harry Lavagetto
8. Whitey Kurowski
9. Ken Keltner
10. Hank Majeski
11. Johnny Pesky
12. Billy Cox
13. Willie Jones

14. Hank Thompson
15. Gil McDougald
16. Al Rosen
17. Bobby Adams
18. Eddie Mathews
19. Don Hoak
20. Clete Boyer
21. Al Smith
22. Ken Boyer
23. Ron Santo
24. Billy Werber
25. Eddie Yost

57. Brother Combinations

1. Vince
2. Wes
3. Mort
4. Norm
5. Virgil
6. Paul
7. Jim
8. Joe
9. Harry
10. Christy
11. Jesus
12. Eddie
13. Frank

14. Billy
15. Ken
16. Emil
17. Bill
18. Tommie
19. Lloyd
20. Hector
21. Fred
22. Dave
23. Faye
24. Ed
25. Charlie

58. No Handicap

1. Red Ruffing
2. William "Dummy" Hoy
3. Mordecai "Three Finger" Brown
4. Pete Gray
5. John Hiller

59. Baseball Tragedies

1. Ed Delahanty
2. Ray Chapman
3. Lou Gehrig
4. Harry Agganis
5. Kenny Hubbs
6. Roberto Clemente
7. Thurman Munson

60. No Untouchables

1. Athletics
2. Giants
3. White Sox
4. Indians
5. Yankees
6. Senators
7. White Sox
8. Dodgers
9. White Sox
10. Red Sox
11. Dodgers
12. Cubs
13. Cardinals
14. Pirates
15. Giants
16. Tigers
17. Cubs
18. Red Sox
19. Pirates
20. Braves
21. Indians
22. Brewers
23. Mets
24. Red Sox
25. Yankees

61. When Did They Come Up?

1930s–1940s

1. Joe DiMaggio
2. Tommy Henrich
3. Joe Gordon
4. Ted Williams
5. Dom DiMaggio
6. Stan Musial
7. Warren Spahn
8. George Kell
9. Eddie Yost
10. Red Shoendienst

1940s–1950s

1. Yogi Berra
2. Jackie Robinson
3. Richie Ashburn
4. Jerry Coleman
5. Whitey Ford
6. Willie Mays
7. Eddie Mathews
8. Al Kaline
9. Hank Aaron
10. Rocky Colavito

1950s–1960s

1. Frank Robinson
2. Roger Maris
3. Ron Fairly
4. Maury Wills
5. Juan Marichal
6. Carl Yastrzemski
7. Ed Kranepool
8. Pete Rose
9. Mel Stottlemyre
10. Catfish Hunter

1960s–1970s

1. George Scott
2. Rod Carew
3. Bobby Bonds
4. Thurman Munson
5. Cesar Cedeno
6. Chris Speier
7. Mike Schmidt
8. Dave Parker
9. Jim Rice
10. Fred Lynn

62. Whom Did They Precede?

1. d
2. c
3. b
4. a
5. c

6. a
7. b
8. d
9. a
10. a

63. Whom Did They Succeed?

1. d
2. b
3. a
4. c
5. d

6. a
7. c
8. b
9. a
10. c

64. Chips off the Old Block

1. George Sisler
2. Mike Tresh
3. Jim Hegan
4. Gus Bell
5. Dolph Camilli

6. Max Lanier
7. Ray Boone
8. Maury Wills
9. Roy Smalley
10. Paul "Dizzy" Trout

65. The Gas House Gang

1. d
2. f
3. h
4. i
5. a

6. j
7. b
8. e
9. g
10. c

66. The Year of _____

1. The Hitless Wonders
2. Merkle's Boner

3. Home Run Baker
4. The Miracle Braves

5. The Black Sox
6. Alex's Biggest Strikeout
7. Murderers' Row
8. The Wild Hoss of the Osage
9. The Babe Calls His Shot
10. The Gas House Gang
11. Ernie's Snooze
12. Mickey's Passed Ball
13. Pesky's Pause
14. Gionfriddo's Gem
15. Feller's Pick-off (?)
16. The Whiz Kids
17. The Miracle of Coogan's Bluff
18. Billy the Kid
19. Mays' Miracle Catch
20. Sandy's Snatch
21. Larsen's Perfect Game
22. The Go-Go Sox
23. Maz's Sudden Shot
24. The M&M Boys
25. The Amazin' Ones

67. The Men at the Mike

1. g
2. i
3. f
4. n
5. j
6. o
7. a
8. m
9. e
10. l
11. b
12. c
13. h
14. k
15. d

68. Infield Inflation

1. Stuffy McInnis
2. Eddie Collins
3. Jack Barry
4. Frank Baker
5. Ira Thomas

1. Ferris Fain
2. Pete Suder
3. Eddie Joost
4. Hank Majeski
5. Buddy Rosar

69. Pen Names

1. Del Rice
2. Wes Parker
3. Fred Winchell
4. Woody Woodward
5. Frank Sullivan
6. Hal Schumacher
7. Dick Williams
8. Pat Meany
9. Art Fowler
10. Jack Graham
11. Carl Reynolds
12. Babe Adams
13. Bill Dailey
14. Don Gross
15. Babe Young
16. Hal Smith

17. Babe Twombly
18. Roxie Lawson
19. Ray Murray
20. Johnny Powers

70. Matching Moguls

1.	l	14.	t
2.	s	15.	c
3.	y	16.	w
4.	i	17.	h
5.	e	18.	d
6.	m	19.	r
7.	u	20.	t
8.	o	21.	j
9.	b	22.	a
10.	z	23.	k
11.	p	24.	x
12.	v	25.	g
13.	n	26.	q

71. A Star Is Born

1.	d	6.	e
2.	f	7.	h
3.	i	8.	a
4.	j	9.	c
5.	g	10.	b

72. The National Pastime

Alabama to Georgia

1.	g	6.	h
2.	i	7.	c
3.	e	8.	d
4.	a	9.	f
5.	j	10.	b

Hawaii to Maryland

1.	c	3.	a
2.	g	4.	f

5. j
6. d
7. b

8. i
9. e
10. h

Massachusetts to New Jersey

1. c
2. e
3. g
4. f
5. j

6. b
7. h
8. i
9. a
10. d

New Mexico to South Carolina

1. j
2. f
3. a
4. h

5. b
6. i
7. c
8. g
9. e

South Dakota to Wyoming

1. g
2. a
3. j
4. e
5. i

6. h
7. b
8. d
9. f
10. c

73. The International Pastime

1. d
2. j
3. g
4. c
5. p
6. r
7. i
8. e
9. m

10. f
11. n
12. a
13. o
14. q
15. k
16. h
17. l
18. b

74. Quick Quizzing the Managers

I.

1. Lou Boudreau (24)
2. Roger Peckinpaugh (23)
3. Joe Cronin (26)
4. Tom Sheehan (66)
5. Burt Shotton (62)

III.

1. e
2. c
3. a
4. b
5. d

II.

1. Casey Stengel
2. Joe McCarthy
3. Connie Mack
4. John McGraw
5. Walter Alston

IV.

1. Joe McCarthy
2. Frank Chance or Billy Southworth
3. Frank Chance or Billy Southworth
4. John McGraw
5. Al Lopez

75. Did They or Didn't They . . . Manage?

1. Joe Adcock
2. Joe Gordon
3. Kerby Farrell
4. Bill Dickey
5. Bucky Walters
6. Phil Cavarretta
7. Christy Mathewson
8. Luke Appling
9. Eddie Joost
10. Mickey Vernon
11. Red Rolfe
12. Ben Chapman
13. Jim Lemon
14. Freddie Fitzsimmons
15. Bob Elliott
16. Eddie Lopat
17. Johnny Pesky
18. Dick Sisler
19. Mel McGaha
20. Eddie Stanky

76. Post-War World Series Winners

National League	*American League*
1. Eddie Dyer	1. Bucky Harris
2. Leo Durocher	2. Lou Boudreau
3. Walter Alston	3. Casey Stengel
4. Fred Haney	4. Ralph Houk
5. Danny Murtaugh	5. Hank Bauer
6. Johnny Keane	6. Mayo Smith
7. Red Schoendienst	7. Earl Weaver
8. Gil Hodges	8. Dick Williams
9. Sparky Anderson	9. Al Dark
10. Chuck Tanner	10. Billy Martin
11. Dallas Green	11. Bob Lemon
12. Tom Lasorda	12. Joe Altobelli
13. Whitey Herzog	13. Sparky Anderson
14. Davy Johnson	14. Dick Howser
	15. Tom Kelly

77. Back-to-Back Pennant Winners

1. Casey Stengel	8. Red Schoendienst
2. Chuck Dressen	9. Earl Weaver
3. Walter Alston	10. Dick Williams
4. Casey Stengel	11. Sparky Anderson
5. Fred Haney	12. Billy Martin
6. Ralph Houk	13. Tom Lasorda
7. Walter Alston	

78. Managers in Search of a Pennant

1. Red Rolfe	6. Bobby Bragan
2. Eddie Stanky	7. Harry Walker
3. Bill Rigney	8. Mel Ott
4. Birdie Tebbetts	9. Gene Mauch
5. Mike Higgins	10. Paul Richards

79. You're Hired to Be Fired

1. e	4. c
2. g	5. a
3. b	6. i

7. h
8. m
9. j
10. l
11. d
12. k
13. f
14. q
15. t
16. p
17. s
18. o
19. r
20. n

80. Managerial Half Truths

1. F (Ed Barrow, 1918)
2. T (1933)
3. T (1948)
4. T
5. T
6. F (Hughie Jennings, 1907–09, too)
7. F (Al Dark, 1962)
8. F (1946, as an interim skipper)
9. F (Tom Lasorda, 1977–78)
10. F (Tommy Lasorda, 1981 also)
11. T (8½ years to 7½ years)
12. T
13. T (1907–08)
14. T
15. F (He was the playing manager.)
16. T (1954 Indians and 1959 White Sox)
17. F (George Stallings, 1914)
18. T (1924–25)
19. T (27)
20. T (660–754)
21. F (Browns, 1933–37 and 1952)
22. T (1961–63)
23. F (3–3)
24. F (1961 Reds)
25. F (John McGraw of the 1911–13 Giants also)
26. T (1906)
27. F (Whitey Herzog, 1982)
28. T
29. T (In 1902, when he won a pennant, the World Series had not yet been established.)
30. F (Paul Owens, 1983)
31. T (.875–.700)
32. T (6)
33. F (Sparky Anderson did it, too.)
34. F (Red Schoendienst, in 1967–68, did it also.)
35. T
36. F (Fred Clarke, 1909; Bill McKechnie, 1925; and Chuck Tanner, 1979)
37. F (Mayo Smith, 1968)
38. T (2–1)
39. F (1976–77 Yankees)
40. F (Billy Southworth, 1942–44)
41. T (1944)
42. T (1974–75)
43. T
44. T (Cardinals, 1942–44; Braves, 1948)
45. F (1920 Indians)
46. F (1–3)
47. F (Joe Cronin)
48. T (1966 Orioles)
49. T (He was 4–3 in 1926, his only series as a manager.)
50. F (Appling did not.)

Chapter Fourteen Answers

81. All-Star Standouts

1. Hank Aaron
2. Brooks Robinson
3. Stan Musial
4. Dwight Gooden (19 years, seven months, 24 days)
5. Satchel Paige (47 years, seven days)
6. Pete Rose (first, second, third, left and right field)
7. Charlie Gehringer
8. Terry Moore
9. Willie Jones
10. Ted Williams
11. Mickey Mantle
12. Joe Morgan
13. Phil Cavarretta
14. Dave Winfield
15. Rod Carew
16. Roberto Clemente
17. George Brett
18. Joe DiMaggio
19. Pie Traynor
20. Tony Oliva
21. Goose Gossage
22. Don Drysdale
23. Lefty Gomez
24. Whitey Ford
25. Atlee Hammaker
26. Tommy Bridges
27. Jim Palmer
28. Steve Garvey
29. Nelson Fox
30. Luis Aparicio
31. Yogi Berra
32. Willie Mays

82. Who's Who

1. Babe Ruth
2. Carl Hubbell
3. Frankie Frisch
4. Lefty Gomez
5. Lefty Gomez
6. Joe Medwick
7. Dizzy Dean
8. Earl Averill
9. Ted Williams
10. Arky Vaughan
11. Mickey Owen
12. Johnny Vander Meer
13. Vince DiMaggio
14. Phil Cavarretta
15. Ted Williams
16. Rip Sewell
17. Vic Raschi
18. Jackie Robinson
19. Roy Campanella
20. Don Newcombe
21. Larry Doby
22. Red Schoendienst
23. Ted Williams
24. Hank Sauer
25. Satchel Paige
26. Al Rosen
27. Stan Musial
28. Ken Boyer
29. Hank Aaron
30. Willie Mays

31. Willie Mays
32. Stan Musial
33. Johnny Callison
34. Maury Wills
35. Tony Perez
36. Ferguson Jenkins
37. Willie McCovey
38. Reggie Jackson

39. Frank Robinson
40. Steve Garvey
41. Carl Yastrzemski
42. Steve Garvey
43. Lee Mazzilli
44. Mike Schmidt
45. Ewell Blackwell
46. Early Wynn

83. From Bando to Washington

1. Claudell Washington (20 years, one month, and five days)
2. Chris Chambliss (1976 Yankees)
3. Bill North (1974–75 A's, 1978 Dodgers)
4. Reggie Jackson
5. Jerry Martin (1978 Phillies)
6. Richie Hebner
7. Jim Palmer (Orioles)
8. Pete Rose (42 years, five months, 24 days)
9. Mickey Rivers (1976–78 Yankees)
10. Jay Johnstone (1976 Phillies)
11. Fred Lynn (1982 Angels)
12. Chet Lemon
13. George Brett
14. Bob Robertson (1971 Pirates)
15. Paul Blair (1969 Orioles)
16. Paul Popovich (1974 Pirates)
17. Steve Garvey (1977 Dodgers)
18. Mike Cuellar (1970 Orioles)
19. Phil Niekro
20. Sal Bando (1974 A's)

84. From Baylor to Wynn

1. Bruce Kison
2. Jim Hunter
3. Dave Giusti
4. Jim Palmer
5. Bert Blyleven (19 years, five months, 29 days)
6. Phil Niekro (43 years, six months, eight days)
7. Cesar Geronimo (1975 Reds)
8. Rusty Staub (1973 Mets)
9. George Brett
10. Don Baylor (1982 Angels)
11. Pedro Guerrero
12. Tony Taylor (1972 Tigers)
13. Davey Lopes
14. Steve Balboni (1985 Royals)
15. Jimmy Wynn (1974 Dodgers)
16. Joe Morgan
17. Hal McRae
18. Reggie Jackson (1972 A's)
19. Pete Rose (right field, left field, third base, first base)
20. Bob Robertson (1971 Pirates)

85. From Anderson to Wynn

1. Billy Martin (1970 Twins, 1972 Tigers, 1976–77 Yankees, 1981 A's)
2. Earl Weaver
3. Sparky Anderson (1970, 1972, 1975–76 Reds; 1984 Tigers)
4. Mike Cuellar (1974 Orioles)
5. Nolan Ryan (1969 Mets)
6. Jim Palmer
7. Dave Stieb (1985 Blue Jays)
8. Tommy John
9. Tug McGraw
10. Steve Carlton
11. Dave Giusti (1971 Pirates)
12. Eric Show (1984 Padres)
13. Jerry Reuss
14. Gaylord Perry (1971 Giants)
15. Jim Hunter
16. Dave McNally (1969 Orioles)
17. Ken Holtzman (1973–75 A's)
18. George Brett
19. Pete Rose
20. Steve Garvey (1978 Dodgers)

86. From Bando to Yastrzemski

1. Fred Lynn (.611 for the 1982 Angels)
2. Brooks Robinson (.583 for the 1970 Orioles)
3. Frank White (.545 for the 1980 Royals)
4. Chris Chambliss (.524 for the 1976 Yankees)
5. Brooks Robinson (.500 for the 1969 Orioles)
6. Tony Oliva (.500 for the 1970 Twins)
7. Sal Bando (.500 for the 1975 A's)
8. Bob Watson (.500 for the 1980 Yankees)
9. Graig Nettles (.500 for the 1981 Yankees)
10. Jerry Mumphrey (.500 for the 1981 Yankees)

87. From Baker to Zisk

1. Jay Johnstone (.778 for the 1976 Phillies)
2. Darrell Porter (.556 for the 1982 Cardinals)
3. Ozzie Smith (.556 for the 1982 Cardinals)
4. Art Shamsky (.538 for the 1969 Mets)
5. Terry Puhl (.526 for the 1980 Astros)
6. Willie Stargell (.500 for the 1970 Pirates)
7. Richie Zisk (.500 for the 1975 Pirates)

88. From Aaron to Staub

1. George Brett
2. Steve Garvey
3. Reggie Jackson
4–8. Any combination of the following: Sal Bando, Graig Nettles, Gary Matthews, Greg Luzinski, and Johnny Bench
9–13. Any combination of the following: Boog Powell, Bill Madlock, Bob Robertson, Ron Cey, and Willie Stargell
14–20. Any combination of the following: Hank Aaron, Rusty Staub, George Foster, Al Oliver, Tony Perez, Pete Rose, and Richie Hebner
21. Jim Rice

89. Championship Series Game Winners

National League

1. Pete Rose
2. Bob Tolan
3. Richie Hebner
4. Manny Sanguillen
5. Johnny Bench
6. Pete Rose
7. Bill Russell
8. Bill Russell
9. Willie Stargell
10. Dave Parker
11. Garry Maddox
12. Jerry White
13. Rick Monday
14. Ken Oberkfell
15. Mike Schmidt
16. Steve Garvey
17. Glenn Davis
18. Lenny Dykstra
19. Alan Ashby
20. Gary Carter

American League

1. Paul Blair
2. Curt Motton
3. Paul Blair
4. Gene Tenace
5. Bert Campaneris
6. Bobby Grich
7. Sal Bando
8. Reggie Jackson
9. Chris Chambliss
10. Thurman Munson
11. Roy White
12. John Lowenstein
13. Larry Harlow
14. George Brett
15. Paul Molitor
16. Cecil Cooper
17. Tito Landrum
18. Johnny Grubb
19. Bobby Grich
20. Dave Henderson

Chapter Sixteen Answers

90. World Series Standouts

I.

1. Yogi Berra
2. Pee Wee Reese, Elston Howard
3. Casey Stengel
4. Babe Ruth (1928)
5. Pepper Martin
6. Bobby Richardson
7. Hank Bauer
8. Lou Gehrig (1928)
9. Willie Wilson
10. Mickey Mantle

6. Athletics
7. Yankees
8. Yankees
9. Yankees
10. A's
11. Reds
12. Yankees

II.

1. Whitey Ford
2. Darold Knowles
3. Christy Mathewson
4. Bob Gibson
5. Bill Bevens
6. Carl Mays
7. Jim Lonborg (1967)
8. Jim Palmer (20)
9. Harry Brecheen
10. Babe Ruth

IV.

1. Al Gionfriddo
2. Billy Cox
3. Willie Mays
4. Sandy Amoros
5. Mickey Mantle
6. Eddie Mathews
7. Bill Virdon
8. Tommie Agee
9. Brooks Robinson
10. Dick Green

V.

1. Harry Brecheen
2. Johnny Podres
3. Don Larsen
4. Lew Burdette
5. Bob Turley
6. Whitey Ford
7. Sandy Koufax
8. Bob Gibson
9. Mickey Lolich
10. Jim Hunter

III.

1. Cubs
2. Athletics
3. Red Sox
4. Giants
5. Yankees

91. World Series Players

1. Richie Ashburn
2. Ted Williams
3. Al Kaline
4. Nelson Fox
5. Harvey Kuenn
6. Johnny Logan
7. Ted Kluszewski
8. Gordy Coleman
9. Vada Pinson
10. Felipe Alou
11. Matty Alou
12. Gus Bell
13. Walker Cooper
14. Ray Sadecki
15. Bob Allison
16. Vern Stephens
17. Satchel Paige
18. Bill White
19. Frank Torre
20. Hank Majeski

92. Two-Team World Series Players

1. Rocky Nelson (Dodgers, 1952; Pirates, 1960)
2. Gino Cimoli (Dodgers, 1956; Pirates, 1960)
3. Rudy York (Tigers, 1940, 1945; Red Sox, 1946)
4. Tommy Holmes (Braves, 1948; Dodgers, 1952)
5. Bill Skowron (Yankees, 1955–58, 1961–62; Dodgers, 1963)
6. Roger Maris (Yankees, 1960–64; Cardinals, 1967–68)
7. Al Dark (Braves, 1948; Giants, 1951 and 1954)
8. George McQuinn (Browns, 1944; Yankees, 1947)
9. Mickey Cochrane (Athletics, 1929–31; Tigers, 1934–35)
10. Reggie Smith (Red Sox, 1967; Dodgers, 1977–78)
11. Joe Gordon (Yankees, 1938–39, 1941–43; Indians, 1948)
12. Johnny Sain (Braves, 1948; Yankees, 1951–53)
13. Enos Slaughter (Cardinals, 1942, 1946; Yankees, 1956–58)
14. Don Hoak (Dodgers, 1955; Pirates, 1960)
15. Orlando Cepeda (Giants, 1962; Cardinals, 1967–68)
16. Bob Tolan (Cardinals, 1967–68; Reds, 1970, 1972)
17. Luis Aparicio (White Sox, 1959; Orioles, 1966)
18. Don Gullett (Reds, 1970, 1972, 1975–76; Yankees, 1977)
19. Dick Groat (Pirates, 1960; Cardinals, 1964)
20. Frank Robinson (Reds, 1961; Orioles, 1966, 1969–71)

93. Mound Classics

1. Johnny Sain
2. Allie Reynolds
3. Preacher Roe
4. Vic Raschi
5. Clem Labine
6. Lew Burdette
7. Bob Shaw, Billy Pierce, and Dick Donovan
8. Ralph Terry
9. Don Drysdale
10. Wally Bunker
11. Dave McNally
12. Jack Billingham and Clay Carroll
13. Bruce Hurst

94. Seventh-Game Winners

1. Johnny Podres
2. Johnny Kucks
3. Lew Burdette
4. Ralph Terry
5. Bob Gibson
6. Bob Gibson
7. Mickey Lolich
8. Steve Blass
9. Ken Holtzman
10. Joaquin Adujar
11. Bret Saberhagen
12. Frank Viola

95. World Series Shorts

Three-Game Winners

1. Stan Coveleski
2. Harry Brecheen
3. Lew Burdette
4. Bob Gibson
5. Mickey Lolich

Individual Records

1. Lefty Grove
2. Whitey Ford
3. Bob Gibson
4. Christy Mathewson
5. Lefty Gomez

Home Run Hitters

1. Mickey Mantle
2. Babe Ruth
3. Yogi Berra
4. Duke Snider
5. Lou Gehrig

Career Records

1. Eddie Collins, Lou Brock
2. Yogi Berra
3. Dusty Rhodes
4. Frank Isbell
5. Bobby Richardson

96. Four Homers in One Series

1. Babe Ruth
2. Lou Gehrig
3. Duke Snider
4. Duke Snider
5. Hank Bauer
6. Gene Tenace
7. Willie Aikens

97. World Series Chronology

1. Jimmy Sebring (Pirates)
2. Christy Mathewson
3. Ed Walsh (White Sox)
4. Harry Steinfeldt
5. Orval Overall
6. Babe Adams
7. Jack Coombs (Athletics)
8. Frank Baker
9. Joe Wood
10. Jack Lapp
11. Johnny Evers
12. George "Rube" Foster
13. Babe Ruth (13⅓)
14. Red Faber
15. Charlie Pick
16. Dickie Kerr
17. Elmer Smith (Indians)
18. Waite Hoyt (Yankees)
19. Art Nehf
20. Babe Ruth (1923 Yankees)
21. Earl McNeely
22. Walter Johnson
23. Jesse Haines
24. Babe Ruth
25. Bill Sherdel
26. Al Simmons
27. Jack Quinn
28. Pepper Martin
29. Tony Lazzeri
30. Mel Ott
31. Frankie Frisch
32. Goose Goslin
33. Carl Hubbell
34. Cliff Melton
35. Red Ruffing
36. Monte Pearson
37. Bucky Walters
38. Whit Wyatt
39. Whitey Kurowski
40. Spud Chandler
41. Mort Cooper
42. Hank Borowy
43. Enos Slaughter
44. Hugh Casey
45. Bob Feller
46. Tommy Henrich
47. Whitey Ford
48. Hank Bauer
49. Johnny Mize
50. Carl Erskine
51. Vic Wertz
52. Gil Hodges
53. Enos Slaughter
54. Lew Burdette
55. Bob Turley
56. Chuck Essegian
57. Roy Face
58. Whitey Ford
59. Don Larsen
60. Harry Bright
61. Tim McCarver (1964 Cardinals)
62. Claude Osteen
63. Dave McNally (Game One)
64. Bob Gibson
65. Mickey Lolich
66. Al Weis
67. Brooks Robinson

68. Roberto Clemente
69. Jim Hunter
70. Ken Holtzman
71. Ken Holtzman
72. Tony Perez
73. Johnny Bench
74. Thurman Munson
75. Brian Doyle

76. Phil Garner
77. Tug McGraw
78. Steve Yeager
79. Robin Yount
80. Eddie Murray
81. Kirk Gibson
82. Bret Saberhagen
83. Ray Knight
84. Frank Viola

98. World Series Multiple Choice

1. c (Yankees)
2. b (Yankees)
3. d (1936–39 Yankees)
4. c (1914 Braves–1928 Cards)
5. b (1965 Twins–1982 Cards)
6. c (1951 Giants–1973 Mets)
7. d (1914 Athletics–1932 Yankees)
8. a (19 years before the 1987 series)
9. d (44 with 1983 Phillies)
10. b (1960–62, 1964 Yankees)
11. b (1972–73 A's)
12. c (1982 Brewers)
13. b (1934–35 Tigers)
14. c (Giants and Cards)
15. a (1934 Tigers)
16. d (1939 Yankees)
17. b (1952, 1955 Dodgers)
18. b (1977–78 Yankees)
19. d (1926–28 Yankees)
20. b (1906 Tigers: four doubles)
21. a (1960 Yankees)
22. d (1925 Pirates)
23. b (1955 Yankees)

24. c (1906–08, 1910 Cubs)
25. b (1929–30 Athletics)
26. c (1972–74 A's)
27. d (1936–39, 1941, 1943 Yankees)
28. a (1964, 1967–68 Cards)
29. b (1955–58 Yankees)
30. d (1905, 1914 Athletics)
31. b (1934 Tigers)
32. a (1949 Dodgers)
33. b (1956 Yankees)
34. d (1924 Senators)
35. b (Yankees)
36. a (Giants and Cards)
37. d (Yankees)
38. b (Yankees)
39. b (Dodgers)
40. d (Yankees)
41. d (Yankees)
42. b (Yankees)
43. d (Yankees)
44. b (27 for the 1924 Senators)
45. a (26 for the 1933 Senators)
46. c (Giants)
47. a (Yankees)
48. c (1925 Pirates, 1928 Cards, 1939–40 Reds)
49. c (Yankees)
50. b

1. Christy Mathewson
2. Red Ruffing
3. Herb Pennock
4. Allie Reynolds
5. Rollie Fingers (1972–74 A's)
6. Moe Drabowski (1966)
7. Max Flack
8. Jim Palmer (1971 Orioles)
9. Ross Youngs
10. Lou Brock (1968 Cards)
11. Emil "Irish" Meusel
12. Burleigh Grimes
13. Paul Molitor
14. Dick Hughes
15. Edd Roush
16. Fred Lindstrom (1924 Giants)
17. Frankie Frisch
18. Dave McNally
19. Goose Goslin
20. Ray Schalk
21. Sherry Smith (Dodgers)
22. Patsy Dougherty (1903)
23. Bill Abstein
24. Red Faber
25. Grove Alexander (Cards)
26. Jesse Barnes
27. Ted Lyons (White Sox)
28. Rogers Hornsby (1926 Cards)
29. Fred Snodgrass
30. Mickey Cochrane (1934–35 Tigers)
31. Mort Cooper (1944)
32. Sparky Anderson (1975–76 Reds)
33. Ken Brett (1967 Red Sox)
34. Sandy Koufax (1965 Dodgers)
35. Lou Brock (Cards)
36. Ken Holtzman
37. Goose Goslin (Senators)
38. Thurman Munson (Yankees)
39. Dusty Rhodes (1954 Giants)
40. Duke Snider (Dodgers)
41. Ed Reulbach
42. Thurman Munson
43. Roger Peckinpaugh
44. Ralph Houk (1961–63 Yankees)
45. Vic Raschi (1949–50 Yankees)
46. Allie Reynolds (Yankees)
47. Bob Kuzava
48. Eddie Plank (Athletics)
49. Mickey Lolich (Tigers)
50. Walter Johnson (Senators)
51. Art Nehf
52. Claude Passeau
53. Bob Nieman
54. Monte Irvin (Giants)
55. Mickey Owen (Dodgers)
56. Yogi Berra (Yankees)
57. Wilcy Moore (Yankees)
58. Bill Bevens
59. Hal Schumacher
60. George Pipgras
61. Clarence Mitchell (1920 Dodgers)
62. Jim Lonborg
63. Mickey Cochrane
64. Ray Kremer

65. Billy Martin (Yankees)
66. Joe Gordon (Yankees)
67. Mort Cooper (Cards)
68. Dick Hall
69. Jim Bagby
70. Jack Billingham
71. Kiki Cuyler
72. Enos Slaughter
73. Harry Walker (Cards)
74. Willie Aikens (Royals)
75. Steve Blass
76. Don Gullett
77. Rusty Staub (Mets)
78. Dave McNally (Orioles)
79. Graig Nettles
80. Dwight Evans
81. Tommie Agee
82. Willie Horton
83. Jim Gilliam
84. Roger Maris (1962 Yankees)
85. Doug DeCinces (Orioles)
86. Joe Pepitone (1963 Yankees)
87. Curt Flood
88. Jimmy Slagle
89. Del Gainor (1916)
90. Joe Bush (1913)
91. Deacon Phillippe (1903 Pirates)
92. Joe Wood (1912 Red Sox)
93. Jack Coombs (Athletics)
94. Claude "Lefty" Williams
95. Benny Tate
96. Fred Merkle (Giants, Dodgers, Cubs)
97. Bucky Harris (Senators)
98. Herb Pennock (1927 Yankees)
99. Yogi Berra
100. Joe Garagiola (Cards)

Chicago Cubs Infielders

1. True (Chance, .296; Cavarretta, .293; and Grimm, .290)
2. True
3. False (1,125–1,259)
4. False (Harry Steinfeldt)
5. True (.304)
6. True (1975–76)
7. Hack Wilson
8. Gary Matthews
9. Bill "Swish" Nicholson
10. Chuck Klein
11. Billy Williams
12. Andy Pafko
13. b
14. c
15. a
16. a
17. b
18. d (1917)
19. c
20. c
21. a (1967–72)
22. d (1906)
23. c
24. b
25. b (1906–08)

Montreal Expos

1. f (1970–74)
2. d (1974–76)
3. a
4. e (1969)
5. c (1970–74)
6. b
7. b (1986)
8. b (1987)
9. a
10. a
11. d
12. c
13. True
14. False (less than one season)
15. True (1985)
16. Ross Grimsley (20 in 1978)
17. Bill Stoneman (1971)
18. Woodie Fryman
19. Jeff Reardon
20. Mike Marshall (1972–73)
21. Carl Morton
22. Bill Stoneman (1969 and 1972)
23. Charlie Lea
24. Steve Rogers
25. Mike Torrez (1974)

New York Mets

1. True (1963)
2. False (Al Weis)
3. False (.238)
4. False (Jim Fregosi did.)
5. True (1962–79)
6. True
7. Rusty Staub (1975)
8. Darryl Strawberry (1987)
9. Cleon Jones (1969)
10. Richie Ashburn
11. Darryl Strawberry (1983–86)
12. Ron Swoboda
13. a
14. b
15. c
16. c (1969 and 1971)
17. a (1972)
18. c
19. b (1965)
20. a
21. b (1986)
22. c (1986)
23. b
24. d
25. a (1984–86)

Philadelphia Phillies

1. False (He did it with the 1941 Dodgers.)
2. False (Juan Samuel had 701 official at-bats in his rookie 1984 season.)
3. True (.305 in 1975)
4. True
5. False (Mike Goliat)
6. False (25–37)
7. Ed Delahanty (all in the 1890s)
8. Gavvy Cravath (1913–15, 1917–19)
9. Chuck Klein (Hack Wilson had a record 190 RBIs that year.)
10. Lefty O'Doul (1929)
11. Dick Sisler
12. Richie Ashburn (1955 and 1958)
13. c
14. b
15. a
16. a (1911)
17. d (1945)
18. c (1909)
19. b (1950)
20. a (266)
21. d
22. c
23. a (1964)
24. b (1972–73)
25. a (1967)

Pittsburgh Pirates

1. Dale Long (1956)
2. Bill Mazeroski
3. Arky Vaughan
4. Pie Traynor
5. Hank Greenberg
6. Honus Wagner
7. f
8. a
9. d
10. c
11. b
12. e
13. a

14. c
15. d
16. False (eephus pitch)
17. False (197–230)
18. True (1960)
19. False (Harvey Haddix)
20. False (Phil Niekro, 1977–80 Braves)
21. True (.750 in 1968)
22. True (3–2 in 1903)
23. False (132–195)
24. True (216–194)
25. True

St. Louis Cardinals

1. a
2. d
3. b
4. c (1964)
5. a
6. b (1950)
7. True (1950–52)
8. True (1937)
9. False (.300)
10. False (Maury Wills stole 104 bases in 1962.)
11. True
12. False (Flood didn't.)
13. Bob O'Farrell

14. Walker Cooper (1942–44)
15. Joe Garagiola (1946)
16. e
17. d
18. i (1931)
19. b (1933–36)
20. h
21. f
22. c (1946)
23. a (The shutouts came in 1968.)
24. j
25. g

Atlanta Braves

1. d
2. d (1973)
3. b (Cardinals)
4. a (1960–64 Yankees)
5. b (1953; Hank Aaron also hit 47 homers in 1971.)
6. c
7. True
8. False (335–398)
9. False (Ralph Garr)
10. True (26–27 in 1982–83)
11. True (1964)
12. True (1975–76 Reds)
13. Joe Torre
14. Earl Williams
15. Ozzie Virgil (1987)
16. b
17. d (1979)
18. e
19. c (209)
20. j
21. h
22. g
23. f
24. a
25. i (Houston, 1979–80)

Cincinnati Reds

1. f (1953–56)
2. c (1975–76)
3. e
4. d
5. b
6. a
7. c
8. b (1976–77)
9. a (1905)
10. a
11. c (1917 and 1919)
12. d
13. True (1970 and 1972)
14. True (1926)
15. True (.306)
16. Johnny Vander Meer
17. Joe Nuxhall
18. Jim Maloney
19. Bucky Walters
20. Paul Derringer
21. Ewell Blackwell
22. Tom Browning
23. Jack Billingham
24. Joey Jay
25. John Franco

Houston Astros

1. Lee May (1972–74)
2. Nellie Fox
3. Denny Walling
4. Doug Rader
5. Joe Pepitone
6. Joe Morgan
7. d (1977)
8. e (1967)
9. f (1967)
10. c
11. b (1979)
12. a
13. a (1963–64)
14. b
15. d (1976)
16. True (21 in 1979)
17. True (1967 and 1969)
18. False (Reds)
19. True (1969)
20. True
21. False (1978 Braves)
22. False (Jim Deshaies did it.)
23. True
24. False (He pitched one for the Angels.)
25. False (J. R. Richard struck out 313 in 1979.)

Los Angeles Dodgers

1. c (1978)
2. d
3. f (1960–65)
4. e
5. a (1949–55)
6. b
7. b
8. a
9. a
10. c (1982–83, 1985)
11. a (1968–70 Senators)
12. a (1962)
13. False (He ended his career with the Twins.)
14. False (Ferguson, .240; Yeager, .229)
15. False (His highest season average was 240; his career mark was .214.)
16. Don Drysdale
17. Fernando Valenzuela
18. Al Downing
19. Orel Hershiser (1985)
20. Don Sutton
21. Tommy John
22. Johnny Podres
23. Ron Perranoski
24. Phil Regan
25. Claude Osteen

San Diego Padres

1. True (38 in 1970)
2. True (1984)
3. False (He led league in intentional passes in 1984 and tied for league lead in 1985.)
4. True (1972 and 1973)
5. False
6. True
7. Tony Gwynn
8. Dave Winfield
9. Ollie Brown
10. Dave Kingman (1977)
11. Kevin McReynolds (1984–86)
12. Bob Tolan
13. c
14. a
15. b
16. a (1976)
17. d (1972 Indians, 1978 Padres)
18. c (1971)
19. c
20. a (1974–76)
21. c
22. c
23. c
24. c (1977–78)
25. c

San Francisco Giants

1. b
2. a (1962)
3. d
4. c
5. b (Giants, Cardinals, and Braves)
6. a (1974–76 in Philadelphia, San Francisco, and Atlanta)
7. True
8. False (Bobby Bonds did it in 1970.)
9. False (51–52)
10. True (before the 1975 season)
11. False (He won one with the Tigers.)
12. True (1963)
13. Tom Haller (1966)
14. Ed Bailey (1962–63)
15. Bob Brenly
16. c (1976)
17. e
18. g (1963–69)
19. h
20. b
21. f
22. a
23. d
24. i
25. j

Baltimore Orioles

1. Jim Gentile
2. Davy Johnson
3. Luis Aparicio
4. Brooks Robinson
5. Mark Belanger
6. Vern Stephens
7. b
8. d (Red Sox, A's, and Padres)
9. f
10. c
11. a
12. e (1977)
13. b
14. a
15. c
16. False (Steve Stone, 25 in 1980)
17. False (Dave McNally)
18. False (Jim Palmer, 20)
19. False (Milt Pappas)
20. True
21. False (He lost 21.)
22. True (1979)
23. True
24. True
25. False (42–36)

Boston Red Sox

1. c
2. e (1960 and 1962)
3. f (the 1944 Browns)
4. d
5. b (1903)
6. a (1955–62)
7. d
8. b
9. c (54)
10. a
11. d
12. b
13. True (1915–16)
14. True
15. True
16. Cy Young (1904)
17. Jim Lonborg
18. Dave Sisler
19. Dick Radatz
20. Denny Galehouse
21. Babe Ruth (1916)
22. Lefty Grove (1941)
23. Red Ruffing
24. Joe Wood
25. Ernie Shore

Cleveland Indians

1. Hal Trosky (1936)
2. Bill Wambsganss
3. Ray Boone
4. Kenny Keltner
5. Bobby Avila (.341 in 1954)
6. Vic Wertz
7. b (in 1905)
8. c
9. e
10. f (Earl Averill, Jr.)
11. d
12. a (1948)
13. b
14. c (Bob Feller, Bob Lemon, Gene Bearden, Mike Garcia, Early Wynn, and Herb Score)
15. d (Russ Nixon, .268; Buddy Rosar, .261; Luke Sewell, .259; and Jim Hegan, .228)
16. True (31 in 1920)
17. False (20–9 in 1956)
18. True
19. True
20. False
21. True
22. False (Nolan Ryan, 5; Feller and Jim Maloney, 3)
23. False (Jim didn't.)
24. True (from 1929–32)
25. True

Detroit Tigers

1. b (1937–38)
2. d (.361 in 1961)
3. a
4. d (.343 in 1949)
5. b (for Cleveland's Rocky Colavito)
6. c
7. True
8. True
9. False (.297)
10. False (Jim Northrup hit the ball.)
11. True (1950)
12. False (Al Kaline, 20)
13. Rudy York (1937)
14. Mickey Cochrane
15. Bill Freehan
16. d (1976)
17. f (1968–69)
18. g (308 in 1971)
19. i
20. e
21. a
22. h (1952)
23. j (1944–46)
24. b (1934)
25. c (He was 21–20 in 1907.)

Milwaukee Brewers

1. True (1975)
2. True
3. True
4. True (1987)
5. False (Paul Molitor hit .353 in 1987.)
6. False (25 in 1977)
7. Hank Aaron (1975–76)
8. Rob Deer (1986)
9. Gorman Thomas
10. Tommy Harper
11. Ben Oglivie
12. Gorman Thomas
13. b
14. a
15. c
16. c
17. d (1986)
18. a
19. a
20. b
21. a
22. b (1981)
23. c (1982)
24. d (1982–84)
25. a

New York Yankees

1. Babe Dahlgren (1939)
2. Billy Martin
3. Phil Rizzuto
4. Frank Baker (1911–14)
5. Aaron Ward (1922)
6. Bill Skowron
7. c (1937 and 1948)
8. f (1958)
9. a
10. b
11. d
12. e
13. a (1936)
14. c (1956)
15. d
16. True
17. False (Dale Mitchell)
18. False (Bob Kuzava)
19. True (10 and 8)
20. False (Wes Ferrell)
21. True
22. True (2)
23. True (1964)
24. False (Reverse Page and Murphy.)
25. False (Lyle didn't.)

Toronto Blue Jays

1. c (1986)
2. d
3. f
4. e
5. b (1978–81)
6. a (Blue Jays and Celtics)
7. c
8. d (1987)
9. b (1987)
10. b (1976)
11. a (1984)
12. c (1977)
13. True (1977)
14. True (1979)
15. False (19 was his high.)
16. Doyle Alexander (1984–85)
17. Dave Stieb (1984)
18. Jimmy Key (1985)
19. Mark Eichhorn (1986)
20. Tom Henke (1985–87)
21. Jim Clancy (1986)
22. Pete Vuckovich (1977)
23. Dale Murray (1975–76 Expos)
24. Bill Singer (1970)
25. Dave Lemanczyk (13–16)

California Angels

1. d
2. b
3. a
4. a
5. d
6. c
7. False (Reggie Jackson, 39 in 1982)
8. False (Mickey Rivers, 70 in 1975)
9. False (Rod Carew, .339 in 1983)
10. False (Bonds was traded to the Angels by the Yankees.)
11. True (1973)
12. True
13. Bob Boone
14. Bob Rodgers (8 years)
15. Jeff Torborg
16. c (1964)
17. d (1962)
18. h (1963)
19. f
20. a
21. b
22. i
23. g
24. e
25. j (1967–68)

Chicago White Sox

1. d
2. b
3. f (1936)
4. e (with 33 homers in 1971)
5. a
6. c (After the 1920 season he was barred from baseball along with the other "Black Sox" players.)
7. d
8. c (1963)
9. b (1921–25)
10. a (1937)
11. d (.353 in 1974 with the Braves)
12. b (188)
13. b (In 1920 Red Faber won 23 games; Claude Williams, 22; Ed Cicotte and Dickie Kerr, 21.)
14. a
15. c (Tom)
16. Charlie Robertson (1922)
17. Ed Walsh (1908)
18. Ted Lyons
19. Monty Stratton
20. Dickie Kerr
21. Claude Williams
22. Wilbur Wood (He was 24–20 in 1973.)
23. Billy Pierce
24. Red Faber (1917)
25. Ed Lopat (1949–53)

Kansas City Royals

1. c (36 in 1985)
2. a
3. b (1971–79)
4. d (1979)
5. d (1986)
6. a
7. True (1969)
8. False (Hal McRae, 1982)
9. True (Thirteen of his first 21 were within the playing confines.)
10. False
11. True (1980)
12. False (Danny Tartabull's father, Jose, did.)
13. Jim Sundberg (1986)
14. Darrell Porter
15. John Wathan
16. b
17. f
18. e
19. c (1977)
20. g
21. d (21 in 1985)
22. j
23. h
24. i (1977)
25. a (1969–74)

Minnesota Twins

1. c
2. b (1982)
3. d
4. a
5. f
6. e
7. d
8. a (1986)
9. d
10. c
11. a
12. b
13. True
14. False (Roseboro, .249; Battey, .270)
15. True (33–26)
16. Jim Kaat (25 in 1966)
17. Bert Blyleven (258 in 1973)
18. Dave Boswell
19. Jim Perry
20. Camilo Pascual (1962–63)
21. Mudcat Grant
22. Dean Chance
23. Ron Perranosky
24. Alan Worthington
25. Pedro Ramos (1961)

Oakland A's

1. Gene Tenace (1972–74 A's, 1982 Cards)
2. Bert Campaneris (1964 Kansas City Athletics)
3. Alfredo Griffin
4. Sal Bando
5. Carney Lansford
6. Bert Campaneris (1965)
7. b (1981)
8. f (1965)
9. e
10. d
11. c
12. a
13. d
14. b (.256)
15. a (19)
16. False
17. True (22)
18. True
19. True (1985)
20. False (He won 21 in 1973.)
21. True (4–1)
22. False (Hunter, 25; Blue, 24)
23. True (0–3)
24. False (Darold Knowles)
25. True (6)

Seattle Mariners

1. True
2. True
3. False (Spike Owen)
4. True (1984)
5. False (Ted Williams, 145 in 1939)
6. False (He struck out a club-record 172 times in 1986.)
7. Phil Bradley
8. Gorman Thomas
9. Tom Paciorek
10. Danny Tartabull
11. Willie Horton
12. Dave Henderson
13. b
14. c
15. a
16. a (1987)
17. c (1987)
18. d
19. a
20. b
21. a (1978 Yankees)
22. d (1982)
23. c (1982)
24. b
25. c

Texas Rangers

1. b (1986)
2. d
3. f (1979–84)
4. a (1978)
5. c
6. e
7. b (32 in 1987)
8. a
9. c
10. a (.305)
11. d
12. d
13. True
14. False
15. True (1980 Royals and 1982 Cardinals)
16. Ferguson Jenkins (1974)
17. Gaylord Perry (1975)
18. Doyle Alexander (Yankees)
19. Bert Blyleven
20. Jim Bibby
21. Charlie Hough
22. Dock Ellis (Pirates, 1971; Yankees, 1976)
23. Greg Harris
24. Mitch Williams (1986)
25. Jim Bibby (1973)

Chapter Eighteen Answers

100. American League Records

1. b (1901 Athletics)
2. c (Tigers)
3. d (1985 Red Sox)
4. c (1929–33 Athletics–White Sox)
5. a (1933–37 Tigers)
6. a (Yankees)
7. d (1981 Rangers)
8. c (1985 Red Sox)
9. c (1926 Indians)
10. b (Senators–Twins–Royals)
11. b
12. a (1987 A's)
13. d (1932 Yankees)
14. d (1959 Indians)
15. b (1964 Athletics)
16. b (1922 Browns)
17. a
18. c
19. c (1946 Indians)
20. a (1937 Tigers)
21. d (1937 Yankees)
22. d (1941 White Sox)
23. c (1936 Yankees)
24. b (1938 Tigers)
25. b (1957 Red Sox)
26. a (Yankees)
27. c (1984 Tigers)
28. b (1932 Athletics)
29. b (1908 Tigers)
30. d (1936–37)
31. d (1968–69)
32. a (1950 Yankees)
33. d (1918–23)
34. c (1961)
35. a (1939)
36. c (1932 Senators)
37. a (1909)
38. c (1916)
39. a (1923 Red Sox)
40. b (1929–32 Athletics)
41. d (1904 White Sox)
42. b (1918 Senators)
43. c (1974 Royals)
44. c (A's–Yankees)
45. a (Tigers)
46. b (1955 Indians)
47. d (1978)
48. b (1938 Indians)
49. a (1965 Tigers)
50. a (1904 White Sox)

101. National League Records

1. c (1925 Cards)
2. c (1930 Phillies)
3. b (1929–33 Phillies)
4. b (1924, 1931 Cards)
5. a (1961 Cards)
6. d (Dodgers and Cubs)
7. a
8. b (Giants and Padres)
9. c (Reds and Pirates)
10. b (1987 Mets)
11. c (1958, 1965 Dodgers)
12. a (1954 Reds)
13. b (1953–61 Braves)
14. d (1949–50 Pirates)
15. c (1954–55 Reds)
16. c (Giants: August 1965)

17. c (1954)
18. a (1972)
19. a (1973)
20. c
21. b (Dodgers)
22. d (1922 Cards)
23. c (Phillies)
24. c (1954 Braves)
25. a (Pirates)
26. c
27. b (1953 Dodgers)
28. d (1943 Giants)
29. a (1950 Giants)
30. b (1976)
31. c
32. d
33. a (1968 Mets)

34. b (1938 Reds)
35. c (Pirates–Dodgers)
36. c (1914 Cards)
37. c (1903 Giants)
38. c (1951)
39. a
40. b
41. b (Cards-Phils-Pirates)
42. c (1938 Reds)
43. a
44. a (1958 Cards)
45. b (1979 Astros)
46. a (1980 Expos)
47. c (1954 Dodgers)
48. d (1971 Astros)
49. c
50. a

102. Major League Records

1. b (165 for the Dodgers in 1962)
2. c (.420 for the Browns in 1922)
3. d (.365 for the Yankees in 1957)
4. a (1939 Yankees)
5. d (1925 Athletics)
6. d (1975 Pirates)
7. a (1933 Senators)
8. b (Astros-Red Sox)
9. b (1953 Red Sox)
10. c (1950 Yankees)
11. b (1957 Red Sox)
12. a (1958–59 Phillies)
13. a (1931 Athletics)
14. c (1927 Pirates)
15. d (1948 Athletics)
16. b (1912 Pirates)
17. c
18. d
19. d (Athletics–Red Sox)
20. b (Braves)
21. a (1927–28 Yankees)
22. d (1942 Braves)
23. b (Indians–Red Sox)
24. c (1961 Yankees)

25. d (1973 Phillies)
26. c (1929 Phillies)
27. c (1954 Cards)
28. a (1968 Giants)
29. c (1976 Phillies)
30. a (1921)
31. b (1926)
32. d (1927 Pirates)
33. a (1922 Cubs)
34. c (1956 Senators)
35. a (1947)
36. d (Indians–Yankees)
37. a (1917 Indians)
38. b (Orioles)
39. b (Dodgers)
40. d
41. a (1985 Braves)
42. a (1974 Dodgers)
43. d (1904 Browns)
44. b (1908 White Sox)
45. d (A's, Padres, Brewers)
46. b (1945 Red Sox)
47. b (1941 Yankees)
48. d (1920 Braves)
49. b (1914 Pirates)
50. c (1978 Orioles)

103. Clues to Cooperstown

I. From Barrow to Youngs

1. Carl Hubbell
2. Lou Gehrig
3. Babe Ruth
4. Johnny Evers
5. Mel Ott
6. Al Simmons
7. George Sisler
8. Bill Terry
9. Hank Greenberg
10. Robin Roberts
11. Jackie Robinson
12. Bob Feller
13. Eppa Rixey
14. Joe Cronin
15. Ray Schalk
16. Frank Baker
17. Bill Dickey
18. Rabbit Maranville
19. Dazzy Vance
20. Ted Lyons
21. Zack Wheat
22. Max Carey
23. Edd Roush
24. Sam Rice
25. Charlie Gehringer
26. Pie Traynor
27. Herb Pennock
28. Frankie Frisch
29. Jimmy Collins
30. Fred Clarke
31. John McGraw
32. Nap Lajoie
33. Ross Youngs
34. Red Faber
35. Goose Goslin
36. Monte Irvin
37. George Kelly
38. Satchel Paige
39. Lefty Gomez
40. Lou Boudreau
41. Chick Hafey
42. Dave Bancroft
43. Harry Hooper
44. Jesse Haines
45. Cool Papa Bell
46. Josh Gibson
47. Branch Rickey
48. Ed Barrow
49. Bob Lemon
50. Heinie Manush

From Aaron To Kell

1. Modercai "Three Finger" Brown
2. Lefty Grove
3. Ty Cobb
4. Roberto Clemente
5. Jimmie Foxx
6. Kiki Cuyler
7. Rick Ferrell
8. Frank Chance
9. Hank Aaron
10. Willie McCovey
11. Yogi Berra
12. Billy Herman
13. Grover Alexander
14. Addie Joss
15. Waite Hoyt

16. Whitey Ford
17. Chief Bender
18. Jack Chesbro
19. Stan Coveleski
20. Walter Johnson
21. Burleigh Grimes
22. Dizzy Dean (1934 Cards)
23. Don Drysdale
24. Jesse Burkett
25. Gabby Hartnett
26. Ed Delahanty
27. Roy Campanella
28. Luis Aparicio
29. Luke Appling (White Sox)
30. Eddie Collins
31. Sam Crawford

32. Earl Averill
33. Mickey Cochrane
34. Jim Bottomley
35. Ernie Banks
36. Earle Combs (1927)
37. Willie Keeler
38. Al Kaline
39. Elmer Flick
40. Rogers Hornsby
41. Joe DiMaggio
42. Hughie Jennings (Tigers)
43. George Kell
44. Travis Jackson (Giants)
45. Harry Heilmann
46. Ray Dandridge
47. Jim Hunter

From Killebrew to Wynn

1. Joe McGinnity
2. Sandy Koufax
3. Early Wynn
4. Rube Marquard
5. Juan Marichal
6. Rube Waddell
7. Christy Mathewson
8. Eddie Plank
9. Warren Spahn
10. Red Ruffing
11. Eddie Mathews
12. Chuck Klein
13. Johnny Mize (1939–40 Cards and 1948–49 Giants)
14. Pee Wee Reese
15. Joe Medwick
16. Mickey Mantle
17. Frank Robinson
18. Ralph Kiner
19. Paul Waner
20. Fred Lindstrom
21. Hack Wilson
22. Willie Mays
23. Duke Snider

24. Harmon Killebrew
25. Joe Sewell
26. Tris Speaker
27. Honus Wagner
28. Stan Musial
29. Lloyd Waner
30. Brooks Robinson
31. Ted Williams
32. Joe Tinker
33. Ed Walsh
34. Bobby Wallace
35. Bill McKechnie
36. Al Lopez
37. Walter Alston
38. Bucky Harris
39. Joe McCarthy
40. Connie Mack
41. Wilbert Robinson
42. Charles Comiskey
43. Casey Stengel
44. Clark Griffith
45. Miller Huggins (Yankees, 1921–23 and 1926–28)
46. Billy Williams

Chapter Twenty Answers

National League

Atlanta

1. Warren Spahn
2. Phil Niekro
3. Eddie Mathews
4. Hank Aaron

Chicago

1. Ernie Banks
2. Billy Williams

Cincinnati

1. Fred Hutchinson
2. Johnny Bench

Houston

1. Jim Umbricht
2. Don Wilson

Los Angeles

1. Pee Wee Reese
2. Duke Snider
3. Jim Gilliam
4. Walter Alston
5. Sandy Koufax
6. Roy Campanella
7. Jackie Robinson
8. Don Drysdale

New York

1. Gil Hodges
2. Casey Stengel

Philadelphia

1. Richie Ashburn
2. Robin Roberts

Pittsburgh

1. Billy Meyer
2. Ralph Kiner
3. Willie Stargell
4. Bill Mazeroski
5. Pie Traynor
6. Roberto Clemente
7. Honus Wagner
8. Danny Murtaugh

St. Louis

1. Stan Musial
2. Ken Boyer
3. Dizzy Dean
4. Lou Brock
5. Bob Gibson

San Francisco

1. Mel Ott
2. Carl Hubbell
3. Willie Mays
4. Juan Marichal
5. Willie McCovey

American League

Baltimore

1. Earl Weaver
2. Brooks Robinson
3. Frank Robinson

Boston

1. Joe Cronin
2. Ted Williams

California

1. Gene Autry

Chicago

1. Nellie Fox
2. Luke Appling
3. Minnie Minoso
4. Luis Aparicio

Cleveland

1. Earl Averill
2. Lou Boudreau
3. Bob Feller

Detroit

1. Charlie Gehringer
2. Hank Greenberg
3. Al Kaline

Milwaukee

1. Hank Aaron

Minnesota

1. Harmon Killebrew
2. Rod Carew

New York

1. Babe Ruth
2. Lou Gehrig
3. Joe DiMaggio
4. Mickey Mantle
5. Bill Dickey
6. Yogi Berra
7. Roger Maris
8. Thurman Munson
9. Whitey Ford
10. Elston Howard
11. Casey Stengel

About the Author

Dom Forker has written seven books, six of which are on baseball. The subjects include *Almost Everything You've Ever Wanted to Know about Baseball* and a series of quiz books. A former college pitcher and a coach at almost every level of amateur play, the author teaches English and creative writing at Delaware Valley Regional High School in Frenchtown, N.J. He is currently at work on a book about the 1949–53 Yankees and a book of poetry on the history of the World Series. He is married and has three sons: Tim, a Met fan; Geoff, a Phillie fan; and Ted, a Yankee fan.